A PLACE
Prepared

Rob Palkovitz

PUBLISHING

New London, Pennsylvania

APlacePrepared.net

A Place Prepared

©2023 by Rob Palkovitz

Cover Design and Layout by Pom Aesthetic, LLC

Editorial Oversight by Nina Groop and Felicia Murrell

All rights reserved. No part of this publication may be reproduced, stored in a retrieval system, or transmitted in any form or by any means, for example, electronic, photocopy, recording, without the prior written permission of the publisher. The only exception is brief quotation in printed reviews.

All Scripture quotations, unless otherwise indicated, are taken from the Holy Bible, New International Version®, NIV®. Copyright ©1973, 1978, 1984, 2011 by Biblica, Inc.™ Used by permission of Zondervan. All rights reserved worldwide. www.zondervan.com. The "NIV" and "New International Version" are trademarks registered in the United States Patent and Trademark Office by Biblica, Inc.™

Scripture quotations marked (AMP) are taken from the Amplified Bible, Copyright © 2015 by The Lockman Foundation. Used by permission.

Scripture quotations marked (ESV) are taken from The Holy Bible, English Standard Version® (ESV®) Copyright © 2001 by Crossway, a publishing ministry of Good News Publishers. All rights reserved.

Scripture quotations marked (MSG) are taken from The Message. Copyright © 1993, 1994, 1995, 1996, 200, 2001, 2002. Used by permission of NavPress Publishing Group.

Scripture quotations marked (TPT) are from The Passion Translation. Copyright © 2017, 2018, 2020 by Passion & Fire Ministries, Inc. Used by permission. All rights reserved. ThePassionTranslation.com

Scripture quotations marked "World English Bible" are from the Public Domain translation of the Holy Bible of that name published at eBible.org and WorldEnglish.Bible. The World English Bible is not copyrighted.

IBSN: 978-0-9970561-8-1   230913

Table of Contents

Chapter 1: Entering In to a Place Prepared 1
Chapter 2: A Place of Deep Love and Acceptance 13
Chapter 3: A Place of Extravagant Belonging 27
Chapter 4: A Place of Everlasting Purpose 35
Chapter 5: A Place of Sure Salvation 43
Chapter 6: A Place of Total Forgiveness and Cleansing 49
Chapter 7: A Place of Secure Family Love 57
Chapter 8: A Place of Unfathomable Plenty 65
Chapter 9: A Place of Total Satisfaction and Contentment 73
Chapter 10: A Place of Everlasting Freedom and Victory 79
Chapter 11: A Place of Constant Goodness 91
Chapter 12: A Place of Increasing Closeness and Care 103
Chapter 13: A Place of Absolute Inclusion and Refuge 111
Chapter 14: A Place of Continual Relationship with God 125
Chapter 15: A Place of Unshakable Union with God 133
Chapter 16: A Place of Oneness in Love 143
Chapter 17: A Place of Power for Life 151
Chapter 18: A Place of Life to the Full 157
Chapter 19: A Place of Transformation and Increasing Maturity 165
Chapter 20: A Place of Divine Destiny 173
Chapter 21: A Place of Absolute Security 181
Chapter 22: A Place of Experientially Knowing God's Constant Goodness . . 193
Chapter 23: A Place Prepared: Living from the Place Prepared 199
100 Biblical Statements, Paraphrased and Personalized 208
Acknowledgments 219
About The Author 221

CHAPTER 1

Entering In to a Place Prepared

In March of 1993, I participated in an academic conference in New Orleans, representing my university and my research program as a professor. The conference corresponded with the beginning of spring break, and upon completion of my conference activities, I planned to meet up with Scott Sheer, a Ph.D. student from our graduate program who lived nearby. Along with being his professor for some of his coursework and supervising his research, we were also friends.

A native of Louisiana from the north side of Lake Pontchartrain, Scott had gone home to spend spring break with his family. After a day together, exploring swamps and some great local food stops, I'd planned for Scott to drop me at a rental car agency so that I could drive to Nashville to join my wife and four young sons to spend the rest of spring break in the Great Smoky Mountains.

Sometime during the afternoon of our adventures in the bayou, Scott asked if it would be okay to drop by and say hi to his family on the way to pick up the rental car. I said sure, but I honestly thought it would just be an imposition on their time. I certainly had no inkling of their anticipation of my arrival, and I surely did not foresee the gift that dropping by would be to me.

When we arrived at Scott's home, we were warmly greeted by his parents, Ray and Anne, his sister Cheryl and brother-in-law Paul, and their young child. It was a heartfelt welcome in the tradition of southern Christian hospitality. Even more than that, decades later, I still remember the experience of entering into a place prepared for me — being warmheartedly and genuinely welcomed, stepping into the fullness of a plan that I had not expected.

After greeting and talking in the front yard, we entered the house and I saw a long table filled with a bounty of amazingly prepared Cajun food, homemade desserts, and beverages. After leading the way along the buffet as "the guest of honor," we all gathered to eat and talk and enjoy one another's company for a few pleasant hours. As the evening came to a close, I was sent off on the rest of my planned journey filled and cared for in many ways beyond what I recognized at that time.

Nearly thirty years later, that experience of stepping into a place prepared for me is still tangible. I felt that I was instantly *familied* — filled in ways that far surpassed the plentiful, lovingly prepared, bounty of food and drink generously provided. The Scheer family clearly put a lot of thoughtfulness, anticipation, planning, preparation, and care into my joining them. I headed toward Nashville, nurtured in body, mind, and spirit. I felt well cared for, loved, accepted, and provisioned for the trip ahead.

That is what it is like to enter a place generously prepared for you, with your best interests in mind. It feeds you in many ways and gives you an abundance of good things to carry with you on your way forward. It provides lasting comforts and resources that you didn't even know you needed, far beyond anything you had imagined. It refreshes you in life-giving ways that have long-lasting beneficial effects.

The place prepared for me by the Scheer family was so much more than food and hospitality. They opened their hearts to me and gave me the opportunity to relate to them in their family. If I had merely come and eaten, though it was a feast, I would have missed their invitation to relationship: heart-to-heart sharing, acceptance, love. Knowing and being known.

If you read through the remainder of this book without mindfully opening your heart to what the scriptures are conveying about God and his heart for you personally, it will simply be an "eat and run" exercise. Of course, reading the scripture will produce some measure of good in you because God's word does not return void. But, if you can trust the words of God and see the invitation, from God himself, to enter more fully into relationship with him, you will not only glimpse the place prepared, but you can allow his Spirit to transform you so that you can experientially live daily life now *from* the place that he has prepared for you.

It is not a matter of just reading, or even studying or proclaiming what the Bible says about you and who you are to God. It is more about giving the love of God, the Father, Son and Spirit permission to make you who he intends you to be. Lingering with him as his word and his love shines truth, light, hope, and healing into your inmost being. Inviting him to bring you into the fullness of what he has planned, created, prepared, and desired for you.

The Bible is the story of God's desire for relationship with us, the reason for our creation and the creation of the entire universe. The New Testament recounts God sending his Son to the people of earth to reveal him to us, to make a way back to relationship with him, and to cleanse us from our sins so that we can return to be with him, to continually live in intimate relationship with him, and to abide with him as his beloved children. It is also the best source of information regarding our place with God, both now and for eternity.

In John 14, Jesus tells his disciples that he is going to his Father's house to prepare a place for them and that he will come back to take them to be with him so they may also be where he is (verses 2–3). If we look for it, the place that Jesus has prepared for us is elaborated throughout scripture to reveal the care, anticipation, and love of God for each one of us, *personally*.

Thinking about the place that Jesus has prepared has caused me to reflect on the idea of *place* in general. These days, we have the opportunity to hear different viewpoints and perspectives concerning various places. From restaurants, Airbnbs, stores, service centers to long-term airport parking lots, the reviews are endless. Although there may be a general consensus regarding a particular place, there is typically a gamut of voices running the spectrum from "excellent" to "don't even think about going there." Whose voices do we trust?

Reviews are not just limited to places; they extend to people as well. Again, there are widely varied opinions regarding how people are doing. Which reviewers sway our thoughts? When it comes to valuable perspective, none can compare with God's. Rather than buying into the vantage point of anyone else, I would prefer to see myself from the viewpoint of the one who desired me, planned me, created me, died for me, and prepared a place for me in order to have fullness of relationship with me. God's thoughts are far more important than those of anyone else who evaluates me. And I would certainly prefer to know God's perspective rather than being influenced by the voice of the enemy of my soul — the father of lies, a liar from the beginning, the one who accuses me and focuses on my failings rather than who I am in Christ. The scriptures hold many verses elaborating God's unchanging viewpoint concerning who we are to God and the place he has prepared for us in relationship with him. The convergence of literally hundreds of verses provides a clear window to God's unrestrained love for us. It provides a true accounting of how God desires us to enter life to the full as his beloved children.

As people living in a three-dimensional space, we are always in *some* place. I can choose to be in the place prepared for me by God no matter where else I may be. From our experiences as humans always in *some* place, we recognize that places can have multiple purposes — shelter, rest, learning, work, creation, repair, fellowship, feeding, gathering, privacy, protection, restoration, communication, conversation, aesthetic beauty, healing. If you think about the most fulfilling or joyous times you have ever experienced and the place you associate with those wonderful times, it is likely that you experienced some of those functions of place. All of that, and more, is available in Jesus in the place he prepared for us.

Let's take a brief look at selected verses from John chapters 14 and 15, with some added emphasis, and then put them together with a compilation of verses from Paul's writings to the early church to understand more about the place Jesus has prepared for us.

Jesus declared, "**In my Father's house** there are many rooms. If it were not so, I would have told you. **I am going there to prepare a place for you.** And if I go and prepare a place for you, **I will come back and take you to be with me that you also may be where I am.** You know the way to the place where I am going" (John 14:2–4).

The Father's house is characterized by many rooms. In most houses, rooms have different "feels" and functions, though places in homes tend to be prepared for a range of specific purposes. What typically happens in your living room may overlap somewhat with what happens in your kitchen, but each room or place in your house is uniquely designed and appointed to facilitate different functions. For example, it is likely that time spent in your living room, relaxing, spending time with others, reading, watching television, eating, enjoying music, or even creating a project staging area, is different from the normal activities and functions that occur in your bedroom, workshop, or shower.

I have read the teachings of Jesus in many different Bible translations. None of the scripture translations I consulted said that Jesus was going to prepare a *room* for me nor do they state that he is building a mansion for me in heaven. In their own manner of expression, every translation says something to the effect that Jesus is going to his Father's house to prepare *a place* for me. In the collectivist Middle Eastern culture of Jesus' time, houses contained a lot of communal family space. A place prepared in the house is not likely a reference to a personal room, but being welcomed into a home has implications for having access to different rooms with different functions. Preparing a place for someone also implies that their arrival is anticipated and welcomed.

John 14 distinctly says that one of the functions of the place that Jesus is preparing is for us to be able to *be with Jesus where he is.* Certainly, when he returns at the end of the age, we will be with him in the place prepared. It is also possible, however, that in the context of John 14, where Jesus was making his friends ready for the coming events of the last few days of his life on earth as a human, he was speaking of his "going" and "coming back" in reference to his death, burial, and resurrection. Several things he says in the next few verses are consistent with this idea.

"**I am the way** and the truth and the life. No one comes **to the Father** except through me (John 14:6). The words I say to you I do not speak on my own authority. Rather, it is the Father, living in me, who is doing his work. **Believe me when I say that I am in the Father and the Father is in me** (John 14:10–11). I will ask the Father, and he will give you **another advocate to help you and be with you forever — the Spirit of truth.** The world cannot accept him because it neither sees him nor knows him. But you know him, **for he lives with you and will be in you.** I will not leave you as orphans; I will come to you. Before long, the world will not see me anymore, but you will see me. **Because I live, you also will live. On that day you will realize that I am in my Father, and you are in me, and I am in you**" (John 14:16–20).

There are several points that are clear in this discourse. Jesus is going to prepare a place for his friends in the Father's house. Jesus is the way to the Father. He declared that he was in the Father and that the Father was in him doing his work. Jesus is telling us he speaks in the authority of the Father. The Spirit, whom the disciples knew because he had been living *with* them, will be in them. Recall that at his baptism, the Holy Spirit descended on Jesus in the form of a dove and remained on him. The Holy Spirit never left Jesus, so the Spirit was literally living with the disciples all the days that Jesus was with them. That is how they knew him. The promised Holy Spirit, after his resurrection, would come to reside in them.

In foreshadowing his resurrection, Jesus stated, "because I live, you will also live." Many scriptures in the New Testament describe who we are "in Christ," and the benefits of his resurrection and life that we will share. We will discuss many of them in the remainder of this book. In John 14:19–20, Jesus states *"and on <u>that</u> day"* (the day he lives) we will realize that he is in his Father, we are in him, and he is in us. Now that is an amazing place — filled by his presence, in him, in the Father.

He continues, "Anyone who loves me will obey my teaching. My Father will love them, and **we will come to them and make our home with them** (John 14: 23). All this I have spoken while still with you. But the Advocate, the Holy Spirit, whom the Father will send in my name, will teach you all things and will remind you of everything I have said to you. Peace I leave with you; my peace I give you. I do not give to you as the world gives. Do not let your hearts be troubled and do not be afraid. You heard me say, **'I am going away and I am coming back to you.'** If you loved me, you would be glad that **I am going to the Father,** for the Father is greater than I. I have told you now before it happens, so that when it does happen you will believe (John 14:25–29).

Remain in me, as I also remain in you (John 15:4). As the Father has loved me, so have I loved you. Now **remain in my love.** If you keep my commands, you will remain in my love, just as I have kept my Father's commands and remain in his love. **I have told you this so that my joy may be in you and that your joy may be complete.** My command is this: Love each other as I have loved you" (John 15:9–12).

The whole chapter of John 14 can be viewed as a discourse on the place Jesus has prepared for us, in him, in the Father, with the Spirit living in us. John 15 continues, encouraging us to *remain* or abide in Jesus, to be with him where he is. In considering a handful of verses from Paul's epistles, we can know where Jesus is as well as where we are spiritually in relationship to him.

Praise be to the **God** and Father of our Lord Jesus Christ, who **has blessed us in the heavenly realms with every spiritual blessing in Christ** (Ephesians 1:3). **I pray that the eyes of your heart may be enlightened in order that you may know the hope to which he has called you,** the riches of his glorious inheritance in his holy people, and his incomparably great power for us who believe (Ephesians 1:18–23). Therefore, **if anyone is in Christ, the new creation has come:** The old has gone, the new is here! (2 Corinthians 5:17). Because of his great love for us, God, who is rich in mercy, made us alive with Christ even when we were dead in transgressions — it is by grace you have been saved. **And God raised us up with Christ and seated us with him in the heavenly realms in Christ Jesus, in order that in the coming ages he might show the incomparable riches of his grace, expressed in his kindness to us in Christ Jesus.** For it is by grace you have been saved, through faith — and this is not from yourselves, it is the gift of God — not by works, so that no one can boast (Ephesians 2:4–9). Since, then, **you have been raised with Christ,** set your hearts on things above, where **Christ is, seated at the right hand of God.** Set your minds on things above, not on earthly things. For you died, and your life is now hidden with Christ in God. When Christ, who is your life, appears, then you also will appear with him in glory (Colossians 3:1–4).

As his followers, we are invited into the place Jesus has prepared. *In Christ, spiritually, we can enter now.* If anyone is in Christ, the new creation has come (2 Corinthians 5:17). We have already been raised with him. We do not need to wait until we are fully united with Jesus, face to face, in our afterlife or after his return to experience the place he has prepared for us. The place prepared holds every spiritual blessing in Christ (Ephesians 1:3). Entering in to experiencing those blessings brings us more completely into living life to the full, which, along with revealing the Father and being the way back to him, is one of the central reasons that Jesus came to the earth (John 10:10). Together, let's explore the depths and breadths and lengths and widths of the love of God for us (Ephesians 3:18), knowing him better, as we survey and experience the place Jesus has personally and uniquely prepared for us.

I have selected one hundred scriptural truths that portray many aspects of the place that Jesus has prepared for us to enter and to remain. I paraphrased, personalized, and grouped the statements to paint a detailed picture of the place that Jesus prepared, making a way for us as God's sons and daughters, our position and inheritance in him, both now and for eternity. The verses are grouped into chapters that focus on a central characteristic of the place that Jesus prepared for us.

> *As we meditate on the scriptures grouped thematically, we see that the place prepared for us by Jesus, the place he wants us to enter with him and remain is:*

- A place of deep love and acceptance
- A place of extravagant belonging
- A place of everlasting purpose
- A place of sure salvation
- A place of total forgiveness and cleansing
- A place of secure family love
- A place of unfathomable plenty
- A place of total satisfaction and contentment
- A place of everlasting freedom and victory

- A place of constant goodness
- A place of increasing closeness and care
- A place of absolute inclusion and refuge
- A place of continual relationship with God
- A place of unshakable union with God
- A place of oneness in love
- A place of power for life
- A place of life to the full
- A place of transformation and increasing maturity
- A place of divine destiny
- A place of absolute security
- A place of experientially knowing God's constant goodness

That is the character of the place Jesus prepared for you.

I have no doubt that there are other functions, other ways to see and experience the place prepared. After all, God, the infinite creative one, planned it. All three members of the Trinity were active in creating it and bringing us access to it.

In Christ, we are invited into the presence of the Father, with the Son, and filled with the Holy Spirit. Invited into life to the full. Complete joy. Abundant fruit. Unity with God remaining in the place Jesus prepared for us. In the Father's house with many rooms for many purposes. We are not intended to just meet with God occasionally and plunge out into the events of our day and our relationships on our own. We are invited to remain in him and _live life from that place._

Besides revealing the characteristics of the place prepared for you by Jesus, the verses also portray who you are to God, our heavenly Father. These verses present the scriptural detail of God's passionate love for you, who you are in Christ, and the relational riches you are invited to in his Spirit. Each statement is listed along with its associated scriptural reference so that you can study it further, in context. When preparing this book, I looked at the context of each verse in at least three different translations (often up to six translations) and gained a lot of insight through comparing the various renderings. If you want to see the nuanced details of the different interpretations of these verses as they were translated from ancient languages to modern English, I encourage you to study them in multiple translations as well. While various translations offer slightly different aspects of the place prepared, they all converge on the central truths of scripture that I have prayerfully reflected on and summarized in one hundred different meditations. Stated simply, although there are nuanced differences among the translations, they are in general agreement in their presentation of the nature of the place prepared.

When beginning this manuscript, I originally thought of each of the hundred entries as a devotional to be read daily. In rewriting and reorganizing the book, I instead grouped them into chapters centered thematically around the essential qualities of the place prepared. In the current rendering, each chapter contains meditations on several scriptural truths that are grouped by a particular trait of the place prepared, such as "a place of deep love and acceptance." At the end of each group of similarly themed verses within each chapter, I have provided a short summary and application section. Of course, how you proceed through this book is up to you. If you like to spend time on brief daily devotions, it can be read as a devotional. Besides the book's opening and concluding chapter, the book presents one hundred reflections on scriptural truths coupled with twenty-one summary and application passages. On the other hand, if you prefer to look at convergent themes that appear in different verses throughout the scriptures, you may prefer to read the book as an offering of thematic chapters with each covering an attribute of the place prepared.

The most important thing is to not reduce the place that Jesus has prepared for you to a mere intellectual understanding. Rather, prayerfully invite the Holy Spirit to reveal and apply God's love for you personally into your inmost being (Romans 5:5). Open your mind, emotions, and spirit to experientially taste and see the love of God that has been richly represented to you through the scriptures. Prayerfully meditate on how God has consistently and extravagantly applied these verses to you personally. Invite him to show you. Sit with the scriptures and with his Spirit as the verses, observations, and meditations reveal more to you regarding your relationship with God.

Compiling this list of scriptural truths and meditating on it in this manner has brought me great freedom, joy, and transformation. Prayerfully reflecting on these statements has helped me to experientially trust and personally encounter the life-changing truth of the scriptures enlivened by the indwelling Holy Spirit. My prayer is that sharing these scriptural truths and my reflections on them will bring you into a deeper intimacy with God the Father as his beloved child so that you can experience and remain in the place he personally prepared for you. I pray that you will encounter more of the Father, Son, and Spirit, and in doing so you will have more of life to the full — the life that he desires for you.

As you read this book, you are likely to think it is a repetition of things that you already know. The challenge for you as a reader is to not shut down simply because it has been mentioned previously in a different context or applied as a principle in a place with different function than the one under current consideration. The place prepared for us by Jesus is infinitely rich in meanings and ways of touching and transforming our lives. The hundred scriptural truths loop around and dovetail with one another in countless ways. Please trust that meditating on the same concepts in different contexts brings deeper integration of their truth and transformative life when we engage them with an open heart. Deciding to prayerfully engage in the recommended activities and contemplations will undoubtedly yield a different outcome than reading through the material without substantive reflection.

God placed us in the world to experience him and relate to him and offers us the place prepared so that we can have life to the full. Jesus made the way. The Holy Spirit comforts us, teaches us, reminds us of all that Jesus said, and he pours the love of God into our hearts. We recognize that we are in Jesus, that he is in the Father, and that he is in us (John 14:20). We are filled by God and immersed in God. That is the place prepared. At its core, the place prepared is being in the presence of God himself. Surrounded. Filled. Saturated.

In his presence, everything is perfect. His presence calms every storm and overcomes every need, circumstance, and lack. When the storm is calmed, we immediately arrive at our destination — being in the presence of God. Like changing water into wine, Jesus turns the ordinary into the extraordinary in his presence. In his presence is total shalom. Peace with God. Peace with oneself. Peace with all others. We truly can have wholeness and peace in all things — body, soul, mind, and spirit.

Before we move forward, let's invite the Holy Spirit to bring us to experientially enter the place that Jesus prepared for us in his Father's house as we meditate on what the scriptures reveal about it.

A Place Prepared

I have paraphrased, personalized, and grouped these hundred biblical statements about the place God has prepared for you. As you read, meditate on the truth of God's Word about his heart toward you and your place in him. Let it transform your inmost being and your relationship with God the Father, Jesus, and the Holy Spirit. Declare the truth of God's Word over yourself.

In Jesus, I am in a place of deep love and acceptance:

In love, I was chosen by God before the creation of the world (Ephesians 1:4). I am set apart, called by God's grace (Galatians 1:15), holy and blameless in God's sight (Ephesians 1:4). I am a dearly loved child of God (Ephesians 5:1). I am fully known by God (1 Corinthians 13:12) and accepted in Christ (Romans 15:7). God loves me with the same love with which he loved Jesus (John 17:23).

In Jesus, I am in a place of extravagant belonging:

I am not my own (1 Corinthians 6:19). I belong with and to Jesus (Romans 7:4). I was bought at a price (1 Corinthians 6:19). God made me alive with Christ even when I was dead in my sins (Ephesians 2:5).

In Jesus, I am in a place of everlasting purpose:
I was once in darkness, but now I am light in the Lord (Ephesians 5:8). I am a chosen person, part of a royal priesthood, a holy nation, a people belonging to God, called out of darkness into his wonderful light (1 Peter 2:9). I am a child of the light and of the day. I do not belong to the night or to darkness (1 Thessalonians 5:5). I am holy; I share in a heavenly calling (Hebrews 3:1).

In Jesus, I am in a place of sure salvation:
By grace, I am saved (Ephesians 2:5). I am saved through faith, and this is not from myself, it is a gift from God (Ephesians 2:8). Christ dwells in my heart through faith (Ephesians 3:17).

In Jesus, I am in a place of total forgiveness and cleansing:
In the Son, I have redemption through his blood (Ephesians 1:7; Colossians 1:14). In the Son, God forgave all my sins (Colossians 2:13, Ephesians 1:7). I am reconciled, holy in God's sight, without blemish and free from accusation (Colossians 1:22). I am washed, sanctified, and justified freely by faith in Christ Jesus and the Spirit of my God (1 Corinthians 6:11; Galatians 3:8, 3:24).

In Jesus, I am in a place of secure family love:
I am a child of God through faith in Christ Jesus (Galatians 3:26). I am lavished in God's love (1 John 3:1). Because I am his child, God sent the Spirit of his Son into my heart, the Spirit that calls out "Abba, Father" (Galatians 4:6). I can receive the full rights of a child of God (Galatians 4:4–5).

In Jesus, I am in a place of unfathomable plenty:
Since I am his child, God has made me an heir (Galatians 4:7). I am called to the riches of his glorious inheritance (Ephesians 1:18). I am not qualified on my own, the Father has qualified me to share in the inheritance of the saints (Colossians 1:12). Surely, I have a delightful inheritance (Psalm 16:6).

In Jesus, I am in a place of total satisfaction and contentment:
The Father has blessed me in the heavenly realms with every spiritual blessing in Christ (Ephesians 1:3). I have been given fullness in Christ. I am complete (Colossians 2:3,10).

In Jesus, I am in a place of everlasting freedom and victory:
I was called to take hold of eternal life (1 Timothy 6:12). I am a child of promise (Galatians 4:28). I am called to be free (Galatians 5:13). It is for freedom that Christ has set me free (Galatians 5:1). I am rescued from the present evil age (Galatians 1:4). The Father has rescued me from the domain of darkness and brought me into the kingdom of the Son he loves (Colossians 1:13). Because I have faith in Christ, I am a victorious overcomer of the world (1 John 5:4).

In Jesus, I am in a place of constant goodness:
I am rooted and established in love (Ephesians 3:17). God's power is at work within me (Ephesians 3:20). I am God's workmanship, created in Christ Jesus to do good works, which God prepared in advance for me to do (Ephesians 2:10). God works in me to will and act according to his good purpose (Philippians 2:13). Jesus chose and appointed me to go and bear much lasting fruit (John 15:5,16). Apart from Jesus, I can do nothing (John 15:5).

In Jesus, I am in a place of increasing closeness and care:
Now, in Christ Jesus, I, who was once far away, have been brought near through the blood of Christ (Ephesians 2:13). My citizenship is in heaven (Philippians 3:20). I am no longer a foreigner or an alien, but a fellow citizen with God's people and a member of God's household (Ephesians 2:12). Through Christ, I have access to the Father, through one Spirit (Ephesians 2:18).

In Jesus, I am in a place of absolute inclusion and refuge:
I am called to one hope, to one faith, to one baptism and to one God and Father of all (Ephesians 4:4–6). I have been baptized into Christ Jesus, baptized into his death (Romans 6:3). I have been crucified with Christ (Galatians 2:20). I died, and my life is now hidden with Christ, in God (Colossians 3:3). I died with Christ to the basic principles of this world (Colossians 2:20). I was buried with Christ in baptism (Romans 6:4). I have been raised in Christ through my faith in the power of God, who raised Christ from the dead (Colossians 2:12). God raised me up with Christ and seated me in the heavenly realms in Christ Jesus (Ephesians 2:6).

In Jesus, I am in a place of continual relationship with God:
I am clothed in Christ (Galatians 3:27) and included in Christ (Ephesians 1:13). I am united with the Lord (1 Corinthians 6:17). I no longer live, but Christ lives in me (Galatians 2:20). In Jesus, I am being built together to become a dwelling in which God lives by his Spirit (Ephesians 2:22). I myself am God's temple (1 Corinthians 6:19).

In Jesus, I am in a place of unshakable union with God:
God's Spirit, whom I received from God, is in me (1 Corinthians 6:19). I am one with God in Spirit (1 Corinthians 6:17). Jesus is in his Father, and I am in Christ, and he is in me (John 14:20). I am marked with a seal (Ephesians 1:13). By the deposit of the Holy Spirit, my inheritance is guaranteed (Ephesians 1:14). The anointing I received from him remains in me and teaches me about all things (1 John 2:27).

In Jesus, I am in a place of oneness in love:
I love because God first loved me, and love comes from God (1 John 4:10,7). I am strengthened with power through the Spirit in my inmost being (Ephesians 3:16). Like living stones, I am being built into a spiritual house (1 Peter 2:5). I am a part of the body of Christ (1 Corinthians 12:27).

In Jesus, I am in a place of power for life:

Grace has been given to me as Christ apportioned it (Ephesians 4:7). His grace is enough for me (2 Corinthians 2:19). In my weakness, he is my strength (2 Corinthians 2:19). I can do all things through him who gives me strength (Philippians 4:13).

In Jesus, I am in a place of life to the full:

God has made known to me the path of life, he fills me with joy in his presence, with eternal pleasures at his right hand (Psalm 16:11). The joy of the Lord is my strength (Nehemiah 8:10). Jesus came so that I may live a new life (Romans 6:4) and have life to the full (John 10:10).

In Jesus, I am in a place of transformation and increasing maturity:

God is pleased to reveal his Son in me (Galatians 1:16). In Christ, I am a new creation, the old is gone and the new has come (2 Corinthians 5:17). I am created to be like God in true righteousness and holiness (Ephesians 4:24). In all things, I am growing up into Christ who is the head (Ephesians 4:15).

In Jesus, I am in a place of divine destiny:

I am destined for glory. When Christ, who is my life, appears I will appear with him in glory (Colossians 3:4). Christ in me is the hope of glory (Colossians 1:27). God gives me the victory through my Lord Jesus Christ (1 Corinthians 15:57). In all these things, I am more than a conqueror through him who loved me (Romans 8:37).

In Jesus, I am in a place of absolute security:

Nothing in all creation will be able to separate me from the love of God that is in Christ Jesus, my Lord (Romans 8:38–39). God is for me, who can be against me? (Romans 8:31). He provides me with plenty and fills my heart with joy (Acts 14:17). God richly provides me with everything for my enjoyment (1 Timothy 6:17). Apart from God, I have no good thing (Psalm 16:2). God has assigned me my portion and my cup (Psalm 16:5). He has made my lot secure (Psalm 16:5). The boundary lines have fallen for me in pleasant places (Psalm 16:6).

In Jesus, I am in a place of experientially knowing God's constant goodness toward me:

God has plans to prosper me, not to harm me, plans to give me hope and a future (Jeremiah 29:11). I will see the goodness of God in the land of the living (Psalm 27:13). I will be like him, for I shall see him as he is (1 John 3:2). I am confident that he who began a good work in me will carry it on to completion until the day of Christ Jesus (Philippians 1:6).

CHAPTER 2

A Place of *Deep Love and Acceptance*

In love, you were chosen by God before the creation of the world (Ephesians 1:4). You are set apart, called by God's grace (Galatians 1:15), holy and blameless in God's sight (Ephesians 1:4). You are a dearly loved child of God (Ephesians 5:1). You are fully known by God (1 Corinthians 13:12) and accepted in Christ (Romans 15:7). God loves you with the same love with which he loved Jesus (John 17:23).

> **In love, you were chosen by God before the creation of the world.**
> **— Ephesians 1:4**

Understandably, our focus is often on the daily experiences of our lives shaped by the day's events and feelings. Yet there is a much bigger picture that supersedes and overwrites our daily experiences, whether we hold it in our consciousness or not.

God Almighty, the creator of heaven and earth, before he created anything, chose you. His thoughts were on you! You are part of his intentionality, his planning. You are not alive because of a set of random events or by mistake. You are chosen in him and by him, in love. You weren't chosen in utility or practicality, or because he needed or wanted you to do something for him. You were chosen in love. And not just any love — his love. The most loving, kind, trustworthy, powerful, richest, protective one ever — the one who brings good from every circumstance — that one chose you.

Your heavenly Father loved you and chose you before he created the world and all that you are experiencing today. Before any of the stuff of earth that takes your attention, focus, work, affection, and time — before any of that existed, your God, your Father, had you in his heart. Chosen. Desired. Wanted. Planned. Positioned. Loved.

God's desire for you, his thoughts about you, and his plans for you are the whole reason creation, the greatest building project in all of history, was started, completed, and exists. In his desire for sharing his trinitarian love with others, he created the universe, all people, and you, specifically. He planned, designed, and created the material universe to give you a place to experience his presence and his love. Before the existence of any of all that we see and experience, God's thoughts of you were in his heart.

We often say, "first things first." Before the creation of the world is about as "first" as you can get! Pause and let it sink into your heart that you are a first priority for God, the Father. Consider the depth of his love for you. It is truly beyond measure. You are a part of his reason for creation, so that you can be with him, in him, in love. Let the enormity of his love settle on you and remain on you as you go through your life in his world today.

Rest in the truth of his word over yourself today: in love, you were chosen by God, your heavenly Father, before the beginning of the world. Pause and take time to consider how it feels to know that you are a first priority to God.

Father, thank you for your love and your care for me personally. Thank you for your desire for me to know you as my loving Father, Abba, Papa. Thank you for your desire for me to know you closely in loving relationship through all my days and for all eternity. Thank you for giving me life and for your perfect care, love, and closeness all my days. This day, I pray for your peace beyond understanding to settle on me and to remain in my heart as I go through the events and feelings I experience. Thank you that you foresaw today and all its circumstances long before you even created the world. Thank you that you saw and chose me from the beginning. I trust you, Father, to go through this day with me, to hold me and to keep me in your perfect loving care. This day, I choose to remain in you.

In Context:
Praise be to the God and Father of our Lord Jesus Christ, who has blessed us in the heavenly realms with every spiritual blessing in Christ. For he chose us in him before the creation of the world to be holy and blameless in his sight (Ephesians 1:3–4).

You were set apart, called by God's grace. — Galatians 1:15

Not only were you chosen by God in his love (Ephesians 1:4), he set you apart from the beginning of your life on this earth and called you by his grace into relationship with him as his child. We do not always like to be set apart — called out from a crowd or group. It can make us feel separated from others, and we may feel self-conscious about the attention, particularly if the focus is on our differences, which is often what being called out is about. But with God, being set apart is distinct. When you are set apart by God, it is in his love.

In contrast to being set apart by other people, being set apart by Father is an honor. It is a testimony of his unique and unchangeable deep love for you personally. It is a function of his individual giving of life, placement, and personal attention and care, directing his thoughts toward you (Psalm 139:17). When God created Adam (Genesis 2:7), he did not do it by speaking him into existence as he did light, or the sun and moon and stars. He did it with his own hands, forming him from the dust of the ground, leaving his fingerprints on Adam and breathing his own breath into him to bring life.

God left his fingerprints on you too. He knit you together in your mother's womb (Psalm 139), giving you individual characteristics. He set you apart as uniquely created. There is no other exactly like you, and his desire is for you to be his child and to call him Father (Jeremiah 3:13). God attended to every detail of your formation, down to numbering the hairs on your head (Matthew 10:30), knowing at any time what their count is. Being set apart by God speaks of his continuous attention to every detail about your life because of his great love for you. This isn't about you as one of eight billion people on earth. This is you personally set apart in his care and his desire for good in your life.

He has been involved in every facet of your life from the beginning, and his attention remains on you and the uniqueness of your life. He knows when you sit and when you rise. He knows what you are going to say before you say it (Psalm 139:2,4). Such attention is not because of his critical scrutiny; it is because of his great love for you and his interest in every detail of your life. It is because he is committed to use everything in your life for good (Romans 8:28), no matter how difficult it seems. The Father, who chose you in love before the creation of the world, set you apart to be born at a particular time and in your unique circumstances. His place prepared for you is one of unfathomable love and care.

He called you by his grace (not by his anger, not to change you, not to correct you). By grace. Grace is undeserved favor, the unmerited or unearned love of God. We often think of being called as being appointed to a task or job in connection with our "calling" as a Christian. But being called also means that we are being summoned into a conversation or to an interaction or event, like being called in from the yard to dinner.

Can you imagine literally receiving a call from God? If your phone rang and it was God Almighty calling, wouldn't you be amazed that he, the one responsible for all of creation and life and existence knew your number and took the time to contact you? Well, he has! He set you apart and called you by his grace. The One who created you in your unique detail loves you so much that he has reached out to you in your circumstances to invite you into relationship with him as your loving Father, Abba, Papa.

Don't dismiss the individual component of this. It's not just that he desires every person on earth to be his child; his word declares that he set you apart — you personally. And he didn't just place a personal call to you once. He calls us continually into a deeper relationship with him as his child.

Meditate on the wonder of this truth about God's personal love for you, and let it settle in your inmost being. "You are set apart, called by God's grace." Reflect on how it feels to understand that God has individually set you apart in his thoughts and affection. Specifically think about how, before you trusted your life into his hands, he pursued you with love.

Father, thank you for creating me and giving me my life. Thank you that you personally attended to every detail of my life from the beginning. Thank you that you continue to care for all the details of my life. Thank you for setting me apart — for your individual attention and personal love for me. Thank you for calling me into relationship with you as my heavenly Father. Thank you for your unearned favor. Thank you that you love me just because you love me. Thank you that you are loving me right now. I choose to receive your love for me and to remain in it. Today, help me to enjoy being set apart by you and relating to you and your unique care and love for me. Thank you for the deep love you have for me in the place you have prepared for me.

In Context:
God, who set me apart from my mother's womb and called me by his grace (Galatians 1:15).

You are holy in God's sight. — Ephesians 1:4

The scriptures declare that we were chosen by God before he began the creation of the universe to be holy in his sight, in Christ. That we can be holy in God's sight is astounding.

As humans, our tendency is to focus on our own efforts and experiences of spirituality. As a result, when we read these words — holy and blameless in his sight — we regard them as something we have to do or be. That may lead us to apply our own diligent effort to grasp holiness and blamelessness, ultimately leading to many instances of falling short of the mark. This creates feelings of failure and a tendency to hide from God, not unlike Adam and Eve when they scrambled to cover their own glaringly apparent nakedness.

When Jesus died on the cross, all our sin and guilt was laid on him. It is no longer held against our account. Every sin, everything unholy, everything worthy of blame, everything we are truly guilty of, every one of our failures was dealt with by his sacrificial death. All our unholiness was atoned for. God no longer sees any of it. As far as the east is from the west, God has removed our transgressions from us (Psalm 103:12).

When God looks at a person who is united to Jesus through faith, he sees the righteousness of Christ. When you accept the sacrifice of Jesus on behalf of your sins, the perfection of Jesus covers you and is applied to your account. Jesus' purity washes over you, cleansing you and making you holy.

The word holy is defined as, "specially recognized as or declared sacred by religious use or authority; consecrated (holy ground). Dedicated or devoted to the service of God, the church, or religion (as a holy man). Saintly, godly, pious, devout (a holy life). Having a spiritually pure quality" (dictionary.com).

It is this living God who made you, set you apart to relate to him, and continues to make you holy. He himself emanates out from you to change you and the very atmosphere around you.

His holiness is a game changer. Apart from him, we are not holy. In him, we are. Recognizing this can help us to see and understand that other people are holy and blameless in God's sight as well — and help us to forgive them as Christ forgave us (Colossians 3:13). Holiness has nothing to do with us and our ability to obey God's commands or to live a pure life through our resolve and perseverance. Holiness has everything to do with the finished work of Jesus and our acceptance of his free gift for us and to us.

In Christ, you are holy, set apart for relationship with your heavenly Father. His holiness brings you into relationship with God, your heavenly Father.

God's holiness in you distinguishes you from the mundane, the everyday, the vulgar, the common, the stained, the condemned. In short, he has finished and accomplished all that you could not: redemption, forgiveness, propitiation. These are all religious terms of beauty, significance, value, and importance. The simple truth is because of Jesus' sacrifice for you and your acceptance of his sacrifice, his Spirit takes up residence in you, marking you as holy and making you holy. That makes you God's child (1 John 3:1). All of this brings you back into fullness of relationship — the original pre-fall desired closeness of walking with God in the garden in the cool of the evening. Our acceptance of Christ and his sacrifice brings us into the place he has prepared for us — a place of deep love and acceptance.

You are set apart, consecrated, forgiven, blessed, and loved as a dear child of God.

Meditate on the vast beauty of this truth about yourself: You are holy in God's sight. Take time to sit in relief from guilt and shame and understand the wonder of being welcomed into relationship with God.

Father, thank you for your holiness and for offering it for me and to me. Thank you that you applied Jesus' holiness to me when I accepted him as my savior and my Lord. Thank you that when you look upon me, you see his holiness, perfection, and beauty, and you attribute it to me. God, you are so generous! Father, your love and kindness are astounding. Let me rest in your presence today as we walk through the gardens of my life together. I pray that I will live my life in a way that reflects your great love.

In Context:
Praise be to the God and Father of our Lord Jesus Christ, who has blessed us in the heavenly realms with every spiritual blessing in Christ.

For he chose us in him before the creation of the world to be holy and blameless in his sight (Ephesians 1:3–4).

You are blameless in God's sight. — Ephesians 1:4

Lifting this short phrase out of the context of the longer scripture likely declares a truth that your mind finds almost too good to be true. You are all too aware of your sins and shortcomings. Blameless? You? What? After all the times you have both knowingly and unknowingly sinned? After all the poor choices you have made across time, and will, no doubt, continue to make despite your best intentions and efforts?

Let's look at this statement in a more inclusive context: "Praise be to the God and Father of our Lord Jesus Christ, who has blessed us in the heavenly realms with every spiritual blessing in Christ. For he chose us in him before the creation of the world to be holy and blameless in his sight (Ephesians 1:3–4)."

Blameless is defined as free from deserving blame; guiltless (dictionary.com). That is amazing news! When you are in Jesus, God does not blame you for the wrong you have done. He fully forgives you, and you are guiltless.

Though things may be a lot "better" in terms of the frequency and magnitude of our poor choices and sins than before coming to Christ, we know that we are still far from perfect, and we fall into sin. We are painfully aware that although we are decreasing in sinfulness over time, we are likely to continue to sin until Jesus returns or we die and go to be with him.

The scriptures teach us that the death of Christ made atonement for your every sin — past, present, and future. They're already paid for. When Jesus died for your sins, all of them were in your future! When you personally accept his sacrifice on your behalf and apply his blood, death, and resurrection to your life, you are fully forgiven. Because you are in Christ, to God you appear without wrinkle, spot, or blemish (Colossians 1:22). This has nothing to do with your own efforts toward right living; it is not by your own power or resolve, but by grace.

There is no better news. What you are completely and utterly unable to do — to make full payment for a single sin, let alone a lifetime of sins — Jesus has already done on your behalf and credited it to your account. He has given you his righteousness in exchange for your sins, leaving you blameless, though you fully deserve blame.

God the Father knew from before the beginning of time that all people, his pinnacle of creation, would eventually and frequently exercise their free will to choose to do things their way instead of his perfect way. He knew that each person would exercise their will to rebel against God.

In his unfathomable love, God chose to provide the only acceptable sacrifice — his Son, God himself, a perfect, sinless one who walked closely with the Father and lived in total unity and harmony with him. His once-and-for-all sacrifice was enough to fully eradicate your every sin. His blood can take on all sins of all people for all time, and fully redeem you, setting you free from guilt, condemnation, and blame. There is a great chasm between the judgment and sentence you know you fully deserve and that which you receive: blamelessness. The place that Jesus has prepared for you is truly a place of deep love and acceptance.

Pause and reflect deeply on this biblical truth about yourself today: In Christ, I am blameless. Thank God for forgiving you from blame.

Thank you, Jesus, for your sacrifice for me. It cost you everything so that your perfect life and sacrifice could be applied on my behalf to make me blameless and allow me access to relationship with you and your heavenly Father. You truly are the Way — the way to the Father, the way to forgiveness, the way to salvation, and the way to life to the full. Your love is boundless and unfathomable. I gratefully receive your love and your sacrifice on my behalf. Thank you for the opportunity to live a new life of love and relationship in you.

In Context:
For he chose us in him before the creation of the world to be holy and blameless in his sight. In love, he predestined us for adoption to sonship through Jesus Christ in accordance with his pleasure and will — to the praise of his glorious grace, which he has freely given us in the One he loves (Ephesians 1:4–6).

You are a dearly loved child of God. — Ephesians 5:1

God is so filled with love that in portraying his personality, virtue, and nature, John, known as the disciple Jesus loved, described God in a single word: love (1 John 4:8). That means you a dearly loved child of love — like father, like child. You can experience (not just know about intellectually or understand some components of his love with your mind) the high and wide, long, and deep (Ephesians 3:18) love of God — the love that nothing can separate you from (Romans 8:39). This love is unending, boundless, and extravagant. It is the love that would send Jesus to earth to live among you and to sacrificially lay down his perfect loving life of relationship to the Father for you. His perfection covers and permeates you, clearing the way for you to enter into fullness of relationship with his Father, and your heavenly Father — a place of deep love and acceptance that settles the longing of your heart to be loved, chosen, desired, wanted, valued. This is true for no reason other than the fact that you are a child of God, not because of what you do or don't do.

Paul's prayer for the Ephesians (Ephesians 3:14–19) was that the eyes of their hearts would be open to intimately know the vastness of God's love. It is God's Spirit that gives you the ability to know and receive this (Romans 5:5). Paul prayed that you could know how high and long and wide and deep the love of God for you is.

For many years, I thought that was simply Paul being eloquent in talking about the dimensions of God's love. However, after reflectively praying his prayer for the Ephesians over myself for about thirty consecutive days, I was in an airplane headed home after a conference, flying at about 30,000 feet altitude and praying this prayer over myself again. In that context, I knew that height is what is above you and depth is what is below you. The breadth and width are self-explanatory. But in thinking about height and depth and breadth and width simultaneously at 30,000 feet above the earth, it was easy for me to see God's love as three dimensional — filling all of existence and extending infinitely in all directions. This led me to experientially know that God's love is to your left and right, in front of you and behind you, above you and below you all of the time, no matter where you are — and that places you directly in the center of God's love!

Truly, you are a dearly loved child of God. Declare that truth over yourself this day! Specifically reflect on the many ways that you have personally experienced the love of God in your life.

Father, God who is so full of love that you are love, thank you for the length and breadth and height and depth of your love for me. Thank you for placing me directly in the center of your love, no matter where I am. Thank you that nothing can separate me from your love for me in Christ. Thank you that I am your dearly loved child. I pray that these realities will grow in my own heart and settle the issues, questions, doubts, fears, and shame that I have harbored in my heart for too long. Thank you that when you look at me, you look at me with the same love that you loved Jesus with. Thank you that your love is inexhaustible, continuous, and toward me always. Thank you that you are loving me right now. I choose to receive your love, and to rest in your love. Thank you that I can freely receive your love. Give me the grace and perseverance to give your abundant love to others that I interact with today. Your love is my delight, Father. Thank you that I am your dearly loved child.

In Context:
Be imitators of God, therefore, as dearly loved children and live a life of love, just as Christ loved us and gave himself up for us as a fragrant offering and sacrifice to God (Ephesians 5:1–2).

You are fully known by God. — 1 Corinthians 13:12

Psalm 139 declares, "You have searched me, Lord, and you know me. You know when I sit and when I rise; you perceive my thoughts from afar. You discern my going out and my lying down; you are familiar with all my ways. Before a word is on my tongue you, Lord, know it completely. ... For you created my inmost being; you knit me together in my mother's womb. ... Your eyes saw my unformed body; all the days ordained for me were written in your book before one of them came to be" (Psalm 139:1–4,13,16). God knows the number of hairs on your head (Matthew 10:30; Luke 12:7).

Even before you were born, God knew all the details about you and your life: when and where you would be born (Psalm 139:16), your going out and your coming in (Psalm 121:7), even your thoughts. He knows your words before you speak them, whether you plan them or speak them thoughtlessly. God knows all about you — right this second, later today, tomorrow, and forever more. This is not invasive surveillance; it is his incredible and pure love, intense and passionate. He is deeply interested in you personally. He cares enough to notice all of this — and to love you in the middle of all of it.

Some people I have spoken with find this level of God's knowledge about them alarming, triggering fear or guilt, hiding, or looking for figurative fig leaves to cover their sinfulness, shortcomings, or failures. But God is love, and love is patient, kind, keeps no record of wrongs, rejoices with the truth, always protects, always trusts, always hopes, always perseveres. Love does not envy or boast; it is not proud, rude, self-seeking, or easily angered. Love never fails (1 Corinthians 13:4–8).

Nothing you do surprises God or leaves him disillusioned with you. The astounding thing about God and his relationship with you is that though he knows everything about you, he fully loves you and accepts you, in Christ. Romans 8 declares that there is nothing that can separate you from his love. There is no deal breaker.

You are fully known by God, and at the same time you are set apart (Galatians 1:15), chosen, blameless, and holy (Ephesians 1:4), regardless of what God knows about you. You are fully known and fully accepted (Romans 15:7).

Everything that you know about yourself pales in comparison. He knows you better than you know yourself! Every self-critical thought you have about yourself stands in contrast to your Father's boundless love, forgiveness, and care for you. Whose report do you choose to believe? His (the all-knowing, all-loving, totally kind one), or yours? As you come to believe what your Papa feels toward you — fully knowing you — it transforms your understanding of who you are in him and to him. Your values change and you begin to think of yourself — and others — less critically and more lovingly. Truly, the place that Jesus prepared for us is a place of deep love and acceptance.

Meditate on this truth: I am fully known by God (1 Corinthians 13:12). Consider the relief that comes from understanding that you do not need to conceal anything from God. He already knows.

Father, thank you that even though you know me better than I know myself, you also love me more than I love myself! Thank you that what you know of me is surpassed by your loving me. Thank you that though you know everything about me, there is nothing that can separate me from your love for me. Father, help me to rest in the assurance of your love for me. Help me to be open with you, You already know everything about me anyhow, so let me be real with you. Thank you that as I approach you, in Christ, that his perfection overwrites all of my imperfection, and that your love for me is the same as your love for him. Thank you that as I confess my sins to you that you are faithful to forgive and cleanse me from all unrighteousness. I pray that knowing the depth of your love for me will transform me to live more intimately with you and to reflect your character in my life.

In Context:
Now we see but a poor reflection as in a mirror; then we shall see face to face. Now I know in part, then I shall know fully, even as I am fully known (1 Corinthians 13:12).

You are accepted in Christ. — Romans 15:7

Christ has accepted you. Acceptance stands in contrast to rejection. To be accepted is to be brought into enrollment or membership. Typically, when you apply to something (such as applying to graduate school or a job), it requires a listing and documentation of your qualifications. In stark contrast, in Christ, you are accepted, but not on your own merit (Colossians 1:12). The Father qualified you and Jesus accepted you.

Frequently when people think about their own qualifications and limitations, they experience imposter syndrome. That is, they feel that they don't really belong in a particular group or position or to be honored. They think, "If only people knew the truth, I'd be rejected, ridiculed, despised." But that's not what God's word says about you. 1 Corinthians 13:12 tells you that you are fully known, and Romans 15:7 says you are accepted.

Fully known and accepted: Those two phrases seldom go together in any context of our lives, other than our relationship with our loving God. Part of the beauty of being God's beloved child is that he fully knows and fully accepts you. Nothing you do changes those facts.

In some ways, acceptance and approval are similar, yet they are distinct in other ways. I can accept things I do not approve. There are still things that will be transformed as you grow in God's unending and unconditional love. There will be changes by his mercy and grace and the power of his Spirit, changes he brings in us through your own humility and weakness, and through depending on him. That never changes his acceptance of you.

Allow the juxtaposition of being fully known and fully accepted to bring rest and peace to your soul. God knows all your actions, emotions, and thoughts. He knows every detail that you may strive to keep hidden from others out of fear of rejection or ridicule. One of the primary tactics of the accuser of the brethren is to whisper into your mind, "If they knew, they'd reject you. If God knew, he'd reject you." These thoughts lead to a prison of fear, isolation, self-doubt, shame, and guilt. But scriptural truth brings great freedom, rest, hope, and joy.

Thoughtfully speak this truth over yourself today: I am accepted in Christ! Meditate on how it feels to be fully known and accepted at the same time.

Jesus, thank you for accepting me. Thank you that my acceptance has nothing to do with my own merit or qualifications. Thank you that while I was dead in my sins, you died for me, and you have accepted me. Thank you for your sacrifice on my behalf. Thank you that though you know everything about me, your love for me is endless. Thank you that nothing can separate me from the love of God that is in Christ Jesus.

In Context:
Accept one another, then, just as Christ accepted you,
in order to bring praise to God (Romans 15:7).

God loves you with the same love with which he loved Jesus.
— John 17:23

The Passion Translation of the Bible renders a portion of Jesus' prayer to the Father this way: "You live fully in me and now I live fully in them so that they will experience perfect unity, and that the world will be convinced that you have sent me, for they will see that you love each one of them with the same passionate love that you have for me" (John 17:23).

The New American Standard Bible and the NIV say, "you sent me … and loved them even as you have loved me."

We don't often focus on the meaning of the word *as*. It is such a small word, yet laden with meaning. *As* means "in the same manner, or in the same way, or to the same degree." *As* is used in comparisons to refer to the degree or extent of something or to emphasize an amount. It is also used to indicate by comparison the way that something happens or is done: "You can do as you wish."

When Jesus says that the Father loves you "even as you have loved me" it means in exactly the same way — even as much as, even to the same amount or degree. Jesus himself declared that the Father has loved each one of us (including you and me) as much as he loves Jesus and with exactly the same love, in the same manner, and to the same amount or degree.

In the gospel of John, Jesus said that he has revealed the Father (17:6) and that he will continue to reveal the Father (17:26). "I know you and will continue to make you known in order that the love you have for me may be in them and that I myself may be in them." Wow.

Can you dare to believe that? Can your heart receive the experiential truth of Jesus' words? The love that the Father has for Jesus is in you and me.

The challenge for us to believe this is that as we compare ourselves to Jesus, we see quite a gap. Clearly, we are not there yet, and we doubt we will ever be. We are in the process of being transformed to be like him, and that transformation will not be completed until we see him face-to-face. We are acutely aware of our shortcomings and focus on that gap. Yet in Jesus' own words, the Father loves you as he loves Jesus. There is no gap in God's love for you.

God is love. His love has no "off" switch and there is no dimmer switch. He is always full-on loving.

As believers in Jesus, we can believe that the Father applies the righteousness of Christ to us. Why is it more of a challenge to our hearts to believe that he appropriates the same love, in exactly the same manner to us that he does to Jesus?

Meditate on this scriptural truth and remind yourself of it often: The Father loves me just as he loves Jesus. Consider the richness of God's love that he directs to you continually: it is the same love that he loves Jesus with.

Lord, we pray for your Spirit of wisdom and revelation so that we can know you better in our inmost being. Give us the ability to experience your boundless love that is flowing to us right now. Father, as we meditate on the vastness of your love — the breadth, the length, the height, the depth of it — help us to know that we are always in the center of your love. Thank you that you are loving me right now. I choose to believe that you love me as you love Jesus and receive the continuous flow of your love for me. I pray that today, I would rest in your love.

In Context:
I in them and you in me — so that they may be brought to complete unity. Then the world will know that you sent me and have loved them even as you have loved me (John 17:23).

A Place of Deep Love and Acceptance: Summary and Application

In love, you were chosen by God before the creation of the world (Ephesians 1:4). You are set apart, called by God's grace (Galatians 1:15), holy and blameless in God's sight (Ephesians 1:4). You are a dearly loved child of God (Ephesians 5:1). You are fully known by God (1 Corinthians 13:12) and accepted in Christ (Romans 15:7). God loves you with the same love with which he loved Jesus (John 17:23).

Taken together, these eight scriptural truths paint the picture of the deepest love and most loving acceptance imaginable. Truly, the words of these scriptures establish that you are doing even better than you know. They clearly show the premeditated planning, longing, and desire God has always had in his heart — his fathomless love for you individually and personally. His boundless investment in creating you and placing you in the exact place he planned and created for you from before the beginning of time. How he chose you and did not hold back anything in order to set you apart and call you into relationship with him. He sent Jesus, his Son, to live among people on earth to reveal the nature of God to you, which at its core is all about his passionate and lavish love. In love, he poured out his unearned favor and grace on you by providing Jesus as a sacrifice for your sin. As you personally accept the sacrifice of Jesus on your behalf, you become holy, set apart, and blameless in God's sight. Jesus, the Way, provided as the only way for us to enter into the Father's presence, and to be his dearly loved child. Loved with the same love that he loves Jesus with, loving you in the same manner and to the same degree as he loves Jesus. Fully known and fully accepted as a dearly loved child of God.

The place that Jesus has prepared for you, by saying what the Father was saying and doing what he saw him doing, is most assuredly a place of deep love and acceptance. As the Holy Spirit pours the love of God into your heart (Romans 5:5), invite him to transform not only your understanding of the depth of God's love for you, but for you to experience it in deeply personal ways. Ask him to help you to know God's love for you in ways that banish the thoughts and fears that you have harbored about your relationship with God. Let the enormity, the lavishness, the consistency, and the strength of his love flood your inmost being until you know, deep in your core, that you are a dearly loved child of God, for that is who you are (Ephesians 5:1). This place of deep love and acceptance is where you were created to live, and move, and have your being. You were made for this place — this place prepared for you — to reside there with the Father, Son, and Holy Spirit and to enjoy the freedoms and fullness of life in their presence.

Prayerfully and joyfully declare these scriptural truths about the place God has prepared for you — a place of deep and love and acceptance:

- In love, I was chosen by God before the creation of the world.
- I am set apart.
- I am called by God's grace.
- I am holy and blameless in God's sight.

- I am a dearly loved child of God.
- I am fully known by God.
- I am accepted in Christ.
- God loves me with the same love with which he loved Jesus.
- I am in a place of deep love and acceptance.

Notes

CHAPTER 3

A Place of *Extravagant Belonging*

You are not your own (1 Corinthians 6:19). You belong with and to Jesus (Romans 7:4). You were bought at a price (1 Corinthians 6:19). God made you alive with Christ even when you were dead in your sins (Ephesians 2:5).

You are not your own. — 1 Corinthians 6:19

You are not your own because you are not on your own. The Holy Spirit, the Spirit of the Father (Matthew 10:20) and the Spirit of Jesus (Galatians 6:4), dwells within you (Ephesians 2:22). He has taken up residence in you; he's not just a casual visitor dropping by for an occasional brief stay. He never leaves or forsakes you. He does not leave you on your own (Matthew 28:20) to care for yourself as an orphan (John 14:10). Though we know that some of Jesus' closest disciples had parents, when he spoke to them about going to prepare a place for them, he said that he would return to them and would not leave them as orphans, or in the same condition as orphans.

An orphan is a person who has experienced the death of one, or usually, both parents, and is therefore deprived of their care, provision, protection, teaching, vigilance, and relationship. Orphans are typically disadvantaged in comparison to their peers, and in many of the details of their lives, orphans need to fend for themselves. Being "orphan minded" refers to having the default mindset that it is necessary to care for yourself, or to "look out for number one," because no one else can be trusted to have your best interest at heart. Sometimes called "orphan spirited," this mindset connotes a belief that it is only one's self-sufficiency and effort that brings what is needed for life and success. In simple terms, it is idolatry to believe that we are more trustworthy in caring for ourselves than God is. Jesus did not leave us as orphans.

In contrast, God has said in Hebrews 13:5, "Never will I leave you; never will I forsake you." In his last words before ascending to be with the Father, Jesus said to his disciples, "surely I am with you always, to the very end of the age" (Matthew 28:20). In John chapter 14 (verses 16–17), Jesus said, "And I will ask the Father, and he will give you another advocate to help you and be with you forever — the Spirit of truth."

Clearly, in God, we are not left as orphans to care for ourselves. Surely, he is with us always. The reality is that your body is a temple of the Holy Spirit (1 Corinthians 6:19). Your body is not just "your house." You have a housemate of unfathomable importance. Your body is the home of God himself.

Jesus declared that he is in the Father, and you are in Jesus and Jesus is in you (John 14:20). We are filled with God and immersed in God. Filled from within and included in and surrounded on the outside. This is a place of extravagant belonging!

Consider the many ways you make provisions or accommodations for your housemates and family members, how you treat your home as shared space and arrange for those you live with to have full access and management of their spaces within the house. With that understanding, how much more should each of us be conscious of welcoming the Holy Spirit to have ownership of his temple — ourselves!

Think about the various things you attend to in your physical living spaces before guests come over. You pick up the clutter, clean, prepare, and arrange. Sometimes, before a prolonged visit, you might repair or renovate a space. To welcome others to your home, you are mindful of offering hospitality: flowers, food, and most importantly, attention and focused conversation. There is time together and planned activities. Have you asked your co-resident dweller — the Holy Spirit of God — whether there are things you could fix up or attend to in order to make his living arrangements more comfortable or accessible to him? I suggest taking a moment or two to ask him about that.

Even when you are physically alone, the Holy Spirit is abiding in you. And he desires you to abide in him. That means to welcome his presence, to attend and converse. You don't want to ignore him or be oblivious to his presence, and you certainly don't want to offend him or behave in a manner hurtful to him. You are not your own because you are (thankfully) not on your own. The Spirit of the living God is living in you.

Consider what would happen if a wealthy king moved into a small, humble, ramshackle house down the block from you. What does he see in that place? No matter what its condition, it becomes much more valuable because he has moved in. It would be more important than places that claim, "George Washington slept here" or "a famous movie was filmed here." Think of your great value being the residence of the Spirit of the living God.

The appraised value of an item may be an expert's estimation of worth, but the true value is determined not by the appraisal, but by what a purchaser is willing to pay. Sometimes in sellers' markets, buyers are willing to pay well beyond the appraised value.

Do you recognize the price that God, our Father, paid for you? The price he paid for you was nothing less than the sacrifice of his beloved, perfect Son. His gruesome torture and death on a cross to redeem you from sin and death and to restore you to relationship with him. You are of inestimable value because God himself paid a ransom so great that no one could place a monetary value on it — priceless. He paid the ultimate price for you and now dwells in you.

Quietly consider this biblical truth about yourself: I am not my own. Meditate on the significance of having ongoing relationship with the God of the universe and having his Spirit abiding in you. How does knowing that you are not on your own change your assessment of a challenge you are currently facing?

Father, thank you for your great love for me, for your grace, and for your mercy. Thank you for sending Jesus to redeem me, and for the presence of your Holy Spirit dwelling in me. I pray for increased awareness of the presence of your Spirit in me at all times. I invite you to transform me to make me a more comfortable and welcoming habitation for your Spirit. I pray that you will fill me with your joy as I experience your presence dwelling in me, and that your love will permeate all that I do and say. I choose to honor you with my body and my life.

> **In Context:**
> Do you not know that your bodies are temples of the
> Holy Spirit, who is in you, whom you have received from God?
> You are not your own; you were bought at a price. Therefore,
> honor God with your bodies (1 Corinthians 6:19–20).

You belong with and to Jesus. — Romans 7:4

You have been chosen, fully known, and paid for. The transaction is wholly completed. It is finished. You belong with and to Jesus — out of love and for freedom (Galatians 5:1). Freedom from sin and death, from rejection, from orphan-hearted fending for yourself. You are redeemed from captivity to sin. In Christ. Home. This is where you belong. This is what you were created for!

The most valuable one ever, the King of Kings, the Holy One of God, gave all of himself in exchange for you. That makes you highly valued and prized. You are well-cared for by the good shepherd, the carpenter, creator, builder, healer, and rabbi. The glorious resurrected One whose name is above all names. The One who will be worshipped by all for all eternity. You belong with and to him! In this context, belonging signifies more than common ownership. You belong in the sense that you are welcomed, loved, and highly valued. And, because Jesus has made himself available to you and has given his all for you, the belonging is mutual. You belong to him and he has fully given himself to you.

He is in the Father, and you are in him, and he is in you (John 14:20). You are greatly beloved. Jesus knows where you are. You are not set aside. You are in a safe place — the safest place ever imagined and created. A place of extravagant belonging. You are rejoiced over with singing (Zephaniah 3:17) and smiled upon. You bring joy to the one who paid an unfathomable price for you, your savior, the eternal Son of God.

Just think of the first two words of this truth — you belong. Not to an organization or to a church or a club, you belong with and to Jesus Christ and to the body of Christ. You are "a member" in him. He is more aware of you than you are of the parts of your own body, and he cares for you in ways that exceed comprehension. He knows when you rise up and when you sit down. He has numbered the hairs on your head. He knows every thought you have. He cares so intensely for you that he truly knows everything about you. The triune God of the universe — Father, Son, and Spirit indwells you.

Who you do belong to has implications for who and what you don't belong to — to sin, to death, addiction, abandonment, rejection. You don't belong to debt, money, or your possessions. You don't belong to slavery, to work, or the circumstances of life. You belong with Christ.

Quietly reflect on the implications of this truth: I belong with and to Jesus, a place of extravagant belonging.

Jesus, thank you that I belong with and to you. I willingly and joyfully give over every bit of ownership of every aspect of my life — body, mind, soul, spirit, time, thoughts, behavior. You are the rightful and righteous owner of all of me and everything about me. You alone are fully trustworthy to bring goodness to every aspect of my life. I invite you to continue to work all things in my life for good. Thank you for your love flowing into me right now, and that your love changes everything. I pray that the fruit of your love in my life will grow, increase, and last.

In Context:
So, my brothers and sisters, you also died to the law through the body of Christ, that you might belong to another, to him who was raised from the dead, in order that we might bear fruit for God (Romans 7:4).

You were bought at a price. — 1 Corinthians 6:20

I am often amazed by what collectors will pay for sports memorabilia, artwork, automobiles, stamps, historic artifacts, or properties. Some of the prices are exorbitant. Millions of dollars for single items — baseball cards, paintings, stamps, coins, cars, toys, technology, books, guitars. Even the most unfathomable price paid for any of these valued items only command such prices because they are considered worth it by someone, and these prices pale in comparison to the price paid for you. Jesus — the perfect sinless one — suffered and died by a horrible unjust execution that your sin and rebellion deserves. He did it for you. He exchanged his perfection for your sin. He valued you that much. The highest price ever paid was paid for you.

It is not logical. Not even when we place it in mere human dealings. Can you imagine the unevenness of the trade if the championship Chicago Bulls had traded Michael Jordan for you? Ridiculous. Can you imagine if a good Samaritan accidentally died while trying to rescue you? You would be overwhelmed with the cost of their sacrifice. Yet, Jesus, fully knowing the unevenness and the full extent of the implications of "the trade," came to earth and intentionally lived for thirty-plus years as a sinless human, walking with his face like flint toward the substitutionary and fully intentional exchange of his life for yours.

This is the perfect one — the Son of God, who lived so intimately attuned to his heavenly Father that he never sinned. He only said what he heard his Father saying, and only did what he saw him doing. The miracle-producing, healing, feeding, teaching messiah. Him. For you. Intentionally. Lovingly. Fully knowing the cost. Unfathomable.

Your value to God is that great. His love for you is that high and deep and wide and long — that you are always in the center of it — and nothing can ever separate you from it. How would you even begin to appraise the value? The cost? You were bought at a price. The fact that scripture leaves it open like that is noteworthy. The Apostle Paul could not begin to declare the value; he just leaves it hanging. There is nothing of greater value to God than you.

In a time of rapid change and uncertainty, take time to meditate on and worship God for his unchangeable, timeless character, and rejoice in the vastness and constancy of his love for us. You are priceless to him. Truly, he has prepared for you a place of extravagant belonging. Meditate on this truth: I was bought at a price. Consider the value of the exchange that God made for you and how that reflects the extravagance of his love for you.

God of all creation — you who are perfect, full of goodness, light, life, and love — thank you for choosing me and saving me out of my separation from you and my sin by sacrificing Jesus on my behalf. You knew the cost to you from before the beginning of creation, yet you chose to create me, to give me life, and to make yourself known to me. You chose to redeem me through the sacrifice of Jesus, and to make me your child, marking me with the seal of your Spirit. Thank you. There is nothing I can say to acknowledge the vastness of your love or your sacrifice for me. I choose to worship you and live the fullness of my life in relationship to you. Increase my closeness to you. Your closeness is total. Bring me nearer to you continually. I desire to be more aware of the place I hold in your heart.

In Context:
Do you not know that your bodies are the temples of the Holy Spirit, who is in you, whom you have received from God? You are not your own; you were bought at a price. Therefore, honor God with your bodies (1 Corinthians 6:19–20).

> **God made you alive with Christ even when you were dead in your sins.** — Ephesians 2:5

It all began with God, who is love. He initiated what is impossible with us, and he did it because of his boundless, unstoppable love. He did it all in love. He continues to relate to you in love.

He gives you the gift of life. In the same way that his power resurrected Jesus after taking on your sin and death, God made you alive in Christ. By bringing you into unity (oneness) with Christ, your sin, the wages of your sin, and your death are eradicated. You are reconciled, justified, atoned for, resurrected. Since you are alive in Christ, you are not a dead person stumbling through a life of futility and drudgery. No. You're a child of the living God invited into the loving eternal relationship of the Trinity.

Nothing can separate you from the love of Christ (Romans 8:39) because you are one with him by virtue of him taking up residence in you. Christ in you, your hope of glory. You don't have to clean up the mess and "get right" with God before he will relate to you. No! He pursues you and comes to you in the midst of your fallenness because of his great love and his rich mercy. You have an invitation into an ever-deepening relationship. You are desired, pursued, chosen, accepted, loved, and cared for. You are never abandoned. You are fully welcomed into this place of extravagant belonging.

Now that you are alive in him, he calls you into profound knowing — intimacy.

In a parable to describe the vast love of the Father (Luke 15:11–31), Jesus says when a wandering son came to his senses and returned to his loving father, the father had to celebrate (compelled by love) "because this brother of yours was dead and is alive again. He was lost and is found." Found. Longed for. Searched for. Pursued. Located. Returned. Enlivened. Celebrated. That is great love and rich mercy. It is that love and mercy that makes you alive in Christ and doesn't depend on you or the impossibility of your attaining perfection. From death (your wages, the consequences due to you for your choices) to life (his gift, his loving power, the only source of life).

Meditate on this truth: God made me alive in Christ, even when I was dead in my sins. This is a place of extravagant belonging.

Father, I choose to celebrate your great love for me with you. I choose to enter into the feast of love going on in the place that you have prepared for me. I choose to experience each day as your child, and to live in awareness of your presence in me and your love flowing into me. Thank you for the consistent intensity of your love for me. I choose to freely receive your love, and to freely give it to others. Father, I pray that you will make me a more effective conduit of your love.

In Context:
But because of his great love for us, God, who is rich in mercy, made us alive with Christ even when we were dead in transgressions — it is by grace you have been saved. And God raised us up with Christ and seated us with him in the heavenly realms in Christ Jesus, in order that in the coming ages he might show the incomparable riches of his grace, expressed in his kindness to us in Christ Jesus. For it is by grace you have been saved, through faith — and this is not from yourselves, it is the gift of God — not by works, so that no one can boast (Ephesians 2:4–9).

A Place of Extravagant Belonging: Summary and Application

You are not your own (1 Corinthians 6:19). You belong with and to Jesus (Romans 7:4). You were bought at a price (1 Corinthians 6:19). God made you alive with Christ even when you were dead in your sins (Ephesians 2:5).

The verses shared in this chapter build on the foundation established in chapter 2. In Jesus, you are in a place of deep love and acceptance. When we personally receive his profound love and acceptance and the sacrifice that he made on our behalf, we are brought into a place of extravagant belonging. The extreme and continual love of God for you personally keeps you from being on your own. His love for you compelled him to pursue you and redeem you and reclaim you as his own. Because of the extravagant price that Jesus paid to redeem you from the spiritual death that your choices rightly earned you and to bring you back into relationship with God as his beloved child, you belong to God. As his beloved child, you belong with him. In his presence. Unreservedly loved. Highly favored. Delighted in. Sung over. Though we are aware of our own sinfulness, faults, and failures, the once-and-for-all sacrifice of Jesus on our behalf means that we do belong. In Jesus, we are home. When we come into Christ, he is literally our residence, dwelling, abode, habitation. Our place in him gives us position, station, standing, rank, class as a deeply loved child of God. There is no more sure place of belonging.

Whenever the enemy of your soul would cause you to think that you don't belong with, in, or to Jesus, it is a lie in contrast to the declared truths of God's holy word. Reject the lying accusation that you don't belong — an accusation designed to kill, steal, and destroy the fullness of life that Jesus purchased for you. Indeed, you do belong. See yourself as belonging and every aspect of your being as alive with Christ. Ask the Holy Spirit to richly pour God's love into your inmost being as you meditate on and declare these truths of scripture over yourself, your life, and position in Jesus.

> **All of creation bears the signature of God. As his child, you bear his image and his fingerprints. Ask God to help you to walk through this life as his image bearer. Ask him to settle the following truths in your inmost being:**

- I am not my own.
- I belong with and to Jesus.
- I was bought at a price.
- God made me alive with Christ, even when I was dead in my sin.
- I am in a place of extravagant belonging.

Notes

CHAPTER 4

A Place of *Everlasting Purpose*

You were once in darkness, but now you are light in the Lord (Ephesians 5:8). You are a chosen person, part of a royal priesthood, a holy nation, a people belonging to God, called out of darkness into his wonderful light (1 Peter 2:9). You are a child of the light and of the day. You do not belong to the night or to darkness (1 Thessalonians 5:5). You are holy, you share in a heavenly calling (Hebrews 3:1).

> **You were once in darkness, but now you are light in the Lord. — Ephesians 5:8**

Light and darkness are distinctly different from one another. Light overcomes darkness and exposes unseen things as they are. Darkness shields the unknown — obstacles and dangers. In the Lord, you are not just in the Light, you are light. The light is not yours, you become light by being a conveyor of the Light of the World. You can overcome darkness by living in the light of Jesus, the Light of the World, living as a child of the light.

There is a greater light than all of us: God. Jesus proclaimed that if you follow him, you will never walk in darkness, but will have the light of life (John 8:12). The fruit of the light is goodness, righteousness, and truth. When you live in these fruits, it can bring enlightenment to others around you who do not live as children of the Light.

On the earth, every twenty-four-hour period includes both darkness and light; the light dispels darkness. The unknown, cloaked in darkness, brings fear to people. Jesus, the Light of the World, takes away the fear of eternal estrangement from God. He came to reveal the Father — to shine light on his character and love. As a Christian, "little Christ," you can do the same. As you mature in Christ and have more and more fruit of his Spirit, you reflect what life in relationship to God is like. You become the light of the world; a city set upon a hill (Matthew 5:14). Just as a lighthouse lights the way for those in a sea of darkness to safely make it to solid ground, you light the way to relationship with God. You are not stuck in the darkness of the blind leading the blind and falling into pits (Matthew 5:14).

In Christ, you are light. Just as the Father has rescued you from the kingdom of darkness and brought you to the kingdom of the Son he loves (Colossians 1:13), your life as a child of the Light can help to lead others to Christ and into fullness of relationship with God. His presence, character, and fruit in you and through you partners with the Spirit of God to extend his kingdom.

Meditate on the following verses. Ask the Lord for his creativity in how you can show his light through your life circumstances and relationships.

John 8:12 — When Jesus spoke again to the people, he said, "I am the light of the world. Whoever follows me will never walk in darkness, but will have the light of life."

John 9:4–5 — "As long as it is day, we must do the works of him who sent me. Night is coming, when no one can work. While I am in the world, I am the light of the world."

Matthew 5:14–16 — "You are the light of the world. A town built on a hill cannot be hidden. Neither do people light a lamp and put it under a bowl. Instead, they put it on its stand, and it gives light to everyone in the house. In the same way, let your light shine before others, that they may see your good deeds and glorify your Father in heaven."

Jesus, thank you that you are the light of the world. Thank you for giving me the light of life and for allowing your light to shine through me to overcome darkness around me. Thank you that darkness cannot overcome your light. I pray that you will continue to enlighten me and that each day I would increase in the clarity and brightness of your light shining through me. I pray for your Spirit of wisdom to lead me as I go through each day. Thank you for giving me everlasting purpose in you to bring light into the darkness. Make clear to me where and how to direct your light and give me grace to see the fruit of your light coming through me as I depend on you.

In Context:
For you were once darkness, but now you are light in the Lord. Live as children of light (for the fruit of the light consists in all goodness, righteousness and truth) and find out what pleases the Lord. Have nothing to do with the fruitless deeds of darkness, but rather expose them (Ephesians 5:8–11).

You are a chosen person, part of a royal priesthood, a holy nation, a people belonging to God, called out of darkness into his wonderful light. — 1 Peter 2:9

The scriptures declare that you are chosen in love (Ephesians 1:4), a citizen of heaven, a holy nation (Philippians 3:20), called out of darkness (Ephesians 5:8), belonging to God (1 Corinthians 6:19; Romans 7:4; Ephesians 1:4).

Jesus is said to be "in the order of Melchizedek," meaning that he is both a priest and a king (see Psalm 110:4 and various verses in Hebrews chapters 5–7). For the first time after his resurrection, Jesus called his followers, who were now children of his Father, "brothers" (John 20:17). Therefore, we are siblings of the priest-king. We are not qualified by the law but chosen and called by God, belonging to him. We don't need a mediator, besides Christ, to enter in and have access to the Father (Ephesians 2:18), living as his lavishly loved children.

God's desire was for an entire nation (not using geopolitical designations like USA), but for a family-nation of people — the body of Christ — to belong with and to God, in his wonderful light, receiving revelation of his love for us. God is bringing further revelation of his calling and pursuing us across time, space, contexts, and events of our lives as he makes us his own dearly loved children (1 John 3:1). The vast implications of his love, desire, and passion for us requires many descriptions, metaphors, and phrases for us to even begin to comprehend the breadth, length, height, and depth of his love for us. It will certainly take all of this lifetime, and perhaps much of eternity, to apprehend the many facets of relationship to him that we can freely enjoy in Christ.

So, yes! Holy. Royal priesthood. Dearly loved children. Citizens of heaven. Members of his household. Living stones. Holy nation. The list goes on and on. In order to help us to comprehend and experience the vastness of his love and what Christ has done for us to bring us into God's family, the scriptures provide many different ways to experientially relate to God's heart toward us. At times, one way might speak to us and at different times, another way. This too is God's kindness and provision.

Quietly reflect on how it feels to have the descriptors chosen person, royal priesthood, holy nation, and belonging to God applied to yourself. How do these designations bring new understanding to your position in the family of God?

Father, thank you that in your great love, you have done what I could never do on my own. You have saved me from myself and brought me into unity with you and your great love for me. I pray that you would bring the reality of all of this more fully into my inmost being. I pray that I would be so rooted and grounded in your love that I would trust you to be with me and for me in all that I face and go through today. I pray that by the grace that Jesus apportions to me, that I would experience the fullness of life as your royal holy priest and as your beloved child.

In Context:
But you are a chosen people, a royal priesthood, a holy nation, God's special possession, that you may declare the praises of him who called you out of darkness into his wonderful light. Once you were not a people, but now you are the people of God; once you had not received mercy, but now you have received mercy. Dear friends, I urge you, as foreigners and exiles, to abstain from sinful desires, which

wage war against your soul. Live such good lives among the pagans that, though they accuse you of doing wrong, they may see your good deeds and glorify God on the day he visits us (1 Peter 2:9–12).

> **You are a child of the light and of the day. You do not belong to the night or to darkness.** — **1 Thessalonians 5:5**

A child of the light and a child of the day. Jesus, who revealed the Father to us, called himself the light of the world (John 8:12, 9:5). As a child of God, you are a child of the light.

Jesus saw what the Father was doing. A child can only see the Father in the light, not in darkness. Darkness is ignorance — not seeing what the Father is doing. From the truth of his scriptures, we know that right now he is loving us, singing over us, working all things together for our good, extending his kingdom on the earth, and preparing for the glorious return of Jesus.

Because you have the Holy Spirit living in you, you have the light of God dwelling in you. When you reflect his glory, you bring light to the world. Because the Spirit reminds you of what Jesus taught (John 14:26), you are enlightened. You are not in darkness, and you are not a child of one who is cloaked or hidden and concealing shameful things. No. You belong with and to one who is glorious in revelation.

In Ephesians 1:18, the Apostle Paul prayed that the eyes of our heart may be enlightened (that is, that we would "see" in our inmost being) in order to know the hope to which he has called us, the riches of his glorious inheritance in his holy people, and his incomparable great power for us who believe. The prayer is for the Father to give us the spirit of wisdom and revelation so that we might know him better. This is about alertness and knowing things in and of the Lord. In the context of the verse, it means we are not sleeping or in ignorance or dulled by drunkenness.

In Jesus, we are enlightened, seeing the Father and coming to know him better. You have been rescued from the domain of darkness by the Father himself and brought into the kingdom of the Son God loves (Colossians 1:13). There has been a transfer of title, deed, ownership, citizenship, dwelling, and possession. In Christ, we are a new creation (2 Corinthians 5:17), a dearly loved child of God (Ephesians 5:1), one with God in spirit (1 Corinthians 6:17), with his Spirit dwelling in us (1 Corinthians 6:19). We do not belong to the night or to darkness, we are children of the light and of the day (1 Thessalonians 5:5). Jesus has prepared a place of eternal purpose for us.

Meditate on how being a child of God changes the way you perceive yourself. Consider how to walk more fully as a child of the light. Ask the Holy Spirit to show you any vestiges of your prior life that he wants to free you from so that you can more fully bring his light into your life and to those you interact with.

God, thank you for instructing my mind to know and understand what your scriptures declare regarding your desires for me and my destiny in you. Thank you for the presence of your Holy Spirit in me, enlightening me, so that I can experience your presence and know you better. Thank you that, in Jesus, I am a child of the light and that you have rescued me from the kingdom of darkness. I pray that your Holy Spirit will continue to reveal more about you and your love for me in my inmost being. I pray that you will open my spiritual eyes to see what you are doing in my life and in the world around me. Give me grace to walk as a child of your light, allowing others around me to see you, your kingdom, and your glory. I pray that your light in me will change people and things around me because of your presence.

> **In Context:**
> But you, brothers and sisters, are not in darkness so that this day should surprise you like a thief. You are all children of the light and children of the day. We do not belong to the night or to the darkness. So then, let us not be like others, who are asleep, but let us be awake and sober (1 Thessalonians 5:4–6).

You are holy, you share in a heavenly calling. — Hebrews 3:1

One meaning of holy is to be set apart for a sacred purpose (see Galatians 1:15; Ephesians 1:4). One of your primary sacred purposes is to have relationship with almighty God forever. This is a place of everlasting purpose — knowing the Father, Son, and Holy Spirit, and growing in intimate relationship as his child. A calling refers to a life's work, the overarching theme that permeates all that we do. As his children, we each have a calling to live in concert with the principles of scripture and to represent him and his character in all that we do.

In his second letter to the Thessalonians (2 Thessalonians 1:11), the Apostle Paul writes, "we constantly pray for you, that our God may make you worthy of his calling, and that by his power he may bring to fruition your every desire for goodness and your every deed prompted by faith." 2 Peter 1:3 tells us that God's divine power has given us everything we need for a godly life through our knowledge of him who called us by his own glory and goodness. Romans 11:29 speaks of the gifts that we have been given by God and that both his gifts and his call are irrevocable. Clearly, God has purposes in our lives, and he has given us all that we need to fulfill them. Just as he gave Adam and Eve meaningful work in the garden before the fall as a gift to them, his calling in our life is a gift as well.

It is significant that the scriptures say that you share in a heavenly calling, you do not have a calling on your own. You receive it from God, it originates in him, and it is only possible in him and with him and through him. Apart from Jesus, you can do nothing (John 15:5). It is possible to do all things through Christ (Philippians 4:13). It is in walking each day in his Spirit that you can begin to live out his calling in your life. Life in partnership with his children was God's desire from the beginning. This is a place of eternal purpose.

Further, we are placed in the body of Christ, made up of every follower of Jesus. Every one of them has received gifts and callings. We are a team of people empowered and led by the Spirit of God to bring forth his kingdom on earth until the return of Jesus and the final establishment of his new heaven and new earth. God has prepared good works for us to do in advance (Ephesians 2:10). As we walk into them, in expectation and dependency on him, we meet him more fully and experience the fulfillment of his creativity, life, and purposes. As we see his hand in our lives and his goodness working in us, we come to know him better, to trust him more fully, and love him more.

It is truly an amazing thing to walk into a moment where you are aware that you were made for such a time as this (Esther 4:14). Fulfilling your divine purpose by allowing/depending on God's Spirit to fill and lead you is as good as it gets in this life. Those moments have been literally thousands of years in the making, being planned and ordained by God himself before you were born (Psalm 139:16). God sees the eternal picture and creates circumstances to equip you step-by-step for the callings, assignments, and purposes he has ordained for your life. I am certain that there are countless purposes in our daily interactions with others and circumstances that are God-ordained appointments that we do not necessarily have awareness of; yet by his grace and power, we fulfill them. Many times, people remind me of things that I have said or done that have changed their lives, and I had no idea. It does make me wonder if we will ever, in eternity, come to understand the fruit of our decisions and activities on earth. Regardless, I am certain that I am holy, set apart, and share in a heavenly calling. The same is true of you.

Prayerfully take a few minutes to reflect on the things in your life that you deeply enjoy doing. Have you considered if or how those things may relate to your personal heavenly callings? Meditate on specific things that you can do to share God's love.

Father, thank you for giving me purpose in this life. Thank you for setting me apart, having plans for my maturing and my life, and giving me the presence of your Spirit to lead me into the adventure of walking each day with you to further your kingdom, both in me and around me, everywhere I go. I pray that your love would so fully permeate me that everyone I meet today would sense you and your care for them. I pray that people would be drawn to you through the things I do and say today, and each day. Thank you for giving me the opportunity to be a conduit of your love, character, and Spirit. I pray that you would increase in me and that all that is not of you would decrease and disappear from my life. I pray that every interaction I have today would be consistent with your character and that your presence in me would change the atmosphere around me for your glory.

In Context:
Therefore, holy brothers and sisters, who share in the heavenly calling, fix your thoughts on Jesus, whom we acknowledge as our apostle and high priest (Hebrews 3:1).

A Place of Everlasting Purpose:

Summary and Application

You were once in darkness, but now you are light in the Lord (Ephesians 5:8). You are a chosen person, part of a royal priesthood, a holy nation, a people belonging to God, called out of darkness into his wonderful light (1 Peter 2:9). You are a child of the light and of the day. You do not belong to the night or to darkness (1 Thessalonians 5:5). You are holy, you share in a heavenly calling (Hebrews 3:1).

The still small voice of God, the voice of the indwelling Holy Spirit, leads you and shows you what God is doing. Quiet the many distracting voices and noises that keep you from hearing God's still small voice. Be still. Attend to the thoughts that scroll across the screen of your mind to become sensitive to God's still small voice. Jesus taught that his sheep know his voice.

In the book of Ecclesiastes, even King Solomon, the wisest of all people, pondered the meaning of life: What's the point? Together, the scriptural truths we have unpacked in this chapter make a clear statement that you have everlasting, eternal purpose. Your purpose is not limited to a fleeting fifteen minutes of fame. In God's view of you, you are not a single-use, disposable, replaceable person. You are uniquely made by him and have been transferred by his boundless love and grace from the kingdom of darkness into his wonderful light. Understanding that you are a child of the light and the day helps to define the activities and character that are consistent with your potential. Knowing that you are set apart and have a heavenly calling may help you to open yourself to God's leading in your life to receive both vision for your future and direction in daily decision-making. One of the best things that you can do is to invite the Holy Spirit to give you understanding and to guide you as you meditate on these truths and pray about their implications for the circumstances you are in now.

Commit to following the promptings you receive as you pray into and pronounce these truths over yourself:

- I am light in the Lord.
- I am a chosen person, part of a royal priesthood, a holy nation.
- I am part of a people belonging to God.
- I am called out of darkness into his wonderful light.
- I am a child of the light and the day.
- I do not belong to the night or to darkness.
- I am holy; I share in a heavenly calling.
- I am in a place of everlasting purpose.

Notes

CHAPTER 5
A Place of *Sure Salvation*

By grace you are saved (Ephesians 2:5). You are saved through faith, and this is not from yourself, it is a gift from God (Ephesians 2:8). Christ dwells in your heart through faith (Ephesians 3:17).

> **By grace you are saved.** — Ephesians 2:5

Galatians 1:15 says that you were called by God's grace — his unmerited favor. Grace entails getting blessings that are not deserved. Grace goes beyond forgiveness or mercy; it is the bestowing of great value, worth, honor, favor and love on you just because our heavenly Father loves you.

Grace is not logical or rational. It is also not our typical experience in everyday life. Grace gives us something valuable and totally beyond our ability to earn, produce, or accomplish.

I once heard an explanation of the difference between mercy and grace that goes like this: Mercy is not getting a punishment you deserve. Grace is getting something of value that you do not deserve. Imagine being pulled over for speeding, doing forty-five miles per hour in a twenty-five miles per hour zone. Mercy would be the police officer telling you that he has decided not to write you a ticket. Grace would be the officer deciding to give you five hundred dollars cash — totally unwarranted and illogical.

The reality is that God's grace abounds far beyond that example. You have inherited every spiritual blessing in Christ (Ephesians 1:3). This means that all the time, at every moment, we get his ever so costly, perfect, pure reward in exchange for our far inferior life. Instead of the punishment, rejection, disqualification, and estrangement from God that we rightly deserve and the death that we have earned through sin, we receive grace — and we are made alive with Christ, included in his family.

Imagine receiving the salary and benefits of a superior by mistake and being concerned that the error will be corrected. In Christ, our switched wages are not an error. God fully intended for us to have every spiritual blessing in Christ. He purposely made the exchange. Our accounts are full beyond measure.

And we have only seen the beginning of it! The scope is far beyond what we can hope or imagine (Ephesians 3:20). This is not about mere economics. It is about the substance of life, eternal pleasures at his right hand (Psalm 16:11) that far surpass a paycheck or benefits or inheritance of even the richest person in the world (and you do know that if we got their earnings for only one day, we would be set for life!). Every moment of every day we have an intimate, loving relationship with God himself. Your loving, all powerful, heavenly Father. Forget none of his benefits (Psalm 103). By grace, you are saved. You are in a place of sure salvation.

Deeply reflect on and then speak this truth out loud: By grace I am saved. Consider how to live each day in a greater degree of awareness of God's grace and in gratitude for it.

Father, thank you for your grace. Thank you for desiring relationship with me, for creating me, making yourself known to me, and for sacrificing your Son to bring me back into relationship with you. Thank you for blessings upon blessings, every good and perfect gift, coming directly from you to me. Thank you for your thoughts toward me, your kindness, and your love. Father, increase my awareness of your presence, your blessings, and your love, and give me the grace to share your goodness with everyone I come into contact with today.

> **In Context:**
> But because of his great love for us, God, who is rich in mercy, made us alive with Christ even when we were dead in transgressions — it is by grace you have been saved. And God raised us up with Christ and seated us with him in the heavenly realms in Christ Jesus, in order that in the coming ages he might show the incomparable riches of his grace, expressed in his kindness to us in Christ Jesus. For it is by grace you have been saved, through faith — and this is not from yourselves, it is the gift of God — not by works, so that no one can boast (Ephesians 2:4–9).

You are saved through faith, and this is not from yourself.
— Ephesians 2:8

You are saved through faith in Christ and his incomparable sacrifice for you, not by faith in yourself or your efforts to be good or any sacrifice that you could offer. Your salvation is totally and utterly dependent on faith in Jesus Christ. In his letters to the early churches, the Apostle Paul emphasizes that as followers of Christ we are set free from fulfilling the law because of his fulfillment of every aspect of the law (the behavioral requirements of the Old Testament). In fact, all those who rely on observing the law are under a curse (Galatians 3:10), because it is written, "Cursed is everyone who does not continue to do everything written in the book of the law" (Deuteronomy 27:26). Galatians 3:11 says, "Clearly no one is justified before God under the law." Later, Paul concludes his discourse on faith and the law by stating, "If you are led by the Spirit, you are not under the law" (Galatians 5:18). But it gets even better. If you are led by the Spirit, you will see an ever-growing increase in the fruit of the Spirit in your life — love, joy, peace, etc. (Galatians 5:22).

The faith I have is certainly not in myself and not even from me. It is faith in Christ. It is a gift from God. If we are not secure in our faith, we can confess, "I believe, help my unbelief" (Mark 9:24) and expect the same mercy, grace, and love to flow from God to us as it did through Jesus in Mark 9 to the one who requested help in his faith.

Truly, God, in his love and desire to relate to us as sons and daughters, has provided all we need — the substitution of Christ's sacrifice on our behalf, bringing justification, redemption, forgiveness, and the way back into relationship with our heavenly Father. God has even provided the faith to believe in and accept the incomparable gift of Christ. He truly does look for us and runs to meet us when we turn to him (Luke 15:20)! This is a place of sure salvation.

Deeply contemplate this scriptural truth today: I am saved through faith, and this is not from myself. Express gratitude to God for his grace and the faith he has provided for you.

Father, thank you for supplying everything necessary to bring me into relationship with you. Thank you for making yourself known to me. Thank you for sending Jesus to reveal you to the world, and for Jesus doing all that is needed to bring my forgiveness. Thank you for supplying my faith. I pray that you will increase my faith in you and my experience of your continual goodness on my behalf. I pray that you will allow my heart to more fully experience the love that you pour into it by your Spirit. Father, let me rest in your goodness, love, and grace toward me.

In Context:
But because of his great love for us, God, who is rich in mercy, made us alive with Christ even when we were dead in transgressions — it is by grace you have been saved. And God raised us up with Christ and seated us with him in the heavenly realms in Christ Jesus, in order that in the coming ages he might show the incomparable riches of his grace, expressed in his kindness to us in Christ Jesus. For it is by grace you have been saved, through faith — and this is not from yourselves, it is the gift of God — not by works, so that no one can boast (Ephesians 2:4–9).

Christ dwells in your heart through faith. — Ephesians 3:17

The faith you have from God, the faith you have in Christ, makes you alive in him and him alive in you. Ephesians 3:17, part of the Apostle Paul's prayer for believers in Jesus, states that Christ dwells (not just visits occasionally) in your heart (inmost being) through faith. The passage continues by praying that you will know that you are "rooted and established (or grounded) in love." That is to say, Paul prays that deep in your inmost being, in your core, you know that you are deeply and completely loved. Christ and his Spirit dwelling in you establish the love of God in your inmost being in ways that nothing else can or does.

Romans 5:5 tells us that "God's love has been poured out into our hearts through the Holy Spirit, who has been given to us." It is the Spirit of God himself, dwelling in you, who pours the love of God into your inmost being.

There is nothing like being in the presence of Jesus. His presence in you makes you a new creation — a human indwelt by the God of the universe, the King of Kings. It is not your behavior or your effort or your purity that brings him into you. It is faith, the gift of God, that brings him to dwell in you. Dwell means to live as a resident. Webster's Dictionary defines reside as "to dwell permanently or continuously: occupy a place as one's legal domicile." Your faith in Christ gives him the legal deed to your inmost being. He dwells in you, and you belong to him. That is a place of sure salvation.

Speak this truth to help your faith increase: Christ dwells in my heart through faith. Meditate on ways that you can more regularly sense the presence of Christ in your inmost being.

Lord, thank you for your presence in my life. Thank you for dwelling in me, never leaving or forsaking me. Thank you for your indwelling Spirit, reminding me of things that Jesus said while he was here on earth as a person and for teaching me all things. I pray that you will increase my awareness of your presence in my life and in my inmost being every day. I welcome you into my heart, my life, my thoughts, and my decisions. There is nothing better than living life with you! Thank you, Father, Jesus, and Holy Spirit for being with me.

In Context:
I pray that out of his glorious riches he may strengthen you with power through his Spirit in your inner being, so that Christ may dwell in your hearts through faith. And I pray that you, being rooted and established in love, may have power, together with all the Lord's holy people, to grasp how wide and long and high and deep is the love of Christ, and to know this love that surpasses knowledge — that you may be filled to the measure of all the fullness of God (Ephesians 3:16–19).

A Place of Sure Salvation: Summary and Application

By grace you are saved (Ephesians 2:5). You are saved through faith, and this is not from yourself. It is a gift from God (Ephesians 2:8). Christ dwells in your heart through faith (Ephesians 3:17).

Thank God that our salvation does not in any way depend on our qualifications or worthiness. The boundless extravagant love of God has moved him to provide, do, and finish all that is necessary for our salvation. While we were yet sinners, God made us alive in Christ. His love and his goodness are the root of all of it. We do not need to clean up our act to come to the cross of Jesus. All we need to do is to place our faith in the completed, once and for all, sacrifice of Jesus on our behalf. And even the faith itself is a gift from God.

Looking at a map of the world, there may be an infinite number of routes that we could take to arrive at any particular place. But Jesus declared that he is the only way to the Father. Jesus is also the only way to the place he has prepared for us — a place of sure salvation.

When we come to Jesus in faith, he comes to permanently remain in our hearts, the core of who we are. When Jesus resides in our inmost being, it is a place of sure salvation. His presence in our hearts gives us full access to our Father. Know that the presence of Jesus in our inmost being means that despite outer circumstances, ultimately everything will be for our good — far beyond good.

> **Meditate on the truth of these statements and ask the Holy Spirit to confirm them to you in experientially tangible ways:**

- By grace I am saved.
- I am saved through faith.
- Christ dwells in my heart.
- I am in a place of sure salvation.

Notes

CHAPTER 6
A Place of Total Forgiveness and Cleansing

In the Son, you have redemption through his blood (Ephesians 1:7; Colossians 1:14). In the son, God forgave all your sins (Colossians 2:13; Ephesians 1:7). You are reconciled, holy in God's sight, without blemish and free from accusation (Colossians 1:22). You are washed, sanctified, and justified freely by faith in Christ Jesus and the Spirit of your God (1 Corinthians 6:11; Galatians 3:8, 3:24).

> **In the son, you have redemption through his blood.**
> **— Colossians 1:14**

The meaning of redemption is to be set free from captivity, slavery, or debt. Baker's Evangelical Dictionary says, "divine redemption includes God's identification with humanity in its plight, and the securing of liberation of humankind through the obedience, suffering, death, and resurrection of the incarnate son."

Redemption is discussed in both the Old Testament and the New Testament. In the Old Testament, redemption most often refers to deliverance from bondage or slavery based on the payment of a price by a redeemer. In the New Testament, redemption refers to the emancipation of people from the captivity of sin solely based on the atoning death of Jesus.

In plain language, redemption is the promise and work of God to deliver us from the power, presence, and debts of sin in our lives. Redemption was accomplished by Jesus coming to live a perfect, sinless life among us as a human and consenting to substitute his suffering and execution for the consequences that our sin justly deserves. While his once-and-for-all sacrifice was sufficient and accomplished all that was needed to set us free, not all aspects of redemption are yet complete in their manifestation. Redemption is the reversal of the consequences of mankind's fall. The Kingdom of God, ushered in by the appearance, life, death, and resurrection of Jesus, is already in progress, but its complete manifestation is yet to come. He will return and reign in the new heaven and the new earth where his followers will be fully united with him, and his kingdom will be fully established. While we still see much evidence of the fallen nature of creation (e.g., disease, war, poverty, environmental hazards), we also experience his kingdom reality now in his presence and foresee the coming of the King and the fullness of his kingdom.

In the Son, you have redemption through his blood. This part of the reversal of the fall is already accomplished. Those who were spiritually dead have been made alive in Christ (Ephesians 2:4), and those who were children of wrath are now children of God (1 John 3:1).

Scripture makes it quite clear that you cannot contribute anything positive to your own redemption; it is utterly dependent on Jesus (Romans 3:23–28). The only one qualified to undo the effects of the fall is Jesus. "And all are justified freely by his grace through the redemption that came by Christ Jesus. God presented Christ as a sacrifice of atonement, through the shedding of his blood" (Romans 3:24–25).

Justification means to be made right or righteous. In math, justification means making two sides of an equation equal. Substituting the sacrifice of Jesus for your sins attributes his righteousness to your account, eradicating your sin and setting the balance equal.

Your personal redemption by Jesus is an astounding gift. Setting you free from bondage of debt for your sins, bringing you back into relationship with your loving heavenly Father, making you a child of God with rights as his child. Both the cost and the implications are enormous.

Though the words redemption and justification can occlude the glorious freedom that is ours because of their theological density and the absence of their familiarity and usage in current language, understanding the completeness of the work and the weight of Jesus' substitution is an important starting point for us to experience the love of God and who we are to him and in Jesus.

In the Son, you have redemption through his blood. Jesus has prepared a place of total forgiveness and cleansing for you. Quietly contemplate this scriptural truth today. Ask the Holy Spirit to indelibly write this truth into your identity as a beloved child of God.

Jesus, thank you for pouring out your blood for me on the cross. Thank you for redeeming and justifying me. Thank you for making me spotless, pure, and holy so that I can have a relationship with Father God. Thank you for freeing me from the kingdom of darkness and bringing me into your kingdom. Help me to live in the fullness of freedom that you have gained for me.

> **In Context:**
> … and giving joyful thanks to the Father, who has qualified you to share in the inheritance of his holy people in the kingdom of light. For he has rescued us from the dominion of darkness and brought us into the kingdom of the Son

he loves, in whom we have redemption, the forgiveness of sins (Colossians 1:12–14).

> **In the son, God forgave all your sins. — Colossians 2:13; Ephesians 1:7**

If we confess our sins, he is faithful and just and will forgive our sins and purify us from all unrighteousness (1 John 1:9). What you cannot do — not in the least, not once, let alone countless times — Christ has done once and for all. He forgave all your sins by his death on the cross, occurring about two thousand years before your birth. Not only did Jesus atone for the sins of your past, but your sins of today and any sins you commit in the future. His once-and-for-all sacrifice centuries ago was applied to your account for the entirety of your life.

This may give me great comfort in knowing that the mistakes and poor choices I make today or in the future are already covered, but that does not give me permission to do as I please and to become callous about sin. Romans 6:1–4 says, "What shall we say, then? Shall we go on sinning so that grace may increase? By no means! We are those who have died to sin; how can we live in it any longer? Or don't you know that all of us who were baptized into Christ Jesus were baptized into his death? We were therefore buried with him through baptism into death in order that, just as Christ was raised from the dead through the glory of the Father, we too may live a new life."

The new life we are to live is one of close relationship with him, following his teachings and obeying his commands. But when we fail, as we inevitably will, we can take comfort in the truth that in the Son, God forgave all our sins.

Once you confess your sins to God, they are forgiven (1 John 1:9) and he, being love itself, keeps no record of wrongs (1 Corinthians 13:5). As far as the east is from the west, he removes your transgressions from you (Psalm 103:12). Once you have applied his sacrifice to you through confessing any sin you are aware of, there is no need to continue to ask for God's forgiveness. It is finished. Any recurring guilt or anguish you continue to feel is not originating from God. It either comes from the accuser of the brethren (Revelation 12:10), who is destined to be hurled down by the authority of Jesus, or from your own unrelenting conscience. Instead, you can choose to receive God's gracious gift of forgiveness and believe that in Christ, you are reconciled, holy in God's sight, without blemish and free from accusation (Colossians 1:22). This is truly a glorious freedom of the children of God! You are brought into a place of total forgiveness and cleansing.

Meditate on the immensity of God's love for you that he demonstrated through Jesus coming to live among us, and willingly dying to bring forgiveness for our sins.

Father, thank you for your forgiveness and for drawing me into close relationship with you. Thank you that your great love and your free grace compel me to live in a manner that is worthy of your name. I pray that your love will empower me to live in unity with you and your ways. I ask you to help me trust in your total and full forgiveness of all the sins that I have confessed to you. Thank you for purifying me from all unrighteousness, making me pure in your sight. I rejoice in the freedom that you have given to me as your child.

In Context:
When you were dead in your sins and in the uncircumcision of your flesh, God made you alive with Christ. He forgave us all our sins, having canceled the charge of our legal indebtedness, which stood against us and condemned us; he has taken it away, nailing it to the cross (Colossians 2:13–14).

In him [Christ] we have redemption through his blood, the forgiveness of sins, in accordance with the riches of God's grace that he lavished on us (Ephesians 1:7–8a).

You are reconciled, holy in God's sight, without blemish and free from accusation. — Colossians 1:22

Looking up reconcile in various dictionaries results in the following range of entries: to win over to friendliness; cause to become amicable, to restore to friendship or harmony (e.g., reconciled the factions: to reconcile hostile persons). To compose or settle a quarrel, dispute, etc., to reconcile differences. To bring into agreement or harmony; make compatible or consistent: to reconcile differing statements; to reconcile accounts. To check a financial account against another for accuracy, to account for. To reconsecrate a desecrated church, cemetery, etc.

Reconciliation with God makes us compatible with him, makes us consistent with him and removes hostilities between us to bring us into harmony with him. His reconciliation clears our account and reconsecrates us.

A blemish can be defined as a mark that detracts from appearance (such as a scar, defect, flaw, stain, or blight). Numbers 19:2 and Leviticus 22:21 say that an offering to God must be without blemish. 1 Peter 1:19 says that Christ was a lamb without blemish. Because the righteousness of Jesus was applied to our account, Ephesians 5:27 says the church is without stain, wrinkle, or other blemish.

Because all our sins are forgiven, we are reconciled — brought back into relationship and invited into the Holy of Holies to commune with God. We may converse with him and reason together with him. We can also experience with new awareness his love being poured on us. Because no accusation against us can stick to Christ, his substitutionary sacrifice and reconciliation of us makes it so that in Christ, we are without blemish and free from accusation. Our account is reconciled — all the debt forgiven. We are alive in Christ instead of dead in our sin. We are not separated from God and not an enemy to God (that idea may be in our minds; it's never in his!). Jesus has already satisfied all the conditions of our reconciliation to God. The equation is balanced. His righteousness freely exchanged for our sin. His perfection for our blemishes. His reputation for the accusations against us.

Once sins are confessed, and we have applied the sacrifice of Christ to them, any residual guilt is the result of allowing the accusations of the father of lies — the accuser of the children of God — to lodge in our minds and emotions. The reality is that in Christ, we have no sin. In Christ, no accusation against us is warranted or true. It is for freedom that Christ has set us free (Galatians 5:1) — free from guilt, accusation, and debt. All of it is gone.

Doubts, fears, inadequacy, condemnation, rejection don't have any place in the life, mind, and heart of a dearly loved child of God. Quarantine it! Block such thoughts and dispose of them. Do not allow doubts to rise in your minds (Luke 24:38). Rest in, take refuge in, relish and be free in the love of your heavenly Father. Things that you know about yourself that cause shame, guilt and disappointment pale in the light of the consistent love of God for you.

Meditate on the good news that in Christ, you are reconciled, holy in God's sight, without blemish and free from accusation. Rejoice! See yourself entering the party with Abba (Luke 15). He has run to meet you and started the party. How does it feel to enter into the joy he has in relating to you?

Father, thank you for your great love and for doing everything necessary to reconcile me back into full relationship with you. Thank you that because I have accepted the sacrifice of Jesus, I am holy in your sight, without blemish and free from accusation. Thank you for giving me the faith to trust in the redeeming sacrifice of Jesus on my behalf. Your love is beyond measure, Father. Please expand my ability to comprehend the vastness of your love and to experience it in my inmost being as I go through this day.

In Context:
Once you were alienated from God and were enemies in your minds because of your evil behavior. But now he has reconciled you by Christ's physical body through death to present you holy in his sight, without blemish and free from accusation — if you continue in your faith, established and firm, and do not move from the hope held out in the gospel. This is the gospel that you heard and that has been proclaimed to every creature under heaven (Colossians 1:21–23).

> You are washed, sanctified, and justified freely by faith in Christ Jesus and the Spirit of God. — 1 Corinthians 6:11; Galatians 3:8, 3:24

The combination of these three words — washed, sanctified, and justified — leaves no doubt. In Jesus, you are cleansed, restored, made right, free from sin, and released from guilt and the debt of sin. The "account" of Jesus covers all your debt and failure. His perfection and the abundance of his account has been exchanged for your account and record.

When something is thoroughly washed, all dirt, stench, and stain is scrubbed clean and rinsed away. It is completely cleansed and renewed, made "white as snow." To be sanctified means to make holy and to be set apart as holy, consecrated as intended before the beginning of time. Consecrated means to be declared and dedicated and set apart for holy purposes. Justified means shown to be just or right, declared innocent or guiltless. Absolved means to be freed from an obligation or the consequences of guilt, acquitted, discharged completely from an accusation or obligation. Justified means leveled and squared, and justification often refers to a sufficient legal reason. In Christ, you have more than sufficient legal reason to be forgiven and set free.

The blood of Jesus was enough, once and for all! The value of being forgiven, in Christ, is of inestimable value.

The trinity of washed, sanctified, and justified presented in this scripture is making it clear. When coupled with the Colossians 1:22 grouping of "reconciled, holy without blemish and free from accusation," there is no question that in Jesus, your case is legally closed. The acceptance of Jesus' sacrifice on your behalf brings you into a place of total forgiveness and cleansing.

Consider how different your present and future would be if Jesus' perfection was not freely attributed to your life. Meditate on what his gift means to you personally.

Jesus, thank you for achieving for me what I could never begin to do for myself. Thank you for applying the sacrifice of your blood, your perfect and sinless life, to my account. Thank you for including me in your crucifixion, death, burial, and resurrection. Thank you for including me in you. Thank you that in you, I am freely washed, sanctified, justified, reconciled, holy, without blemish and free from accusation. I pray that your Spirit would continually remind me of who I am in you and how our Father sees me in you. I pray that you would keep me from entertaining the accusations and lies of the enemy of our souls, and that I would remain free in you by trusting your grace and not my own effort.

In Context:
And that is what some of you were. But you were washed, you were sanctified, you were justified in the name of the Lord Jesus Christ and by the Spirit of our God (1 Corinthians 6:11).

Scripture foresaw that God would justify the Gentiles by faith, and announced the gospel in advance to Abraham: "All nations will be blessed through you."…So the law was our guardian until Christ came that we might be justified by faith (Galatians 3:8, 3:24).

A Place of Total Forgiveness and Cleansing:

Summary and Application

In the Son, you have redemption through his blood (Ephesians 1:7; Colossians 1:14). In the Son, God forgave all your sins (Colossians 2:13; Ephesians 1:7). You are reconciled, holy in God's sight, without blemish and free from accusation (Colossians 1:22). You are washed, sanctified, and justified freely by faith in Christ Jesus and the Spirit of your God (1 Corinthians 6:11; Galatians 3:8, 3:24).

In Jesus, we are brought into a place of total forgiveness and cleansing. To be redeemed, forgiven, reconciled, holy, without blemish, free from accusation, washed, sanctified, and justified leaves no doubt that for those who are in Christ, there is no condemnation (Romans 8:1). The totality and enormity of his forgiveness and cleansing is astounding.

There is not an adequate metaphor to help us grasp the absolute release from our deserved guilt. Power washing, bleaching, scrubbing, sterilizing, decontaminating — none of these captures the complete restoration to wholeness that is ours in Christ. As far as the east is from the west, so far has he removed our transgressions from us (Psalm 103:12). Gone. In the place of our sinfulness, the righteousness of Jesus, the perfect, sinless, Lamb of God, is credited to us.

If you are aware of any unconfessed sins, take time now to give them to the Lord, to ask his forgiveness and to apply the blood of his sacrifice to your account. Regularly invite the Holy Spirit to remind you of unconfessed sin so that you can accept the free gift and perfect atonement of Jesus in your life. If your mind returns to sins that you have already asked his forgiveness for, know that it is not the Lord convicting you of already forgiven sins. Do not let the voice of the accuser convince you that you are guilty once you have asked God for forgiveness and have committed to change and walk in consistency with his character. In Hebrews 8:11, God says,

"For I will forgive their wickedness and will remember their sins no more." God also states in Isaiah 43:25, "I, even I, am he who blots out your transgressions, for my own sake, and remembers your sins no more." Scripture clearly teaches that God chooses to forgive and forget confessed sins. Since this is articulated various ways through many verses, if confessed sin continues to concern you, the concern is not inspired by God. It is either the voice of the accuser or your own guilt not trusting the goodness of God to forgive you. 1 John 1:9 states, "If we confess our sins, he is faithful and just and will forgive us our sins and purify us from all unrighteousness." Look at the convergence of the verses you have meditated on in this chapter: God has done everything necessary to totally forgive and cleanse you. Ask the Holy Spirit to transform your thinking, to renew your mind, and to deposit the love and forgiveness of God into your inmost being. Ask him to allow you to experience a sense of his forgiveness and total cleansing fully and finally.

> **Meditate once again on the truth of his words about the place he has prepared for you, a place of total forgiveness and cleansing.**

- I have redemption through his blood.
- God forgave all my sins.
- I am reconciled, holy in God's sight, without blemish and free from accusation.
- I am washed, sanctified, and justified freely by faith in Jesus and the Spirit of my God.
- In Jesus, I am in a place of total forgiveness and cleansing.

Notes

CHAPTER 7

A Place of *Secure Family Love*

You are a child of God through faith in Christ Jesus (Galatians 3:26). You are lavished in God's love (1 John 3:1). Because you are his child, God sent the Spirit of his Son into your heart, the Spirit that calls out, "Abba, Father" (Galatians 4:6). You can receive the full rights of a child of God (Galatians 4:4–5).

> **You are a child of God through faith in Christ Jesus.**
> **— Galatians 3:26**

In John 14:6, Jesus declared, "I am the way, the truth and the life." The way to what, or to who? The Father. A father is only a father in relationship to a child. A son or a daughter is a son or daughter in relationship to a father, and in the case of Jesus, the Father. He spent all his days as fully human on this earth, worshipping the Father in spirit and in truth. Jesus showed us how to trust the Father and to defer to him in all things — how to talk with him, to say what he was saying, and to do what he was doing.

Living as a child of God is the life to the full that Jesus came to give us (John 10:10). The fullness of life that Jesus demonstrated is available to us, as children of God of the universe, as well. We do not have to wait until we die to be united with Jesus and enter the place he has prepared for us. We can live our lives on this earth from the place that Jesus has prepared for us. Walking with God, our heavenly Father.

Contemporary social science research has established that a child learns a great deal about who she or he is by relating to their father. The quality of father-child relationships contributes significantly to a child's sense of identity. Father-child relationships inform how to live. There is no such thing as a fatherless child. Though the child's human father may be absent or minimally or negatively involved in the child's life, all children do have a father. Without a father, there is no birth. If a father is present, children substantively depend on their father for provision, protection, and creating opportunities across many domains. Positively engaged human fathers gain love, joy, pride, and a sense of purpose in their fathering.

Children who experience positive father relationships demonstrate self-assurance and tend to be characterized by can-do attitudes. They are centered, experientially knowing that they are loved. These attributes are central to their identity because they are rooted and grounded in love. The quality of father-child relationships is foundational, a central basis for many other life issues. Fathers mold ways to "carry" the self. They influence beliefs about what you are capable of and where you are headed.

God was always Father — the perfect loving Father. He did not suddenly become Father in a moment in time because the Father, Son, and Holy Spirit always coexisted in mutuality before the beginning of time. Opening ourselves to being his child changes everything. Every little thing is going to be alright.

The sacrifice of Jesus was and is, a flawless, ironclad plan and provision. Perfect love. When Jesus said, "it is finished," it echoed back to before the beginning of time when you were first desired, planned as a child of God. The way to the Father is provided for you to be a fully loved, accepted, known child of God, lavished in Father's love.

All that Father has is yours because you belong to him as a child (John 16:15). Being a child has legal status and associated rights: support, inheritance, authority, one with Christ, and co-heirs of his glorious inheritance (Romans 8:15–17). As a co-heir with Christ, consider, what is not available to Christ? Jesus declared that all that belongs to the Father is his (John 16:15). Because the Holy Spirit lives in you, all that the Father has is revealed, declared, and disclosed and transmitted to you (John 16:15 AMP). More importantly, being a child of a loving father yields relational components — love, pride, play, counsel, prayer, well-being, well-doing, reciprocity of relationship. Relish the status and relational reality of being a child of God. Jesus has prepared a place of secure family love for you to enter.

Quietly consider what it means for you to be a beloved child of God. Take a few moments to ask God's Spirit to help you to experience a greater measure of God's love for you. Ask God to work healing in your heart for past disappointments and hurts that you experienced with your earthly father. Ask the Holy Spirit to keep wounds from your relationship with your earthly father from creating distance in your relationship with God.

Father, thank you for desiring and planning me from before the beginnings of the cosmos. Thank you for sending Jesus to seek and to save all who were lost or dead in their sin and estranged from you, including me. Thank you for the sacrifice of Jesus on my behalf to serve as the way back into relationship with you, giving me full freedom, love, and acceptance as your child. I pray that I will more fully and tangibly experience your love and live in a greater depth of relationship with you as your beloved child.

In Context:
So in Christ Jesus you are all children of God through faith (Galatians 3:26).

> **You are lavished in God's love.** — 1 John 3:1

In him, we have redemption through his blood, the forgiveness of sins in accordance with the riches of God's grace (Ephesians 1:7), the love he lavished on us.

Lavish can be defined as expending or bestowing profusely; expended or produced in abundance, marked by profusion or excess, using a large amount of something, given in large amounts, having a rich and expensive quality. Extravagant.

You are lavished in grace and love. Everywhere you look, you are centered in it (and it is infinitely high, deep, long, and wide). Everywhere you go. Timeless. Since before the beginning of time and onward throughout eternity. All encompassing. Consuming. Ever-present. All expenses paid. Covered. Boundless. Beyond pampered. Obsessed over. The target of infatuation.

How can we miss it? If this kind of attention and love was from a person in your everyday life, this would smother you. But God's love is perfect, not self-serving or manipulative. It is mature. It does not require reciprocation. In fact, it is so far beyond any hope of proper reciprocation, it should undo you. No expense spared. It is poured into your heart by the indwelling Spirit of God himself (Romans 5:5).

Have you ever seen a flooding rain so vast that the ground becomes fully saturated and the overflow simply cannot be contained? That is how profuse and continuous and complete is God's love. We cannot contain its extravagance. We are being continually flooded by torrents of his love. We love because he first loved us this way. Love, by its nature, gives itself away. As we receive the continuous flow of God's love into our hearts, it will fill us, and spill out to others.

God is loving you right now. Being loved as a human child brings attachment, the secure bases for exploration, trust, and positive assumptions about how the world and others work. How much more the love, attachment, presence, closeness, care, and synchronized dance of the Heavenly Father. There is no scarcity, and his love is not intermittent.

Meditate on the reality of the immensity and constant availability of his love for you. As God's child, you are in the place of secure family love.

Father, thank you for the vastness, the consistency, and the extravagance of your love for me. Thank you that your love is continually directed to me personally, knowing all the details of my life, my well-being, and my needs. Thank you that your love causes all things to work together for good in my life. It is a joy to experience your love, to see your hand in my life, and to know that I am your lavishly loved child. Father, I choose to trust in you and to rest in your love as fully as I can. I pray that you will increase my capacity to know the vastness of your love for me.

In Context:
See what great love the Father has lavished on us, that we should be called children of God! And that is what we are! The reason the world does not know us is that it did not know him. Dear friends, now we are children of God, and what we will be has not yet been made known. But we know that when Christ appears, we shall be like him, for we shall see him as he is (1 John 3:1–2).

> **Because you are his child, God sent the Spirit of his Son into your heart, the Spirit that calls out "Abba, Father". — Galatians 4:6**

When you accepted Jesus as your savior, God, the Father became your Father, so he sent the Spirit of Jesus, who came to reveal the Father into your heart. This is the Spirit that calls out, "Papa!" This is the Spirit fully attached to his loving Father and who is always tuned into and aware of the Father. His Spirit dwells in your heart. Just as the Spirit descended like a dove and rested on Jesus at his baptism and remained in him for the rest of his time on earth as a man, once you accept Jesus' sacrifice on your behalf, the Spirit of God comes into your heart and remains.

The Spirit marks you with a seal — a seal of authenticity — of sonship because it is the Spirit of his beloved Son. This is better than "made in the USA" or "official MLB." This is not merely a stamp, it's a living Spirit, the Spirit of the Son that relates fully to Papa. That Spirit. He continually reveals more of Papa to your heart. The Spirit always looks toward and draws near to Papa. The Spirit loves, trusts, obeys, desires, and honors Papa. The Spirit of unity with Papa produces the unified, singular fruit of the Spirit — the very character of Papa. This is God's DNA in you — love, joy, peace, patience, kindness, goodness, gentleness, and self-control. The Spirit of sonship has the same character as Papa and plants it into you as a living and life-giving Spirit to bring transformation. The Spirit is the yeast that works through the whole lump.

The calling out from his indwelling Spirit is a beckoning, an invitation to closeness — a seeking, a hunger, a deference, a dependency. It produces proximity, reunion, and mutual delight between you and your Father. The Spirit in you turns your thoughts toward all that is true, noble, right, pure, lovely, admirable, and praiseworthy (Philippians 4:8).

Secure attachment with God is the antidote for the orphan spirit, striving to do things on your own because in your core, you do not fully trust God. Resting in God's continual love and presence brings you into the transforming reality that you were made for — living as his greatly valued child. Our relationship with him mirrors regularly walking with him through the gardens of your life in the cool of the evening.

It is the Spirit of the Son that reveals the Father to your heart and teaches you to live as his deeply loved child by calling out to Papa. Meditate on that truth and let it rest in your inmost being. In Jesus, you are a dearly loved child of God in a place of secure family love.

Father, I thank you for sending the Holy Spirit to dwell in me, to remain in me, and to reveal to me more about you, your love for me, and your continual care for me. I pray that I will be ever more sensitive to the small still voice of your Spirit in me as he pours your love into my inmost being. I pray that I will be more attentive to his voice as he reminds me of your holy scriptures that declare who I am in you, and the vastness of your love and compassion for me. I choose to rest in your presence, your care, and your love as your child, with your Spirit dwelling in my heart.

In Context:
But when the set time had fully come, God sent his Son, born of a woman, born under the law, to redeem those under the law, that we might receive adoption to sonship. Because you are his sons, God sent the Spirit of his Son into our hearts, the Spirit who calls out, "Abba, Father." So you are no longer a slave, but God's child; and since you are his child, God has made you also an heir (Galatians 4:4–7).

You can receive the full rights of a child of God.
— Galatians 4:4–5

The scriptures describe some of the full rights as children of God to include freedom from following the law. Freedom to live by the Spirit. Freedom to be a full heir of an unfathomable heavenly inheritance. What does this mean? You're a child of promise. You can cultivate and mature the fruit of the Spirit (God's character). You can keep in step with the Spirit.

The parable of the lost son in Luke 15 conveys that the love of the Father motivates him to be on the lookout for you as you choose to reduce the distance you have put between yourself and God and return to him. When you do, he runs to you. You are hugged and kissed by the Father and given a robe, ring, and sandals of the Father's household. You are fed in the Father's house — celebrated at an extravagant feast. You are welcomed into Papa's home and family.

Accepting the love and grace of the Father makes us children who receive rights as children. He sent Jesus to live as a human under the law to fulfill the law and be a way to him and into fullness of free relationship with him and full rights of sons (not servants). The son allows the father to direct servants to welcome and care for children. In Jesus' parable in Luke 15, the older son didn't receive the father's care that was continually available to him. His life was dominated by orphan mindedness. He depended on his own faithfulness and laborious striving, which prevented him from seeing the Father's love and grace. In contrast, the younger son had the realization that he had no rights, so he gave up to return to the father and live in his household.

Present yourself to the Father as you are, and then receive what he gives in response. His ways are not our ways; they are higher. His invitation is to sonship, far beyond living as a servant. It is living in the same extravagant love the Father has toward his Son.

The Trinity is and has always been perfectly harmonious, balanced, characterized by full-out love, honor, respect, care, and deference to one another. Much of the content of scripture is the story of how they extended their love to birth and invite humans into relationship — completed by Jesus being the way back to relationship with the Father — providing the revelation of the Father and the sufficient once and for all sacrifice to be the way to the Father. Then, the Father gives the Spirit of his Son into our heart, the Spirit that calls out Abba Father. We are brought into the company of occupation of the Trinity and into the presence of Father. It is the Spirit of the Son and the Holy Spirit that brings us to the Father.

You can receive full rights as God's child. Let that truth settle in your inmost being. Meditate on how God has prepared a place for you in secure family love and how he welcomes you into that place.

Father, thank you for your unending love that characterizes all you do. Thank you for desiring relationship with me and making a way for me to come into fullness of relationship with you. Thank you for sending Jesus as a way to you, and for giving your Holy Spirit to me to dwell in me. Thank you that you never leave or forsake me and for your generous heart toward me. I pray that I will increase in experiencing your love in all aspects of my life, that you would open my heart to know you more fully, and that you would enlighten my spiritual eyes to see the continual and countless ways that you run to me to immerse me in your love. I pray that my experience of your love will transform me to live in the fullness of relationship that you desire for me.

> **In Context:**
> But when the set time had fully come, God sent his Son, born of a woman, born under the law, to redeem those under the law, that we might receive adoption to sonship. Because you are his sons, God sent the Spirit of his Son into our hearts, the Spirit who calls out, "Abba, Father." So you are no longer a slave, but God's child; and since you are his child, God has made you also an heir (Galatians 4:4–7).

A Place of Secure Family Love: Summary and Application

You are a child of God through faith in Christ Jesus (Galatians 3:26). You are lavished in God's love (1 John 3:1). Because You are his child, God sent the Spirit of his Son into your heart, the Spirit that calls out "Abba, Father" (Galatians 4:6). You can receive the full rights of a child of God (Galatians 4:4–5).

This set of verses clearly establishes that in Jesus, we are in a place of secure family love. Decades of social science research robustly demonstrate that in contemporary culture, experientially knowing secure family love brings a cascade of positive developmental contexts that change lives for the better. Secure attachment with a benevolent caregiver sets children on a different pathway than insecure and anxious attachments. Secure attachment is associated with the development of trust, the fountainhead of positive social, emotional, and mental health. Secure child-parent attachment also predicts a whole host of positive developmental resources for children to utilize in navigating the challenges of daily life.

Whether you have experienced positive relationships with parents and significant others or not, as a follower of Jesus, you are brought into a place of secure family love. As his beloved child, you are loved by God himself with the same love with which he loves Jesus. You are brought into fullness of relationship with God, who is love, the one who works all things together for good in your life (Romans 8:28). This is the God who knows all that you truly need and unrestrainedly supplies it in love and joy, singing over you. You have the benefit of every spiritual blessing in Christ with which to face daily challenges.

Recent fathering research has established that men who are positively engaged with their children over time experience pride, love, joy, and satisfaction in watching their children grow. Can you imagine the positive feelings of God himself, your perfect heavenly father, as he lovingly relates to you as you draw near to him?

When the angel of the Lord appeared to Moses in the burning bush and God spoke, he told him to take off his sandals because the place where he was standing was holy ground. The presence of God makes a place holy. In the new covenant, accepting the sacrifice of Jesus on your behalf and trusting your life to him keeps you in intimate proximity with him everywhere you go. He is with you, in you, ahead of you, around you. You are on holy ground. He is for you. You are not left as an orphan. His goodness and love provide more than the secure attachment you need. His love and presence are transforming. It truly changes everything.

Pray that the Holy Spirit will make you increasingly aware of the presence and the love of God in every aspect of your life. Pray for greater ability to trust in the Lord with all of your heart and to not lean on your own understanding. Make it your goal to acknowledge him in all of your ways and to give him glory as he makes your paths straight. Recognize the place of secure family love that God has placed you into.

Meditate on and declare the following truths about who you are in Jesus:

- I am a child of God.
- I am lavished in God's love.
- Because I am his child, God sent the Spirit of his Son into my heart, the Spirit that calls out "Abba, Father."
- I can receive the full rights of a child of God.
- I am in a place of secure family love.

Notes

CHAPTER 8

A Place of Unfathomable Plenty

Since you are his child, God has made you an heir (Galatians 4:7). You are called to the riches of his glorious inheritance (Ephesians 1:18). You are not qualified on your own, the Father has qualified you to share in the inheritance of the saints (Colossians 1:12). Surely you have a delightful inheritance (Psalm 16:6).

> **Since you are his child, God has made you an heir.**
> **— Galatians 4:7**

An heir is a person who inherits or has the right of inheritance in the property of another. In common law, an heir is a person who inherits all the property of a deceased person by descent, relationship, will, or a legal process. In civil law, an heir is a person who legally succeeds the place of a deceased person and assumes the rights and obligations of the deceased and the liabilities for debts or possessing rights to their property. Essentially, an heir is a person who inherits or is entitled to inherit the rank, title, or position of another. An heir can also be a person or group considered as inheriting the tradition or talent of a predecessor.

In any case, an heir receives what they did not earn. They receive it both as a gift and as a right. All that they inherit comes as the result of the life of the one who passes it on. It is the legacy of their benefactor. It comes from their predecessor's achievement and generosity and their desire to gift the heir.

As children of God, we are heirs of the unfathomable riches of God. The inheritance we receive is not limited to just material wealth; it includes spiritual gifts, talent, tradition, character, and ways of relating.

As children of God, we take on the ways of our heavenly Father. We get the "deposit" of his Spirit, marking or sealing our inheritance. It is like a down payment now, transforming us from glory to glory, and when we see him face to face, we will be like him. Then the full inheritance will be received, the transaction fully completed, resulting in our finished transformation into the likeness of our loving God. For now, we are given the invitation and the ability to experience life to the full, receiving full rights as his children. Later, we enjoy the full inheritance of eternal life. All of this exists in relationship to the Father as his beloved sons and daughters. To be an heir of God, the maker of the entire universe, puts us into a place of unfathomable plenty.

Reflect on how your status as a child of God changes your hope for the future. Consider the characteristics of the fruit of the Spirit (Galatians 5:22) that you have seen most clearly demonstrated in your relationship with God so far, and think about those that you long to see more of in your daily life and relationships.

Father, I thank you for the depth of your generous heart toward me. Thank you for gifting me with every spiritual blessing in Jesus. Thank you for attributing his life, character, and sacrifice to me. Thank you for placing me as your child. I choose to trust and receive the inheritance your scriptures declare are mine as your beloved child. Father, as your child, I choose to live each day of my life in the fullness of what you declare is mine and I look forward to seeing you face to face and being fully transformed to relate to you for all eternity. I long for more of your character in my daily life. Thank you, thank you, thank you. Your lovingkindness endures forever.

> **In Context:**
> But when the set time had fully come, God sent his Son, born of a woman, born under the law, to redeem those under the law, that we might receive adoption to sonship. Because you are his sons, God sent the Spirit of his Son into our hearts, the Spirit who calls out, "Abba, Father." So you are no longer a slave, but God's child; and since you are his child, God has made you also an heir (Galatians 4:4–7).

You are called to the riches of his glorious inheritance.
— Ephesians 1:18

The best news is that being an heir of God does not depend on the death of God. He has always been alive and he will live forever. Jesus, as a human, died once to be raised to sit at the right hand of the Father. His inheritance is available to us while he is alive, as in the parable of the prodigal son (Luke 15). Our inheritance in him is both for now and forever. We have been blessed with every spiritual blessing in Christ (Ephesians 1:13). His death and resurrection released his inheritance to us as his heirs.

We have received the Holy Spirit, who pours out the love of God into our hearts (Romans 5:5). Romans 8:16–17 says, " The Spirit himself testifies with our spirit that we are God's children. Now if we are children, then we are heirs — heirs of God and co-heirs with Christ, if indeed we share in his sufferings in order that we may also share in his glory."

The riches of God are unfathomable. Sharing them with every co-heir will never diminish their amount or availability to you personally. The riches of God are without limit. When we think of inheritance, we tend to think about goods or property or money. These are the least of our inheritances in the kingdom. The most valuable of all is the welcoming we receive into the fullness of eternal relationship with Father, Son, and Holy Spirit, beginning now and lasting throughout all time.

Meditate on the amazing reality of inheriting the fullness of all that God has designated for you, bringing you into a place of unfathomable plenty. Invite the Holy Spirit to enlighten the eyes of your heart so that you may experientially know the hope to which he has called you.

Father, Jesus, and Holy Spirit, thank you for the richness of relationship that you have given to me. I pray for the ability to abide in you, to always be aware of your loving presence, and to trust in you to lead me in all aspects of my life now and into eternity. I choose to receive the spiritual and the tangible blessings that you continually shower on me. Thank you for the abundant provision of all that I need for life to the full. Your love and generosity are truly astounding.

In Context:
I pray that the eyes of your heart may be enlightened in order that you may know the hope to which he has called you, the riches of his glorious inheritance in his holy people, and his incomparably great power for us who believe. That power is the same as the mighty strength he exerted when he raised Christ from the dead and seated him at his right hand in the heavenly realms, far above all rule and authority, power and dominion, and every name that is invoked, not only in the present age but also in the one to come (Ephesians 1:18–21).

> **You are not qualified on your own, the Father has qualified you to share in the inheritance of the saints.**
> **— Colossians 1:12**

It is the Father who has qualified you to share in the inheritance that he has designated for you. The Father has rescued us from the dominion of darkness and brought us into the kingdom of the Son he loves. In Christ, we have redemption, the forgiveness of sins. It is the forgiveness of sins and our redemption that qualifies us.

Webster's Dictionary defines dominion as supreme authority, sovereignty, legal absolute ownership. The kingship of Jesus is eternal, never to be overthrown or shaken again. The kingdom of Jesus is the realm in which God's will is perfectly fulfilled. In this kingdom, Jesus holds the preeminent position, having paramount rank, dignity, and importance, and his authority is final.

Your acceptance of the sacrifice of Jesus on your behalf has brought about a legal change in your citizenship. You are no longer under the dominion of darkness and you are a citizen of heaven. You are now a new creature, a living vessel housing God himself! You are in Christ, Jesus is in the Father, and he is in you. His presence in you qualifies you to share the inheritance of the saints, all who are children of God.

The unity of the scriptures that reveals the tapestry of God's artful and skillful plans is astonishing. The unified agency of God, in his trinitarian nature, planning for you, providing for you, redeeming you, and rescuing you from the domain of darkness while you were yet a sinner is awe-inspiring. In all this, he has given you an eternally planned, secure, abundant, and custom-tailored inheritance. You are in a place of unfathomable plenty.

This is something you could never begin to accomplish with a few hundred thousand years of full-time work, but by faith you receive it as a gift and so do I. Selah. I am so grateful that I do not need to qualify for the inheritance that God has designated for me. He himself has qualified me.

As you meditate on the love and generosity of God, let it settle in your inmost being that all that he desires for your relationship with him for eternity is secured in his unshakable authority, power, and love. They are inseparable.

Father, Jesus, and Holy Spirit, thank you for your love, compassion, and generosity toward me personally. Thank you for desiring to have me know you, and for making yourself known to me. Lord, I pray that I will increase in intimately knowing you and your thoughts toward me, and that I would see and trust in the details of your care for me. Even this day, I pray that you will draw near to me as I draw near to you. Thank you that you have qualified me to receive all of the good and perfect gifts that you have designated for me, and that as I trust in you, I will see your faithfulness and goodness to me in your perfect timing.

> **In Context:**
> For this reason, since the day we heard about you, we have not stopped praying for you. We continually ask God to fill you with the knowledge of his will through all the wisdom and understanding that the Spirit gives, so that you may live a life worthy of the Lord and please him in every way: bearing fruit in every good work, growing in the knowledge of God, being strengthened with all power according to his glorious might so that you may have great endurance and patience, and giving joyful thanks to the Father, who has qualified you to share in the inheritance of his holy people in the kingdom of light. For he has rescued us from the dominion of darkness and brought us into the kingdom of the Son he loves, in whom we have redemption, the forgiveness of sins (Colossians 1:9–14).

Surely you have a delightful inheritance. — Psalm 16:6

The Lord himself has determined what you inherit. Every good and perfect gift comes from him (James 1:17). The amount, the extent, and nature of it are all set by him. Then he secures the whole lot, every item, down to the last detail. It is all delightful. There is no sense of contention for another inheritance; yours was custom planned, purchased, and transferred to you by your creator. This is down to the details of your portion and your cup, and likely, when, and how, to release it to you. It is all pleasant. The Bible doesn't say it specifically, but I wonder if my inheritance was recorded in the Lord's book at the moment he recorded every day of my life, before the beginning of time. It is consistent with God's goodness, love, and character that he would have planned every detail of my provision and inheritance when he desired and designed me. Whether he recorded it before my beginning or not, the scriptures clearly declare that he secured my inheritance.

In God we trust! This is much more than an inscription on U.S. currency. Long before the existence of the United States or any contemporary nations, David, the psalmist, declared that it is God who gives us a delightful inheritance and makes our lot secure. While nations rise and fall and much of the future is not knowable, you can fully trust that you have a delightful inheritance.

Meditate on the reality that God himself, your unshakable, eternal, and loving Father, has secured that inheritance for you. Consider how this guarantee changes your perspective of challenges you are currently facing and your priorities.

Father, thank you for your faithfulness, your lovingkindness, and your goodness. Thank you that you have specifically directed your thoughts to me and that you have designated a delightful inheritance for me. Thank you that you yourself have secured it and determined and overseen all of its details. Thank you for your thoughts toward me, and your desire to draw me into close relationship with you, now and forevermore. Father, I choose to trust in you and your goodness toward me personally. Thank you that you are loving me right now. I pray that you will open my spiritual eyes to see the depth and details of your goodness toward me, and that I will grow in love toward you, security in you, and love for others. I pray that I would enjoy the bounty of the delightful inheritance that you have designated for me.

In Context:
Lord, you alone are my portion and my cup; you make my lot secure. The boundary lines have fallen for me in pleasant places; surely I have a delightful inheritance (Psalm 16:5–6).

A Place of Unfathomable Plenty: Summary and Application

Since I am his child, God has made me an heir (Galatians 4:7). I am called to the riches of his glorious inheritance (Ephesians 1:18). I am not qualified on my own, the Father has qualified me to share in the inheritance of the saints (Colossians 1:12). Surely, I have a delightful inheritance (Psalm 16:6).

Imagine receiving a phone call telling you that you have just been named heir to a huge estate of an extremely wealthy person. Can you imagine how fortunate you would feel? What would your thoughts be? Would you think, "What did I ever do to deserve this?" Just like salvation is not based on our qualifications, neither is being a child or an heir. The Father has qualified us to become his heirs. The scripture says, "Since you are his child." Since implies that there is a direct link or cause. You are his child, and so you are his heir.

The inheritance is abundantly glorious and rich. In his sermon on the mount, as Jesus was talking to those gathered about many of the issues of life, he said, "Therefore I tell you, do not worry about your life, what you will eat or drink; or about your body, what you will wear. Is not life more than food, and the body more than clothes? Look at the birds of the air; they do not sow or reap or store away in barns, and yet your heavenly Father feeds them. Are you not much more valuable than they? Can any one of you by worrying add a single hour to your life?" (Matthew 6:25–27). He clearly stated his Father's care for birds of the field, and by extension, his greater care for us. He challenged those gathered to recognize that their worries, anxiety, and striving does not result in an extension of life. It is reliance on God's care that relieves us from worries and brings us into position to receive his generous provision.

One characteristic of the place that Jesus has prepared for us is that it is a place of unfathomable plenty. Even the most cursory reading of the life of Jesus shows the continual abundance of the Father's provision for him and through him to others. Feeding thousands. Providing healing. Bringing the kingdom of God to earth. In every event and circumstance recorded in the life of Jesus, he never lacked anything that was truly needed. Jesus knew the total provision of the Father. In John 16:15, he declared, "All that belongs to the Father is mine."

Being an heir of God brings us into the place of unfathomable plenty. Consider what it means to be blessed in the heavenly realms with every spiritual blessing in Christ (Ephesians 1:3).

Meditate on the following truths and speak them into your life:

- Since I am his child, God has made me his heir.
- I am called to the riches of his glorious inheritance.
- The Father has qualified me to share in the inheritance.
- Surely I have a delightful inheritance.
- I am in a place of unfathomable plenty.

Notes

Notes

CHAPTER 9

A Place of Total Satisfaction and Contentment

The Father has blessed you in the heavenly realms with every spiritual blessing in Christ (Ephesians 1:3). You have been given fullness in Christ. You are complete (Colossians 2:3,10).

> **The Father has blessed you in the heavenly realms with every spiritual blessing in Christ.** — Ephesians 1:3

We may not focus on this often, or to the extent that we should, because we live in a material world that occupies a lot of our attention and energy. Yet the spiritual realm is just as real and has eternal characteristics that far exceed the temporality of the material world and our life in it. In a brief passage in his letter to the Ephesians, the Apostle Paul lists some (not all) of the spiritual blessings we have been blessed with by the Father. Many of these are ones that we have already focused on in previous meditations. Putting them together and reading them in the Amplified translation of the New Testament (with some of the blessings below in a bold font) brings emphasis to the astounding realities of our Father's love for us personally. Reading over this passage slowly and prayerfully and meditating on it will bring great encouragement, understanding of our identity in Christ, and the depth and extent of the personal love of our heavenly Father toward us. Ask the Holy Spirit to speak his encouragement into your inmost being as you reflect on this passage:

Blessed and worthy of praise be the **God** and Father of our Lord Jesus Christ, who **has blessed us with every spiritual blessing in the heavenly realms in Christ**, just as [in His love] **He chose us in Christ** [actually selected us for Himself as His own] before the foundation of the world, **so that we would be holy** [that is, consecrated, set apart for Him, purpose-driven] and **blameless in His sight**. In love He predestined and **lovingly planned for us** to be adopted to Himself **as [His own] children** through Jesus Christ, in accordance with the kind intention and good pleasure of His will — to the praise of His glorious **grace and favor, which He so freely bestowed on us in the Beloved** [His Son, Jesus Christ]. **In Him we have redemption** [that is, our deliverance and salvation] through His blood, [which paid the penalty for our sin and resulted in] the **forgiveness and complete pardon of our sin**, in accordance with **the riches of His grace which He lavished on us**. In all wisdom and understanding [with practical insight] He **made known to us the mystery of His will** according to His good pleasure, which He purposed in Christ, with regard to the fulfillment of the times [that is, the end of history, the climax of the ages] — to bring all things together in Christ, [both] things in the heavens and things on the earth. In Him also **we have received an inheritance** [a destiny — we were **claimed by God as His own**], having been predestined (chosen, appointed beforehand) according to the purpose of Him who works everything in agreement with the counsel and design of His will, so that **we who** were the first to **hope in Christ** [who first put our confidence in Him as our Lord and Savior] would **exist to the praise of His glory**. In Him, **you** also, when you heard the word of truth, the good news of your salvation, and [as a result] believed in Him, **were stamped with the seal of the promised Holy Spirit** [the One promised by Christ] **as owned and protected** [by God]. The Spirit is the guarantee [the first installment, the pledge, a foretaste] of our inheritance until the redemption of God's own [purchased] possession [His believers], to the praise of His glory (Ephesians 1:3–14, AMP).

Meditate on how this passage of scripture articulates a place of total satisfaction and contentment. Consider how to bring the comforts of these scriptural truths into the challenges you face on a regular basis.

God, our Father, I am so thankful for all of the blessings that you have given me. I know that it cost Jesus dearly to "freely give" this to me. I pray that you will increase my awareness of the blessings that you have already granted me through your grace. I pray that as I go through today, and every day, in the tangible, material world, that your Holy Spirit would remind me of the spiritual blessings that are presently available to me as well as those that I will enjoy for eternity in your presence. I pray that the reality of these blessings would overshadow every thought, feeling, event, and circumstance of this world. I pray for increased faith to remain in awareness of your presence and your provision of all of these blessings. Thank you for your rich grace and unending love and generosity toward me.

> **In Context:**
> Praise be to the God and Father of our Lord Jesus Christ, who has blessed us in the heavenly realms with every spiritual blessing in Christ. For he chose us in him before the creation of the world to be holy and blameless in his sight. In love he predestined us for adoption to sonship through Jesus Christ, in accordance with his pleasure and will — to the praise of his glorious grace, which he has freely given us in the One he loves. In him we have redemption through his blood, the forgiveness of sins, in accordance with the riches of God's grace that he lavished on us. With all wisdom and understanding, he made known to us the mystery of his will according to his good pleasure, which he purposed in Christ, to be put into effect when the times reach their fulfillment — to bring unity to all things in heaven

and on earth under Christ. In him we were also chosen, having been predestined according to the plan of him who works out everything in conformity with the purpose of his will, in order that we, who were the first to put our hope in Christ, might be for the praise of his glory. And you also were included in Christ when you heard the message of truth, the gospel of your salvation. When you believed, you were marked in him with a seal, the promised Holy Spirit, who is a deposit guaranteeing our inheritance until the redemption of those who are God's own people — to the praise of his glory (Ephesians 1:3–14).

> **You have been given fullness in Christ. You are complete.**
> **— Colossians 2:3,10**

Fullness is full. Full means that all that can be contained is contained. There is no lack. Fullness brings satisfaction, completeness. It implies that there are no gaps and no need for anything else. Think of a fully stuffed suitcase or a moving truck that cannot hold anything else.

The fullness the Deity lives in Christ (Colossians 2:9), all of God that there is, and you have been given fullness in Christ. As Christ dwells in you, containing the fullness of the Deity, he fills you. You are full of the Spirit (without measure). In Jesus, you are filled with streams of living water, filled to overflowing (John 7:39).

The fullness of the Deity lives in Christ in you! The scriptures never say that you need to understand all of this for it to be true. As the Holy Spirit reveals the truth of God's word into your inmost being, you come to experience more fully what it is to experientially know God.

The Word says that you have been given fullness in Christ. Jesus said that he came that you could have life to the full (John 10:10). The fullness of God is not available to you merely to fix you or to make you better for the sake of someone else. The fullness of God is available to you so that you can fully relate to him.

I don't think that receiving his fullness is a one-time event. To me, the scriptures indicate that it is a continuous (glory to glory) bubbling up of the springs of living water that fill me and overflow me and fill me again. Jesus shouted out to those in the temple (John 7:37–38), "Let anyone who is thirsty come to me and drink. Whoever believes in me, as Scripture has said, rivers of living water will flow from within them."

Quietly consider places in your life where you thirst for more of God's presence. Drink him into those places. Jesus has prepared a place of total satisfaction and contentment for us.

Jesus, thank you for coming to earth to live as a person. Thank you for showing us what a life lived in fullness of relationship with the Father looks like. Thank you for inviting us into that relationship and offering to quench our thirst through your Spirit. I pray that I will choose to come to you to drink of your Spirit, character, and love instead of trying to fill myself with other things. I welcome your presence and choose to make more room in my life for you to flow into, inhabit, and overflow.

In Context:
My goal is that they may be encouraged in heart and united in love, so that they may have the full riches of complete understanding, in order that they may know the mystery of God, namely, Christ, in whom are hidden all the treasures of wisdom and knowledge… For in Christ all the fullness of the Deity lives in bodily form, and in Christ you have been brought to fullness. He is the head over every power and authority (Colossians 2:2–3, 9–10).

A Place of Total Satisfaction and Contentment:
Summary and Application

The Father has blessed you in the heavenly realms with every spiritual blessing in Christ (Ephesians 1:3). You have been given fullness in Christ. You are complete (Colossians 2:3,10).

In my final weeks of working on the manuscript for this book, I was fortunate to be the guest of friends at their lake house. It is a spacious and wonderfully furnished home outfitted with everything to make your visit to the lake relaxing and fulfilling. It is decorated in lake motif with numerous plaques and sayings. One of them reads, "If you are lucky enough to live at the lake, then you are lucky enough."

That is a pretty descriptive saying to help us recognize the completeness offered by the place that Jesus has prepared for us and the contentment we experience in the presence of God. All else pales in comparison. In John chapter 15, Jesus commands his followers, "Remain in me as I also remain in you." If we are fortunate enough to be in the place prepared for us by Jesus, then we are fortunate enough. 1 Timothy 6:6 says, "Godliness with contentment is great gain."

I think that part of our inability to remain in awareness of the Spirit's presence in us and our place in Jesus is due to the distractions of the "urgency" and priority of things in our daily life — the worries of this life, the deceitfulness of riches, and the desire for other things (Mark 4:19). Though we are frequently bombarded with marketing and media that convey that we need many products or experiences in order to be happy, we can consciously decide to limit the time and effort we invest in things that exacerbate the worries of life, the deceitfulness of riches, and the desire for other things. We don't want to allow these things to choke the word of God in our lives, making it unfruitful. Antidotes include deciding to be content with the things that God richly supplies for our needs, being content to remain in the places that he has prepared for us, deciding to stay in his presence, partaking of what he is doing, and seeking to remain in step with the Father, Son, and Holy Spirit and what they are saying and doing in any circumstance.

Invite the Holy Spirit to show you where you have allowed the worries of this life, the deceitfulness of riches, and the desire for other things to take your attention away from the place of total satisfaction and contentment that Jesus has prepared for you.

Prayerfully reflect on the following truths:

- The Father has blessed me in the heavenly realm with every spiritual blessing in Christ.
- I have been given fullness in Christ.
- I am complete.
- I am in a place of total satisfaction and contentment.

Notes

Notes

CHAPTER 10

A Place of Everlasting *Freedom and Victory*

You were called to take hold of eternal life (1 Timothy 6:12). You are a child of promise (Galatians 4:28). You are called to be free (Galatians 5:13). It is for freedom that Christ has set you free (Galatians 5:1). You are rescued from the present evil age (Galatians 1:4). The Father has rescued you from the domain of darkness and brought you into the kingdom of the Son he loves (Colossians 1:13). Because you have faith in Christ, you are a victorious overcomer of the world (1 John 5:4).

> **You were called to take hold of eternal life.** — 1 Timothy 6:12

Taking hold of eternal life entails letting go of the things we cling to (which are worthless idols) so that our hands are open to take hold of eternal life through relationship with God. In the most recent NIV translation, Jonah 2:8 reads, "Those who cling to worthless idols turn away from God's love for them." In the 1984 edition, the NIV rendered this verse to read, "Those who cling to worthless idols forfeit the grace that could be theirs." The Amplified version reads, "Those who regard and follow worthless idols turn away from their [living source of] mercy and lovingkindness."

Sometimes our clinging is subconscious. It is "just the way we are" because of our upbringing, our culture, our family culture, or our habitual patterns formed over many years. Bringing our clinging into consciousness allows us to make intentional decisions to release our grasp on things that distract us from the things that really matter. Keeping our hands empty so that we can take hold of eternal life is a posture of the heart that plays out in the habits of our trust and dependency on God as opposed to trusting money, circumstances, health, or other relationships. Seeking God first entails holding our hearts open to and for him first and foremost. That brings us into life to the full, being his beloved, bountifully loved, child. It is a posture that leads us into taking hold of eternal life. When our hands (and hearts and minds) are filled with other things, it is difficult to take hold of the eternal life to which we are called.

1 Timothy 6:6–8 points us toward these higher values. "But godliness with contentment is great gain. For we brought nothing into the world, and we can take nothing out of it. But if we have food and clothing, we will be content with that." Similarly, in the Old Testament, Moses declared the word of God to the children of Israel (Deuteronomy 30:19–20). "This day I call the heavens and the earth as witnesses against you that I have set before you life and death, blessings and curses. Now choose life, so that you and your children may live and that you may love the Lord your God, listen to his voice, and hold fast to him. For the Lord is your life, and he will give you many years in the land he swore to give to your fathers, Abraham, Isaac, and Jacob."

John, the "apostle that Jesus loved," writes, "Do not love the world or anything in the world. If anyone loves the world, love for the Father is not in them. For everything in the world — the lust of the flesh, the lust of the eyes, and the pride of life — comes not from the Father but from the world. The world and its desires pass away, but whoever does the will of God lives forever" (1 John 2:15–17).

Comparison, desiring other things, and focusing on the self and what you do and do not have are all things that make us unfruitful in following the word of God. Jesus said, "Still others, like seed sown among thorns, hear the word; but the worries of this life, the deceitfulness of wealth and the desires for other things come in and choke the word, making it unfruitful. Others, like seed sown on good soil, hear the word, accept it, and produce a crop — some thirty, some sixty, some a hundred times what was sown" (Mark 4:18–20). And Hebrews 10:36 says, "You need to persevere so that when you have done the will of God, you will receive what he has promised."

You are finding rest for your soul. As you trust more in God and his love for you, you can rest in him. That gives you rest from the troubles of this world (rather than depending on things of the world to bring you rest). That is relationship! That is knowing God, which is the basis of eternal life (John 17:3). That is what it means to be called to take hold of eternal life.

You cannot take hold of anything if you keep your grasp on things you were never intended to cling to. Orphan-hearted thinking keeps things in your hands that do not belong there. That is a heavy load to hold on to that keeps you from holding on to God. Taking hold of eternal life means opening your hands to prevent the pride of life from filling your hands, mind, effort, heart, attention, and affection and making you weary in the process. Seeking God first — with all your heart, mind, soul — is light in comparison, and it brings relationship, which is the basis of eternal life.

Ask the Holy Spirit to reveal to you anything that you are striving to grasp in your own power that prevents you from more fully experiencing the fullness of life that he intends for you. Take time to consider the things that come to mind and prayerfully invite God's loving goodness to replace your self-striving.

God, thank you for calling me to eternal life. Thank you for giving many accounts in your Word for what that means and how to achieve it. Thank you that true relationship with you is the gateway to all that brings fullness of life as your children. I pray that your Spirit, dwelling in me, would show me, in your way and time, things that I am holding on to that are worthless idols. Help me trust the grace that you yourself apportion to me to open my hands and let go of the worthless things that I cling to in my life. I choose to take refuge in you, God.

In Context:
But you, man of God, flee from all this, and pursue righteousness, godliness, faith, love, endurance and gentleness. Fight the good fight of the faith. Take hold of the eternal life to which you were called when you made your good confession in the presence of many witnesses (1 Timothy 6:11–12).

You are a child of promise. — Galatians 4:28

Being a child of the promise is being a child of God, whose promises are always the same, whose promises never fail, whose promises are for you and not against you, and whose promises are yes and amen. His promises are recorded in his unfailing Word, where not a single stroke of the scribe's pen will fall to the ground unfulfilled. His promises always come true. There is nothing that can stand against them. Being a child of the promise means that you can trust him and believe him because of his character (who he is).

Being a child of the promise also means that you can make choices. One of the promises throughout scripture is that God gave men and women, created in his own image, free choice. Part of the promise is that you have the freedom to choose. When you choose in accordance with his will, his promises, his best for you comes out of it. He said in Deuteronomy 30, "See, today I lay before you life and death, the blessing, and the curse. Choose life." An inalterable doctrinal truth is that as a person, you do have a choice. Whenever you choose poorly, when you disobey, when you choose components of life driven by the orphan spirit, when you choose your thinking as better than his, it invokes in the law of sowing and reaping. You are basically sowing to the flesh when you don't follow his Spirit. When you sow to the flesh, you reap in the flesh. It is a promise, it is true. Hebrews chapter 11 names people of faith, and it says their faith was reckoned to them as righteousness because they acted upon it. Although they did not see the full benefit of choosing to believe and follow God, it was reckoned to them as righteousness because God has the best plan. They are now reaping the benefits of their faith. The law of sowing and reaping also works for you when you choose to believe God, believe his provision of Jesus Christ, believe that his way is the best way, and love him with all of your heart, mind, soul and strength. Sowing to the Spirit yields life and the fruit of the Spirit. It's similar to what social scientists talk about when they discuss positive developmental cascades — or positive ripple effects. Simply stated, when you put good things into a system, more good things happen across the system. Conversely, negative elements introduced into the system yield destructive outcomes.

When you sow to the flesh, the consequences of your own choices keep you from attaining the fullness of the promises of God. When you choose to live according to his promises, they eventually come into manifestation. It is for freedom that God set you free. You are free from the old covenant, you are free from the law of sin and death, but you need to choose life. Just as the Old Testament saints had to choose life and it was counted to them as righteousness, you still need to choose life in your daily decisions.

What does it mean to be a child of promise? God's promise to crush Satan's head under the heel of Jesus? Being a child of God's new covenant? To be one who hears and receives the gospel, the good news of God? One who receives the promised Holy Spirit? To receive a promised inheritance as sons and daughters of God? Things hoped for, but not yet received? Increasingly seeing signs of God's kingdom coming? The invitation to enter into fullness of relationship with God? Perhaps these are all aspects of being a child of promise.

Living in expectation of the fulfillment of God's promises is far better and different than hopelessness. But it is also different than living in the fruition, completion, or experience of promises in finished form. It is both "kingdom now" — experiential glimpses of the fullness ahead that bring hope, faith, and adhering to the promise — and "kingdom come," when at the return of Jesus, we will not be limited to partial glimpses, and all things will be made new and the fullness of life as God intended will manifest forever more. At that time, God "will wipe every tear from their eyes. There will be no more death or mourning or crying or pain, for the old order of things has passed away" (Revelation 21:4).

Hebrews 11:13–16 recounts the heroes of faith stating, "These heroes all died still clinging to their faith, not even receiving all that had been promised them. But they saw beyond the horizon the fulfillment of their promises and gladly embraced it from afar. They all lived their lives on earth as those who belonged to another realm. For clearly, those who live this way are longing for the appearing of a heavenly city. And if their hearts were still remembering what they left behind, they would have found an opportunity to go back. But they couldn't turn back for their hearts were fixed on what was far greater, that is, the heavenly realm!"

Hebrews 11:33–40 (The Passion Translation) continues to describe the relationship between promises and faith: "Through faith's power they conquered kingdoms and established true justice. Their faith fastened onto their promises and pulled them into reality! It was faith that shut the mouth of lions, put out the power of raging fire, and caused many to escape certain death by the sword. Although weak, their faith imparted power to make them strong! Faith sparked courage within them and they became mighty warriors in battle, pulling armies from another realm into battle array. These were the true heroes, commended for their faith, yet they lived in hope without receiving the fullness of what was promised them. But now God has invited us to live in something better than what they had — faith's fullness!"

Living now as lavishly loved children of God (1 John 4:3) gives you a "kingdom now" foretaste of the kingdom to come, when as a child of promise, you will forever experience the fullness of all that God intends for you. Now, seeing as in a mirror dimly (1 Corinthians 13:12), you experience aspects of the fullness of relationship with God that lies ahead. Entering into the place prepared for you by God is both a kingdom come and a kingdom now experience. I urge you not to wait until Jesus returns to establish the new heaven and the new earth to enter into the place he has prepared for you.

Jesus has prepared a place of everlasting freedom and victory for you. Consider areas of your life that are not yet characterized by the fullness that scripture portrays, but do not remain focused on what you currently lack. Choose instead, that as much as it is up to you, to enter the place prepared now and experience life to the full in his presence. Invite the Holy Spirit to lead your meditations.

Father, thank you for making me a child of your promise. Thank you that every one of your promises will come to pass and that at the end of the age, you will restore all things to the fullness of living in unity with you that you intended from before the sin and rebellion of each of us. Thank you that your kingdom is advancing and that the return of Jesus is drawing closer. I pray that you will give me increasing faith to pull your promises into fruition. Thank you that your power, your love, and your goodness ensure that all you desire to happen will happen. Thank you that you are loving me right now and that in your love you are working all things together for my good. I choose to trust your promises and to rest in you as you bring them into my experience and reality.

> **In Context:**
> Now you, brothers and sisters, like Isaac, are children of promise. At that time the son born according to the flesh persecuted the son born by the power of the Spirit. It is the same now (Galatians 4:28–29).

You are called to be free. — Galatians 5:13
It is for freedom that Christ has set you free — Galatians 5:1

Experiencing freedom implies being set free from something, which allows you to engage in and experience other things as a result of your freedom. In Jesus, you are set free from sin, condemnation, guilt, elementary principles of the world, keeping every detail of the Old Testament law, slavery, decay, human rules, and the dominion of darkness. Trusting in Jesus brings freedom from the orphan spirit, fending for yourself and relying on your own "strength" or "goodness." Focusing on the place that Jesus has prepared for you to enter can bring freedom from fear, anxiety, depression, and hopelessness. You now have freedom to enter into relationship with the living God, receive from him, rest in him, enjoy his presence, and live by his Spirit. You are free to approach God with freedom and confidence (Ephesians 3:12). You are free to depend on his goodness and receive his love, presence, and life. You are free to gain life to the full. You are free to enter into the experience of living through each day and its challenges as his child.

Lack of freedom stunts our hope, our ability to dream, and our potential to grow, explore, and create. Being tied to a whole set of the "have tos" dictated by others results in a total lack of discretionary time or energy. Dutifully living a life of obligation is stifling.

Freedom brings unbounded choice. Freedom brings possibility to express creativity, to enjoy good things, to rest, to love others, and to have dominion over choices. Living in the freedom of Christ, you can become the director of time and what you want to do with it. Freedom not to strive for love and approval. Freedom from rejection. Freedom from a meaningless life.

How many of us experience the freedom to which we are called while we are bound to the realities and the demands of everyday life, work, and chores? It is possible! In Jesus, we are invited to be restored to experience and enjoy life in the garden, walking with God in the cool of the evening. We are invited to enter the place he has prepared for us.

In Luke 15, misuse or abuse of freedom is represented by the younger son, who wanted to live in a place far away from relationship with his father. Freedom brings responsibility — to choose well, to live by the Spirit. Deciding to live in the freedom of being generously loved by the God of all creation is life giving.

Meditate on this freedom that is a great gift with boundless possibility. It is for freedom that Christ has set you free. You are free to enter with him into his place of everlasting victory and ultimate success.

God, thank you for setting me free from myself and dependency on my futile ways. Thank you for setting me free from the law of sin and death. Thank you that you give me freedom in so many regards. I pray that I will use the freedom you have given me to enter into the life that you have desired for me to receive in your love. I pray that my life and my choices will be known because I use my freedom to do the wonderful things that you have prepared for me to do in advance, doing them in your love.

> **In Context:**
> It is for freedom that Christ has set us free. Stand firm, then, and do not let yourselves be burdened again by a yoke of slavery... You, my brothers and sisters, were called to be free. But do not use your freedom to indulge the flesh; rather, serve

one another humbly in love. For the entire law is fulfilled in keeping this one command: "Love your neighbor as yourself" (Galatians 5:1,13–14).

> **You are rescued from the present evil age.** — Galatians 1:4

Because Jesus gave himself for your sins, you are rescued. Here are just a few things you are rescued from: sin and death, eternal separation from God, rejection, condemnation, guilt, bondage to sin, fending for yourself as an orphan, division, futility, stuckness, repetition of ineffective efforts, monotony, hopelessness, weariness, bondage, illness, and isolation. You are rescued from all of this.

Recent news coverage of global conflict and oppression have made us aware of the plight of refugees. To pursue freedom and life, they must leave behind everything to come to a place where they entrust themselves to governments and institutions that offer better options than the oppressive conditions they have fled from. Refugees are fully at the mercy of others to gain entrance to a new land and to receive what they need to pursue life in freedom from their former oppressors.

Scripture makes it clear that we are all refugees, depending on God to receive us and to transfer us from the domain of darkness into his kingdom and relationship with him. Our rescue was the Father's will. Jesus accomplished it.

Though we cannot possibly reciprocate, how do we show our appreciation and honor our rescuer? Living "for" him. With him. In him. Praising him. Giving glory and honor to him. Loving him. Living in accordance with his Word. Living in the freedom that he has bought for us at an inestimable price to himself. By choosing not to return to Egypt (things that enslaved us in the past) or our own vomit (2 Peter 2:22). By choosing not to increase our knowledge of evil and good through comparing ourselves to others or making judgments against ourselves or others.

The basic principles of the world do not apply to you because you died with Christ (Colossians 2:20). In Christ, you are rescued from strict adherence to the traditions of man. There is no need to subject yourself to fallen people and their practices. You are free from reciprocity because you can never repay the vast debt God freed us from. You are free from religious systems.

Your rescue from the present evil age makes you free to seek refuge in and pursue Christ, and the things over which he presides. This is relationship, not rules. The end of your story on earth is not the end of your story. The present age, with its evils, is not your destiny. You are able to transcend the futility of life because you are the Father's abundantly loved child.

2 Timothy 4:18 says, "The Lord will rescue me from every evil attack and will bring me safely to his heavenly kingdom. To him be glory for ever and ever.

Amen." The World English Bible translates 2 Timothy 4:18 like this: "And the Lord will deliver me from every evil work, and will preserve me for his heavenly Kingdom. To him be the glory forever and ever. Amen."

Psalm 16:1–2 says, "Keep me safe, my God, for in you I take refuge. I say to the Lord, 'You are my Lord; apart from you I have no good thing.'" The Passion Translation renders these verses: "Keep me safe, O mighty God. I run to you, my safe place. I said to Yahweh, 'You are my Maker and my Master. Any good thing you find in me has come from you.'" We can choose to take refuge in God and experience more fully the place of everlasting freedom and victory — ultimate success.

Quietly consider places where you feel that you are still stuck in circumstances that keep you from experiencing the fullness of life that Jesus has prepared for you. Prayerfully invite more of his presence in each thing that comes to mind and trust him to work all things together for your good (Romans 8:28).

God, thank you for your plan and desire to rescue me from the present evil age. Thank you that beyond having thoughts of doing it, you accomplished all of it through the life, death, and resurrection of Jesus. Thank you for including me in him and attributing his righteousness and freedom to me so that I am free to enter into fullness of relationship with you as your extravagantly loved child. I pray that this day, your Spirit would clearly lead me so that I would be aware of your promptings on where I am to conform to the needs, desires, and expectations of others and where you are leading me to lovingly express my freedom in you to resist conformity to things of contemporary culture and circumstances. I choose to trust you to speak into my awareness through all of my circumstances today and to appropriate grace to walk in your Spirit through all that I experience. Thank you for freeing me from the present evil age and all of the ways that I have been stuck in it.

> **In Context:**
> Grace and peace to you from God our Father and the Lord Jesus Christ, who gave himself for our sins to rescue us from the present evil age, according to the will of our God and Father, to whom be glory for ever and ever. Amen (Galatians 1:3–5).

The Father has rescued you from the domain of darkness and brought you into the kingdom of the Son he loves.
— Colossians 1:13

God almighty has rescued you; he has done on your behalf what you were not able to achieve through your best effort. Rescue often requires a decision and an action that is risky and costly to the self. Rescuers get down and dirty, sweaty; their efforts are often heroic. Rescue involves restoration — transfer from a state of danger and despair to safety, refuge, hope, and peace. Rescue brings you out of a place or circumstance where you have been captive, stuck, broken down, or in utter need of heroic intervention and assistance beyond the self. Rescue achieves what you cannot do on your own. We hear of rescue efforts on behalf of people who are lost, trapped in a fire or car crash, kidnapped, or held hostage. If we could honestly look at your spiritual condition before accepting Jesus, that was us. Every one of us. Because of our sin, we were captive in the domain of darkness and could not even see our way out. People in darkness cannot clearly see their own state of affairs and the lurking dangers that surround them. They are in the domain of the evil one, where the father of lies, the one who steals, kills, and destroys, has dominion.

The Father brought us out of there and into the kingdom of the Son he loves. Think about that change of atmosphere. Order not chaos. Love and life rather than hate and death and decay. Participation and meaning instead of isolation and despair. Sowing to the Spirit instead of sowing to the flesh. Life to the full instead of slavery. Hope and joy for hopelessness and depression.

Acceptance of the sacrifice of Jesus on your behalf is not merely a "life improvement hack." This is so far beyond being upgraded from coach to first class. It is more like going from a place of lack, imprisonment, and deception to palatial living in close friendship with the King. As a believer, you can recognize the extent of the rescue, holding both immediate and eternal consequences. The place that Jesus has prepared for you is a place of everlasting freedom and victory.

Meditate on places where the Lord has already brought you freedom and new life. Express your gratitude to him and trust that he will continue to walk with you through difficulties you currently face.

Father, thank you for rescuing me. Thank you for making the effort, paying the cost, and accomplishing what I could never do. Thank you for rescuing me from traps and dangers beyond what I could ever comprehend. Thank you for bringing me into the kingdom of your Son, whom you love. Thank you for including me in the kingdom of heaven, under the rulership of the most loving, benevolent, and trustworthy being ever. I pray that my status as a citizen of your kingdom would be tangible and real to me. I pray that my heart would be filled with gratitude to you for the rescue you completed on my behalf, and I pray that I would be sensitive to the prompting of your Spirit when you are urging me to participate in the rescue of others who have not yet seen or comprehended the dangers they are ensnared in. I pray for your compassion for them and your wisdom in how to partner with your Spirit to bring them into the kingdom of the Son you love.

In Context:
For he has rescued us from the dominion of darkness
and brought us into the kingdom of the Son he loves,
in whom we have redemption, the forgiveness of sins.
— Colossians 1:13–14

> **Because you have faith in Christ, you are a victorious overcomer of the world.** — 1 John 5:4

In John 16:33, Jesus said, "I have told you these things, so that in me you may have peace. In this world you will have trouble. But take heart! I have overcome the world."

Jesus overcame the world. He left you peace for the trouble that you face. Your faith in him and choice to live in obedience to his commands makes you an overcomer. Overcoming in this sense is not as a conqueror. Webster's Dictionary elaborates that overcome includes the ability to surmount difficulties or to overwhelm. For example, you can be overcome by the heat. To overcome means to gain superiority or win. For example, "strong in the faith that truth would overcome."

Your faith in Christ, not in your behavior or righteousness, is the victory that overcomes the world. Your faith comes with the love of God, which originates in him and from him — and that is what gives you the ability to obey his commands and to follow the promptings of his Spirit. All together, these things keep you above the troubles of this world, making you a victorious overcomer. Together, they give you the freedom to choose to go through life without being dragged down by worries and the desire for other things (Mark 4:19). Your faith in Christ holds you to a different standard that compels you to behave differently than "the world," those who have not yet chosen the freedom of living as a child of God.

To overcome the world is to live by love — love from God that is freely received and then freely given to those you encounter. That makes you an overcomer of the world's systems, values, beliefs, and behavior. Victory for the kingdom acts like yeast, first to transform you, and then it flows through you to shape atmospheres and expand God's kingdom around you. The place prepared is truly a place of everlasting freedom and victory — ultimate success.

Quietly reflect on the provision of God that gives you the resources you need to overcome the challenges of this life. Meditate on his love for you and his heart for your well-being.

Jesus, thank you that I have been born again in you. Thank you for making me a new creation in you, a person in whom the Spirit of God dwells. Thank you that you overcame the world so that in you, I too can be an overcomer. God, I pray that you will continue to work in and through me, transforming me more and more into your image so that as I walk through this life as your child, I will release your overcoming Spirit into all that I do and say.

In Context:
In fact, this is love for God: to keep his commands. And his commands are not burdensome, for everyone born of God

overcomes the world. This is the victory that has overcome the world, even our faith. Who is it that overcomes the world? Only the one who believes that Jesus is the Son of God (1 John 5:3–5).

A Place of Everlasting Freedom and Victory: *Summary and Application*

You were called to take hold of eternal life (1 Timothy 6:12). You are a child of promise (Galatians 4:28). You are called to be free (Galatians 5:13). It is for freedom that Christ has set you free (Galatians 5:1). You are rescued from the present evil age (Galatians 1:4). The Father has rescued you from the domain of darkness and brought you into the kingdom of the Son he loves (Colossians 1:13). Because you have faith in Christ, you are a victorious overcomer of the world (1 John 5:4).

God has invited us to his place of refuge in Jesus. As we choose to come to him, to trust in the sufficiency of his love, grace, and sacrifice on our behalf, we enter into the place that he has prepared for us. It is a place of refuge. It is a place of resting in the shadow of the Almighty (Psalm 91:1). We are refugees from the domain of darkness and welcomed as children of God.

Take time to quiet yourself regularly, to be still and know that God is God. Listen for his voice to speak into your life. Ask in the Spirit, where am I? What is the nature of the place that you have me in now? What are you doing in this place? What is it time for? What can I do to partner with you in this place now?

Choosing to be aware of God's presence with you and his desires for you in the place where he has you opens you to opportunities to let his nature overflow you to bring changes to the places where you are. Choose to depend on him. Take refuge in him.

> **Invite the Holy Spirit to apply the freedom and substance of these biblical truths in your life:**

- I was called to take hold of eternal life.
- I am a child of promise.

- I am called to be free.
- It is for freedom that Christ has set me free.
- I am rescued from the present evil age.
- The Father has rescued me from the domain of darkness and brought me into the kingdom of the Son he loves.
- Because I have faith in Christ, I am a victorious overcomer of the world.
- In Jesus, I am in a place of everlasting freedom and victory.

Notes

CHAPTER 11

A Place of *Constant Goodness*

You are rooted and established in love (Ephesians 3:17). God's power is at work within you (Ephesians 3:20). You are God's workmanship, created in Christ Jesus to do good works, which God prepared in advance for you to do (Ephesians 2:10). God works in you to will and act according to his good purpose (Philippians 2:13). Jesus chose and appointed you to go and bear much lasting fruit (John 15:5,16). Apart from Jesus, you can do nothing (John 15:5).

> **You are rooted and established in love.** — Ephesians 3:17

This truth comes in the context of Paul's powerful prayer for the believers in Ephesus. Wow! What a prayer! And because it is Holy Spirit inspired scripture, it is God's desire, so praying it over yourself brings God's fruit into your life. I recommend praying this prayer over yourself regularly. Try praying it every day for thirty days, I expect you'll be surprised by how God roots and establishes you in his love. I have done this in the past, and I repeat the discipline on occasion because I have experienced the good fruit of his Word transforming my life.

As briefly described earlier, I used to think Paul was just being eloquent by saying God's love is high and deep, but the first time I spent a month praying this prayer over myself, I experienced something remarkable as I was mindfully praying through the prayer on the way home from a business trip. Looking out of an airplane from my window seat, I looked up and down through three-dimensional space and realized something about the width and length, the height and depth of Christ's love. It was a selah moment at 30,000 feet that has changed my experiential understanding of the love of Christ. Quite simply, in an airplane, it becomes obvious that height is what is above you and depth is what is below you. Because of the vastness of Christ's love, its infinite nature, when we meditate on the width and length and height and depth of it simultaneously, we come to the revelation that we are directly in the center of his love! Anything that extends to infinity in all directions away from you places you in its middle.

Christ's love is so vast that no matter where you are, you are right in the middle of it — right in its crosshairs. You are the target and recipient of God's boundless love. You can never traverse or walk out of it. That revelation of being rooted and established (some translations say rooted and grounded) "grounded" me at 30,000 feet.

Roots are the source of life to a plant. Besides anchoring the plant, all nourishment for life comes through the roots. To be rooted in God's love means that his love is your anchor and stability, what keeps you grounded. In love, you were chosen by God (Ephesians 1:4) before all of creation, set apart, and called by God (Galatians 1:15). If that's not "rooted" in God's love, I don't know what is! That is how you were established.

Let the experience of God's vast love for you personally feed and support you. Roots draw from the soil that the plant is grounded in. You are rooted and grounded in love. Being rooted and grounded in something or someplace establishes the entire basis for your life. From the roots come fruits. A good tree does not produce bad fruit (Matthew 7:17–18). Root pruning stunts a plant. Plants that reproduce from root cuttings are always the same stock as the parent plant. Because you are rooted in God's love, his love becomes your core character trait.

Romans 11:18 says, "Consider this: You do not support the root, but the root supports you." Colossians 2:6–7 elaborates: "So then, just as you received Christ Jesus as Lord, continue to live your lives in him, rooted and built up in him, strengthened in the faith as you were taught, and overflowing with thankfulness." You are rooted and established in love. The place that Jesus has prepared for you is a place of constant goodness.

Meditate on ways that God's love for you roots and establishes you. Consider how it has grown in your identity since you first invited Jesus into your life. Reflect on ways that you have experienced being in the center of God's love in the past and what that means for the challenges you face now.

Jesus, thank you that I am rooted and grounded in your love. Thank you that no matter where I am, I am in the center of your love and that your love is boundless and continuous. Thank you that there is nothing I can or must do to increase your love for me, and thank you that there is nothing I can do that would make you love me less. I pray that as your Spirit pours your love into my heart that I would experience your love more fully and continually throughout each day of my life. Help me to take time to receive and reflect on the vastness and security of your love. I pray that experiencing more of your love will transform me to be more like you.

> **In Context:**
> I pray that out of his glorious riches he may strengthen you with power through his Spirit in your inner being, so that Christ may dwell in your hearts through faith. And I pray that you, being rooted and established in love, may have power, together with all the Lord's holy people,

to grasp how wide and long and high and deep is the love of Christ, and to know this love that surpasses knowledge — that you may be filled to the measure of all the fullness of God (Ephesians 3:16–19).

> **God's power is at work within you.** — Ephesians 3:20

You can rest in God's power. It works in you and will bring about his ways in you, through you, and on your behalf. Whatever circumstances or negative forces are influencing you or that you face, God's power in you is there to counteract them and to overcome them. What is stronger or superior to God's power? What can prevail against it? His power is pure, good, and perfect. His power is sufficient. His power will persevere and overcome. His power is never "off" or "out." God's power is at work in you, right now. You can rest assured that his power will also be at work in you tomorrow. His power can be applied to overwriting the wounds we have received in the past.

The truth of this is so important for us to grasp that God has addressed it through many verses distributed through several portions of scripture. Here is a small sampling: The power of life (John 5:26) and to move and have my being comes from God (Acts 17:28). He gives you power so that you can have great power and endurance and patience (Colossians 1:11). His power renews in knowledge of his image (Colossians 3:9). Your existence depends on him. Apart from him you can do nothing (John 15:5). He gives you power for all.

2 Peter 1:3 says, "His divine power has given us everything we need for a godly life through our knowledge of him who called us by his own glory and goodness."

Ephesians 3:20 says "Now to him who is able to do immeasurably more than all we ask or imagine, according to his power that is at work within us …" Wow! You did not ask, imagine, or hope near enough! His power is at work in you. In Jesus, you are truly in a place of constant goodness.

Meditate on specific ways that you have experienced the power of God in your life already. Invite him to expand your awareness of his power working on your behalf. Ask for his power to be enough for obstacles you are experiencing today.

God, thank you that you, the all-powerful one, have made your power available to me and that you work your incomparable power on my behalf. I pray that I will be more aware of your power flowing toward and into me. I pray that I would ask for and depend on your power more than on fending for myself. I pray that I would trust you to be with me and for me in every situation that I face. God, I choose to trust your power over my own tendency to live independently.

In Context:
Now to him who is able to do immeasurably more than all we ask or imagine, according to his power that is at work within us, to him be glory in the church and in Christ Jesus throughout all generations, for ever and ever! Amen (Ephesians 3:20–21).

You are God's workmanship, created in Christ Jesus to do good works, which God prepared in advance for you to do. — Ephesians 2:10

This verse directly follows Ephesians 2:9, which tells us that we are saved by grace, not works. Our works are not the basis of our salvation. Yet God, our creator, invites us to co-participate with him by engaging in good works that he prepared for us to do in advance.

You are the living, changing product of the workmanship of the greatest master craftsman ever! The creator of the entire universe, who made everything in perfection, harmony, beauty, and completeness. He does great work! Though we are well-aware of our failures, flaws, shortcomings, and weaknesses, the truth is that we are fearfully and wonderfully made (Psalm 139:14) in the image of God himself. His power continually works in us from his heart of love and goodness and wise perfection.

God has had elaborate plans for your life from before the beginning of time. He created you with the ability to do what he dreamed for you. He set the path to prepare you and arranged everything for your success.

My wife, Judy, has been an art teacher for many years. During the recent pandemic, I video recorded art project lessons that she shared with her students online. That experience taught me a valuable set of truths. When an arts and crafts teacher does a project with a child or a group of children, they plan everything, coming to the session with objectives and goals. They assemble everything needed for successful completion of the project. They provide instruction, encouragement, and coaching, but they also desire each child's creative ideas to personalize the project. The advance planning and provision along with the character of a loving teacher, nearly guarantees the success of every child on every project. In many ways, it is very much a co-participation. The teacher could have done the craft alone at a much more advanced level than the kids. But the teacher takes delight in seeing the children participate, experiment, learn, create, and become more experienced and accomplished. The teacher helps to birth and mature students' giftings, personal confidence, and skills through planned works — prepared in advance. In many ways, the project that the children take to their homes is not the main project. The child's development is the main project. Good works, prepared in advance, birth and hone development of those who complete them.

How much more has God prepared our good works? How much more does he coach, encourage, and supply everything needed for our success in the good works he prepared for us to do? The result of participating in the good works that God so lovingly prepared for you personally — custom made for your giftings, callings, and personal development — is that you become God's workmanship. You are a work of his art, his own masterwork, fulfilling the destiny he planned for you because you are joined to Jesus.

When Jesus walked the earth as fully human, he fulfilled his destiny by saying what his Father was saying and doing what he saw him doing. He came for more than to live sinlessly and be a perfect sacrifice for our sins through a horrific death. The Father prepared miracles and teachings and relationships and conversations in boats and by wells and over meals for him to experience and add his own creative participation to. When we think about this and the great love of the Father toward Jesus, don't be fooled into thinking that God does less for us. He loves us with the same love he loved Jesus with (John 17:23)! He has given as much forethought, preparation, and provision into our good works — our craft projects — as he did for Jesus. What he has prepared for each of us is unique to our giftings and callings, destiny, and growth as his child. As we participate in the good works God prepared in advance for us to do, we more fully enter the place prepared for us — a place of constant goodness.

Reflect on ways that you have grown in relationship with God by doing things you have felt prompted by him to do. Consider whether he is beginning to plant fresh vision in you to partner with him in new endeavors. Invite him to guide you in the timing and other logistics of partnering with you in new projects to share his love.

God, thank you for caring for me so personally that you have written all the days of my life in a book before one of them came to pass. Thank you for custom designing good works for me to do and for preparing them in advance, down to every detail, so that when I co-participate in those good works with you, I become your master work. Thank you for the opportunities you bring to me every day to partner with you in extending your kingdom on earth, both in me and through me. I pray that today I will recognize some of the opportunities you have designed in advance for me to do, and that I will do them with you and in your character. I pray for the lasting fruit that you desire to bring into my life and to others through the good works that you have prepared for me to do with you.

In Context:
For it is by grace you have been saved, through faith — and this is not from yourselves, it is the gift of God — not by works, so that no one can boast. For we are God's handiwork, created in Christ Jesus to do good works, which God prepared in advance for us to do (Ephesians 2:8–10).

> **God works in you to will and act according to his good purpose.**
> — Philippians 2:13

God's purpose is fully good. His purpose is rooted and grounded in love, because love is at the core of who God is. His love continually flows toward you and into you. But not just to you. God works in you through the indwelling of his Holy Spirit, who is the Spirit of Truth (John 14:17). He, living in you, keeps you from being left in the same situation as an orphan (John 14:18). In John 16:13–15, Jesus declared, "But when he, the Spirit of truth, comes, he will guide you into all the truth. He will not speak on his own; he will speak only what he hears, and he will tell you what is yet to come. He will glorify me because it is from me that he will receive what he will make known to you. All that belongs to the Father is mine. That is why I said the Spirit will receive from me what he will make known to you."

Proverbs 19:21 says, "Many are the plans in a person's heart, but it is the Lord's purpose that prevails." In the New Testament, Romans 8:26–30 elaborates these truths in the following manner: "In the same way, the Spirit helps us in our weakness. We do not know what we ought to pray for, but the Spirit himself intercedes for us through wordless groans. And he who searches our hearts knows the mind of the Spirit, because the Spirit intercedes for God's people in accordance with the will of God. And we know that in all things God works for the good of those who love him, who have been called according to his purpose. For those God foreknew he also predestined to be conformed to the image of his Son, that he might be the firstborn among many brothers and sisters. And those he predestined, he also called; those he called, he also justified; those he justified, he also glorified."

It is time to begin to trust the thoughts, promptings, and leadings that come to you (and are consistent with God's word and his character) as coming from him to you — as his working in you and through you to act according to his good purpose. This is how he will lead you into the good works that he prepared in advance for you to do (Philippians 2:13). Is it possible that when God is working all things together for our good that includes him prompting you to be a conduit of his love and his character in the situations you are in? Beyond being a professional designation (such as pastor) for some, full-time ministry is a lifestyle for all of God's children.

Life to the full, or living the adventure, entails believing that God works in you and through you to change atmospheres and make kingdom differences in the earth — right where you are. It involves being salt and light. It involves being leaven. These are things that change everything. They can bring sudden changes (signs and wonders) or subtle changes (covert prayer walking, interjecting positive God words or perspectives into conversations). So we do not grumble and complain. We do not highlight the pain and suffering that are part of this fallen world, and we certainly don't intentionally do things to increase it. Instead, we bring God's character and the fruit of his Spirit into every context of our lives. We are invited to walk in relationship with our God in a place of constant goodness.

Meditate on the Galatians 5:22–23, which lists the fruit of the Spirit: love, joy, peace, patience, kindness, goodness, faithfulness, gentleness and self-control. How have you seen growth in these characteristics of God's Spirit bring good fruit in your life? Invite him to increase the harvest of his fruit in your life.

God, thank you for humbling yourself to come to earth and to dwell in and to work in me. I pray for greater sensitivity to the prompting of your Holy Spirit. I pray that the things that you are speaking to me and the things that you are leading me to do and say would be more prominent in my life than my own perspectives, desires, and ways. I trust you to work in me to fulfill your good purpose in me and through me.

In Context:
Therefore, my dear friends, as you have always obeyed —
not only in my presence, but now much more in my absence —
continue to work out your salvation with fear and trembling,
for it is God who works in you to will and to act in order to
fulfill his good purpose. Do everything without grumbling
or arguing, so that you may become blameless and pure,
"children of God without fault in a warped and crooked
generation." Then you will shine among them like
stars in the sky as you hold firmly to the word of life
(Philippians 2:12–16).

> **Jesus chose and appointed you to go and bear much lasting fruit. — John 15:5,16**

God chose you (Ephesians 1:4)! You are chosen for a particular job (or jobs) lovingly prepared in advance for you to do (Ephesians 2:10). He gives you the will to do them (Philippians 2:13) and has his power working through you (Ephesians 3:20). This is a master plan for success. Good fruit comes from loving one another with the love with which he first loved you. Because you are rooted and grounded in love (Ephesians 3:17), you are fruitful in Christ if you remain in him and do not attempt to do the appointed tasks apart from him.

Chosen and appointed by Jesus. Webster's Dictionary defines appointed in the following manner: "1) Chosen for a particular job. An appointed official. 2) Officially fixed or set. At the appointed time. 3) Provided with complete and unusually appropriate or elegant furnishings and equipment. A beautifully appointed room."

You have been chosen and appointed for the specific job, officially set at an appointed time, and provided with complete and unusually appropriate and elegant ability to bear much lasting fruit in God's kingdom. You have been appointed with his desire, authority, and ability to partner with him as he does what only he can do. Let these thoughts register in your spirit and soak in for a few moments.

How amazing to be wanted and chosen by God. How life-altering to be given the opportunity to partner with him to do the things that are on his heart and have been since before the beginning of time. How wonderful to know that his zeal accomplishes all of this in you and through you, and that his love for you does not change based on your ability or failures. What a fulfilling life to walk in relationship with our God in a place of constant goodness.

Meditate on ways that fruit trees and other food crops bear fruit. What parts can you facilitate in your life, and how must you remain dependent on God for the provision, growth, and preservation of fruit?

God, thank you for choosing and appointing me to partner with you to bear good fruit that will last. Thank you for giving me opportunities to further your kingdom in my life and through the things you have prepared in advance for me to do. Thank you for having me in mind and making room and opportunity to be a part of your eternal desires and plans. I pray that through all of my experiences and interactions today I would respond from your perspective of loving others, expanding your kingdom, and bearing fruit. All life and every good and perfect gift comes from you, and apart from you, I can do nothing. I choose to depend on you to bring life and the fullness of lasting fruit as I walk through this day in relationship to you. Fill me with your love and let your love flow through me into all that I do and say today.

> **In Context:**
> Remain in me, as I also remain in you. No branch can bear fruit by itself; it must remain in the vine. Neither can you bear fruit unless you remain in me. I am the vine; you are the branches. If you remain in me and I in you, you will bear much fruit; apart from me you can do nothing… You did not choose me, but I chose you and appointed you so that you might go and bear fruit — fruit that will last — and so that whatever you ask in my name the Father will give you. This is my command: Love each other (John 15:4–5,16–17).

Apart from Jesus, you can do nothing. — John 15:5

Love gets it done. The Love of God, where all of life originates, is flowing into you and through you to others. Without his love, presence, and guidance, you can do nothing. Nothing loving, nothing lasting, nothing life giving, nothing bearing good fruit. He is the alpha and the omega (Revelation 22:13) — the source, the lasting one, the beginning and the end. Remaining in him allows his character, love, and power to transform you in lasting, fruitful ways. Love wins.

In many western cultures, there is a high value placed on independence and being your own person. The life of self-sufficiency is not just a culturally fueled developmental drive, it is a deception of Satan. A desire for independence is what brought original sin. Through the introduction of sin came broken relationship with God and the introduction of death. The wages of sin still bring death.

Apart from him, you can do nothing because apart from him, you are not cleansed and you cannot enter God's presence. God is the source of life, love, light, and power for good. It is foolish to think that you could depend on yourself instead. It is vain to think that you have anything to offer that even remotely approximates good in comparison. Placing yourself ahead of God to act independently is acting out of an orphan-hearted spirit. It brings sinfulness and leads to barking up the wrong tree. It releases the fruit of the tree of knowledge of good and evil, perpetuating characteristics of the fall initiated in the original sin of Adam and Eve.

God's desire is for you to produce much good fruit that will last, which depends on you depending on and remaining in Jesus. Apart from him, you can do nothing. Understanding the futility of independence and the importance of asking the Father in the name of Jesus positions us to co-participate with God to bring the good, lasting fruit of his love into fruition. The creation of good, lasting fruit is God's work, not a human enterprise. Having opportunity to participate in God's work in his way brings his fruit in you and to others. Trusting in him with all of your heart and leaning not on your own understanding positions you in a place of his constant goodness.

Consider whether there are areas in your life where your natural talents and abilities make it nearly automatic for you to do well. Traits that you have that frequently bring good results when you use them. Consider how you can appreciate and use the abilities that God has given you while truly depending on him for outcomes.

God, thank you for your heart of love and your desire to bring good into all things in the lives of all people. Thank you for the opportunities you create for me to walk through each day with you and to be a part of advancing your kingdom and your glory. I pray that today I would experience more of your love, choose to remain in you, and do what you are doing and say what you are saying in order to bear the fruit of your kingdom. God, help me to be slow to act on my own and quick to invite you into all that I experience today.

In Context:
Remain in me, as I also remain in you. No branch can bear fruit by itself; it must remain in the vine. Neither can you bear fruit unless you remain in me. I am the vine; you are

the branches. If you remain in me and I in you, you will bear much fruit; apart from me you can do nothing...You did not choose me, but I chose you and appointed you so that you might go and bear fruit — fruit that will last — and so that whatever you ask in my name the Father will give you. This is my command: Love each other (John 15:4–6, 16–17).

A Place of Constant Goodness: *Summary and Application*

You are rooted and established in love (Ephesians 3:17). God's power is at work within you (Ephesians 3:20). You are God's workmanship, created in Christ Jesus to do good works, which God prepared in advance for you to do (Ephesians 2:10). God works in you to will and act according to his good purpose (Philippians 2:13). Jesus chose and appointed you to go and bear much lasting fruit (John 15:5,16). Apart from Jesus, you can do nothing (John 15:5).

Because God is good, and your place prepared is in him and in relationship with him, the place prepared is a place of constant goodness. Romans 8:28 declares the working of God's goodness in all aspects of your life and circumstances: "And we know that in all things God works for the good of those who love him, who have been called according to his purpose." Note that it says all things. Whether they were things done to you, intended for your harm, or the result of your own poor choices, or just the way things are because of the state of the world, God works for good. The constant and overwhelming goodness of God, grounded in his incomparable love and power, works things proactively and everything retroactively to create a complete tapestry of blessing. There is nothing in all of creation that can separate you from the love of God that is in Jesus, our Lord (Romans 8:39). In his love for you, he uses his goodness to bring everything in your life together for good.

Your worries, anxieties, and self-striving apart from him do nothing of lasting value. In fact, they can cause you to forfeit the grace that could be yours (Jonah 2:8). 1 Peter 5:7 says, "Cast all your anxiety on him, because he cares for you." To cast something means to throw it off or away from yourself. Casting all your anxiety on him implies that you are not to hold on to any of it. Instead, you are to completely give worries over to him, trusting him to provide all that you need to successfully navigate the challenges you face. You trust in him, not your own understanding, effort, or merit. The preceding verses say, "God opposes the proud but shows favor to the humble. Humble yourselves, therefore, under God's mighty hand that he may lift you up in due time." This is not a prescription for inactivity and being irresponsible. God does give you things to do, and to do diligently. He could have easily provided Noah with an ark, but God told him to build it. Biblical scholars estimate that the construction would have taken around a hundred years. That's diligent labor. A lot of diligent labor. But it is also clear that apart from the grace and health and strength and direction from God, Noah would have failed. The hand of God is also evident in bringing all the animals to the ark at the right time in the right numbers and pairings. These verses help us to see that there is a continual interplay between humility, trusting dependence on God, and diligent and responsible obedience to the direction he provides. Being humble releases the favor of God.

The life of Jesus also shows that the place of God's goodness and direction does not result in an easy life free from trials and suffering. It shows that awareness of God's presence and provision of all that is needed allows one to overcome the world, in love. Being in the place of God's constant goodness certainly provides the best alternative to toughing it out on your own in your feeble self-reliance. Pray that the Holy Spirit will shape your thoughts and expectations regarding the ways to walk through the challenges of this life. Pray for him to show you the fullness of the place that Jesus has prepared for you, a place of constant goodness.

Meditate on the following truths:

- I am rooted and established in love.
- God's power is at work within me.
- I am God's workmanship, created in Christ Jesus to do good works, which God prepared.
- God works in me to will and act according to his good purpose.
- Jesus chose and appointed me to go and bear much lasting fruit.
- Apart from Jesus, I can do nothing.
- In the Lord, I am in a place of constant goodness.

Notes

CHAPTER 12: A Place of *Increasing Closeness and Care*

Now, in Christ Jesus, you, who were once far away, have been brought near through the blood of Christ (Ephesians 2:13). Your citizenship is in heaven (Philippians 3:20). You are no longer a foreigner or an alien, but a fellow citizen with God's people and a member of God's household (Ephesians 2:12). Through Christ, you have access to the Father, through one Spirit (Ephesians 2:18).

> **Now, in Christ Jesus, you, who were once far away, have been brought near through the blood of Christ.** — Ephesians 2:13

Let's hear what the scripture has to say about being brought near. Colossians 1:19–20 says, "For God was pleased to have all his fullness dwell in him, and through him to reconcile to himself all things, whether things on earth or things in heaven, by making peace through his blood, shed on the cross." And 2 Corinthians 5:18–21 says, "All this is from God, who reconciled us to himself through Christ and gave us the ministry of reconciliation: that God was reconciling the world to himself in Christ, not counting people's sins against them. And he has committed to us the message of reconciliation. We are therefore Christ's ambassadors, as though God were making his appeal through us. We implore you on Christ's behalf: Be reconciled to God. God made him who had no sin to be sin for us, so that in him we might become the righteousness of God."

The shed blood of Jesus has sanctified us, cleansed us from our sins, and has reconciled us to God through his initiative and his plan. Reconciliation has brought us near to God. Sin separated us because of our own rebellion and wrong-headed decision-making. By our own decisions, doubts, fears, and lack of belief and trust, we were not in God's kingdom or family, and we were not cultivating his presence. We were not in regular close relationship with our creator and the lover of our soul. Christ's sacrifice changed everything for us. Jesus himself is our peace with God.

You are in him, and he is in the Father. Being brought near is such an understatement of the total immersion of God you have in Christ. Meditate on this reality: In Jesus, you are in a place of increasing closeness and care.

Father, thank you for desiring me, creating me, and pursuing me across all time and space until I "found you." Thank you for making yourself and the depth of your love known to me. I pray that more and more I would experientially know and rest in your love. Thank you for continual access to you. I choose to remain in you and give you praise for your great love.

> **In Context:**
> But now in Christ Jesus you who once were far away
> have been brought near by the blood of Christ. For he
> himself is our peace ... He came and preached peace to
> you who were far away and peace to those who were near.
> For through him we both have access to the Father by
> one Spirit (Ephesians 2:13–14, 17–18).

Your citizenship is in heaven. — Philippians 3:20

Webster's Dictionary says that a citizen is an inhabitant of a city, town, or nation, especially one entitled to the rights and privileges of a freeman; a member of a state; a person who owes allegiance to a government and is entitled to protection from it. Your citizenship is in heaven.

Citizenship has implications for the location of a primary residence and the allegiance one has to that place as well as to those who provide leadership and legal decisions, such as the governor of your place of residence. Citizens are governed by its rules and regulations, but also are benefactors of its freedom and leadership. Citizenship gives you rights and privileges and responsibilities. Being a citizen of heaven gives you immunity to the elementary principles of this world. The new heaven and the new earth will be your eternal residence where the rule and reign of God's kingdom — established and planned in the awesomeness of his goodness and character — will remain forever. His perfect plan without deviation or dissent will be fully carried out. You get to dwell in it, partake of it, and participate in it as you are united in relationship with the supreme ruler, provider, and protector. All of the resources of this kingdom are available to you in Christ.

Various agencies and organizations rank countries by creating composite scores of safety, infrastructure, economy, freedoms, education, healthcare, and similar resources (including the peace and happiness of their citizens). Even the greatest places in the world to live pale by comparison to being a citizen of heaven where we will be eternally in relationship with God himself in the perfection of his planned new heaven and new earth. No tears, no pain, no death, no suffering. Eternal fellowship and feasting with him and his children. God himself has prepaid and provided all of the costs, taxes, and fees. Citizenship in heaven far surpasses the greatest all-inclusive resort ever. A visit to a resort provides a time-limited respite from the realities of everyday routines of life, and not everything that you "enjoy" while there contributes positively to your health. In contrast, citizenship in heaven is life-giving and eternal. Everything that is part of the kingdom of heaven brings good fruit and joy. There is no part of it that brings disease, sorrow, or death. This is life to the full.

A person's citizenship and a sense of their homeland forms a part of their identity. Knowing that we are citizens of heaven changes the way we walk through each day in this life. Awareness of being a citizen of heaven causes us to see that the place prepared for us is a place of constant goodness, the goodness of God himself. As we grow in relationship with him, we also recognize that it is a place of increasing closeness and care.

Meditate on ways that your everyday decision making would be different if you remained continually aware of being a citizen of heaven and in the presence of the King of Kings. Invite the Holy Spirit to frequently remind you of your citizenship.

Father, thank you that you have declared that I am a citizen of heaven. Thank you for providing all I needed to attain citizenship. Thank you that my status as a citizen is finished in Christ and sealed by your Spirit. Thank you for the security of knowing my destiny and future for all of eternity. Thank you that beyond being a citizen of heaven, as your child, you have made me a member of your own household. I pray that I will never lose sight of this as I go through each day on earth in this life. Thank you that I am truly an alien in this world. Thank you that the trials and struggles of this world are temporary. I ask for your grace to face them in your character. I pray that knowing my citizenship is in heaven will resound in my identity and in the way I live each day until we are face to face.

In Context:
For, as I have often told you before and now tell you again even with tears, many live as enemies of the cross of Christ. Their destiny is destruction, their god is their stomach, and their glory is in their shame. Their mind is set on earthly things. But our citizenship is in heaven. And we eagerly await a Savior from there, the Lord Jesus Christ, who, by the power that enables him to bring everything under his control, will transform our lowly bodies so that they will be like his glorious body (Philippians 3:18–21).

> **You are no longer a foreigner or an alien, but a fellow citizen with God's people and a member of God's household.**
> **— Ephesians 2:19**

A foreigner is one who has not been immersed in the customs, language, rules, and "inside scoop" of the place they are visiting. Permission is required to enter and to stay when visiting foreign countries. Currency exchange is necessary, and it can be challenging for a foreigner to feel at home or to feel at ease in the country they are visiting. Sometimes, foreigners or aliens long to return to their home country.

A foreigner does not have the same rights as citizens. They often have lower status and may face various forms of legal restrictions, discrimination, challenges, or hurdles. Stating that you are no longer a foreigner means that you once were, but that is now in the past. Your status has changed in Christ.

Being in Christ, you are a fellow citizen with God's people. You share status with all of his children. As his children, we are all siblings. There is a sustaining combination of fellowship, acceptance, rights, and life-giving principles. We also enjoy the protection of God's law, rule, and presence as well as his authority, power, and wisdom. Being a citizen of his kingdom is different than being a citizen of any earthly kingdom. His kingdom continually provides a reliable and stable government that has our best interest at heart.

As if that weren't enough, it gets even better. We are members of God's household. Being children in the household is far different than being foreigners or even citizens. Children have rights and power and access and intimacy. These do not negate the rights of citizenship but far exceed the rules, laws, and privileges of citizens. Citizens can make requests through writing or other formal channels (such as contacting a representative) to have a time-limited meeting with a ruler for a specific purpose. Children can have an ongoing relationship with their papa. They can sit on his lap, play on the floor, or sit at the table and share a meal. Wow. As his dearly loved children, we are in a place of increasing closeness and care.

Quietly reflect on how you can remain more aware of being in God's household. How does your place in his family change your approach to things you are facing today?

God, thank you for placing me as a citizen under your authority and rulership. Thank you for the benevolence and trustworthiness of your government. Thank you that beyond making me a citizen of your kingdom that you have placed me as your child in your household. I pray that you would continue to reveal to my heart, through your Holy Spirit, the security, closeness and tenderness of your love and presence as I walk through each day. More and more, I pray that I would come to know that as your child and a citizen in your kingdom, I am a foreigner in this life. I pray that I would walk through all that you have planned for me in awareness of representing you, my Father and my King, to all I come into contact with today.

> **In Context:**
> He came and preached peace to you who were far away and peace to those who were near. For through him we both have access to the Father by one Spirit. Consequently, you are no longer foreigners and strangers, but fellow citizens with God's people and also members of his household, built on the foundation of the apostles and prophets, with Christ Jesus himself as the chief cornerstone. In him the whole building is joined together and rises to become a holy temple in the Lord (Ephesians 2:17–21).

> **Through Christ, you have access to the Father, through one Spirit.** — Ephesians 2:18

So often we read a scriptural truth without allowing the fullness of what it is declaring to register in our spirit and permeate us. We see familiar words in shallow ways, not thinking through the richness of meaning that the Spirit of God was desiring to communicate to us through the words recorded in scripture. That is why the dictionary definitions of common words are frequently included in the meditations on the scriptures.

Webster's Dictionary defines access as "permission, liberty, or ability to enter, approach or pass to and from a place or to approach or communicate with a person or thing. Freedom or ability to obtain or make use of something. A way or means of entering or approaching. An increase by addition. A sudden access of wealth." Think about what this means for having access to the Father through one Spirit through Christ. Allow each of those meanings of access to register in your thinking and in your spirit.

Jesus taught us to pray directly to his Abba. He said you should ask him directly. You have permission to approach and communicate with God himself (1 John 4:8). Your access is through Christ. The veil of the temple tore in two from top to bottom. Because you are holy and blameless and judged to be righteous in Christ, it is through him that you have access to a holy God. Your Father desires you to approach. You are members of his household. Members of households regularly interact. They do not ignore one another or avoid talking together unless there is a major disruption to the relationship. You should not ignore God by not abiding with him. At the very least, praying continually means conversing often.

Just imagine if your child brought a friend of theirs to your home and he or she ignored you or feared you. How hurtful and disappointing would that be? It would clearly communicate the misunderstanding they have regarding how welcomed they are into the household, and the wrong beliefs they hold regarding your character and desire to interact with them.

You have freedom in Christ to freely approach and communicate with your Father. He gives you direct access. This is better than having his private, direct number on speed dial with a smart phone on WIFI! Use the access you have been given to call him. Come in and sit and reason with him. Come to the table with him. Enter his presence. You are in Jesus, Jesus is in the Father, the Spirit is in you. Enter through Jesus into his presence. Take the time right now to sit in that place. Experience the place of increasing closeness and care.

Jesus, thank you for being the way, for giving me access to God, for restoring me to relationship, and for bringing me into the beauty of knowing you. I choose to know you better, to believe what your scriptures declare concerning your love for me, and to trust your desire to welcome me into your presence, to indwell me, and to relate to me for eternity.

In Context:
He came and preached peace to you who were far away and peace to those who were near. For through him we both have access to the Father by one Spirit. Consequently, you are no longer foreigners and strangers, but fellow citizens with God's people and also members of his household (Ephesians 2:17–19).

A Place of Increasing Closeness and Care:

Summary and Application

In Christ Jesus you who were once far away have been brought near through the blood of Christ (Ephesians 2:13). Your citizenship is in heaven (Philippians 3:20). You are no longer a foreigner or an alien, but a fellow citizen with God's people and a member of God's household (Ephesians 2:12). Through Christ, you have access to the Father, through one Spirit (Ephesians 2:18).

In previous chapters, we have discussed how God transferred us from the kingdom of darkness to the kingdom of the Son he loves. In accepting the sacrifice of Jesus and applying it to our lives personally, we become Christians, or a "little Christs." Change of name brings change of identity. The gospels record Jesus changing the name of several of his followers. In John 1:42 Jesus says, "You are Simon, son of John. You will be called Cephas," which, when translated, is Peter.

Taking another's name in marriage or adoption is a common example of changes in contemporary life situations that have associated identity shifts. In social sciences, a major life change is sometimes referred to as a life-course transition. In addition to marriage, other examples include the birth of a child, moving, and retirement. It is important to recognize that it is not the event itself (like the wedding), that brings the life-course transition. Typically, the transition is triggered by the event, but real transitions take time. True transitions require a simultaneous change in identity and in consistency of behavior that reflects the new identity. A married person no longer sees themselves as single, but married, and they behave in a manner that is consistent with being a marital partner.

When we become followers of Jesus, we become new creations, the old is gone and the new has come (2 Corinthians 5:17). All of this is from God. Still, it takes time for us to mature in our new identity as sons and daughters of God, to bring our conduct into compliance with the principles of scripture, and to decide diligently and purposefully to do all that is necessary to enter his rest (Hebrews 4:11). The place prepared is a place of rest and trust where we lean on God, knowing that his yoke is easy and his burden is light (Matthew 11:30).

> As we cast our anxieties on him, trust in him, and choose to enter his presence and rest, we can experience that the place that Jesus prepared for us as a place of increasing closeness and care.

- In Christ Jesus, I, who was once far away, have been brought near through the blood of Christ.
- My citizenship is in heaven.
- I am no longer a foreigner or an alien.
- I am a fellow citizen with God's people.
- I am a member of God's household.
- Through Christ, I have access to the Father, through one Spirit.
- I am in a place of increasing closeness and care.

Notes

Notes

CHAPTER 13

A Place of *Absolute Inclusion and Refuge*

You are called to one hope, one faith, one baptism and one God and Father of all (Ephesians 4:4–6). You have been baptized into Christ Jesus, baptized into his death (Romans 6:3). You have been crucified with Christ (Galatians 2:20). You died, and your life is now hidden with Christ, in God (Colossians 3:3). You died with Christ to the basic principles of this world (Colossians 2:20). You were buried with Christ in baptism (Romans 6:4). You have been raised in Christ through faith in the power of God, who raised Christ from the dead (Colossians 2:12). God raised you up with Christ and seated you in the heavenly realms in Christ Jesus (Ephesians 2:6).

> **You are called to one hope, to one faith, to one baptism and to one God and Father of all. — Ephesians 4:4–6**

A clear part of this verse is that you are called. You may have various experiences with calls, like a phone call, a call to dinner, or an invitation. Less commonly in contemporary usage, being called can also refer to a destiny, a particular purpose in life. Taken together, it is clear that being called to one God and Father of all means that you are clearly desired, chosen, and summoned by God himself. God came after you! He reached out to you. He loved you first.

If you look up call in Webster's Dictionary, it says "shout, make a request or a demand (called for an investigation), to get communication by telephone, to make a brief visit, to announce or read loudly authoritatively. To command or request to come or be present (called to testify) to cause to come to bring (calls to mind) to summon a particular activity, employment, or office (called to active duty) convoke (call a meeting) rouse from sleep or summon to get up. A divine vocation or strong inner prompting to a particular course of action. The attraction or appeal of a particular activity, condition, or place (the call of the wild)."

All of this converges to establish that to be called is to be pursued, wanted, desired, and beckoned. God initiated the call — that same God and Father of all who is over all and working in all and permeating all. You are called by him.

Being called to one hope when there are so many — salvation, forgiveness, relationship, eternal life — makes it clear that each of those hopes is grounded in one ultimate source: our Father. It is our ongoing, living relationship with God, through and in Christ, that encompasses and establishes all of these other hopes. He is the one hope to which we are called. This verse comes embedded in the context of discussions of unity and humility. One faith is our faith in the triune God and his love as presented in his word; it is the only faith that produces good fruit. One baptism represents submersion in God and his Spirit; scriptures refer to multiple baptisms that are each subsumed in him: baptism in water, the Spirit, death, life. One baptism entails being submerged in God and flooded by him.

This verse makes it clear that there is no hope or fruitful trust in other things; they are all worthless idols. God is the only unchangeable one. He is over all, and he is the same yesterday, today, and tomorrow. He is our hope. He baptizes us. Our faith brings salvation, forgiveness, eternal life, sonship, and life to the full. We are called to these things — called by him — so his desires for our lives will come into reality as we give ourselves to him. He is working all things together for our good (Romans 8:28). The place Jesus prepared for us is a place of absolute inclusion and refuge.

Invite the Holy Spirit to bring to mind how your call to life in relationship with God brings hope to the specific challenges you are facing now. Ask him to increase your trust in the hope that he offers.

Father, thank you for calling me. Thank you for providing Jesus, the way to enter relationship with you. Thank you for the hope I have in you, for providing the faith to trust you, and for immersing me in your presence, your love, and your Spirit. I pray that I will keep my hope centered in you and not in worthless idols. I choose to depend on you and the sufficiency of all that you have already done on my behalf as well as on your constant provision and the way you are growing me into who you designed me to be.

> **In Context:**
> There is one body and one Spirit, just as you were called to one hope when you were called; one Lord, one faith, one baptism; one God and Father of all, who is over all and through all and in all (Ephesians 4:4–6).

> **You have been baptized into Christ Jesus, baptized into his death.** — Romans 6:3

Webster's Dictionary defines baptize as to "purify or cleanse spiritually, especially by purging. Initiate. To give a name to: Christen. A decision with an accompanying action."

Christ was sacrificed for our sins. Being baptized into him appropriates his sacrifice to us. You are credited with his account. His death "counts" for you. Because you are baptized into him, submerged in him, permeated by him, your old nature was crucified with him and atoned for (Galatians 2:20). By Jesus, and in him, you are cleansed and made spotless and blameless. In the Spirit, when you accept the sacrifice of Jesus on your behalf, you are actually crucified with him. His righteousness is substituted for your sinfulness.

A secondary meaning of baptized is "initiated." Initiated into Jesus implies the beginning of involvement, increasing engagement with his Spirit, and growing in his character. Baptism in Jesus and in his Spirit brings the fruit of his Spirit in increasing measure: love, joy, peace, forbearance, kindness, goodness, faithfulness, gentleness, and self-control (Galatians 5:22–23). It brings us a gift of his Spirit (1 Corinthians 7:7).

Deciding to be baptized into Christ and into his death means that you have decided to depend on him for your forgiveness, purification, justification, and reconciliation with God. It means that you have decided to have your subsequent actions conform to his commands, principles, and character. Being baptized in his Spirit initiates ongoing growth into maturity of his character shaping your decisions, actions, and words.

Baptism in Jesus means that you are submersed in Christ. When you are submersed into the waters of baptism, you are fully surrounded by the water, symbolizing the complete surrounding of Jesus. This is total cleansing — not leaving any part of you dirty or dry. When you emerge from the water, you are soaked and you're in a different state than when you entered. The scriptures make it clear that being baptized in Jesus brings you into all he gained and accomplished on your behalf through his death and resurrection. Being baptized in Jesus "christens" you, naming you as a child of God. The presence of his Spirit continues to work through all aspects of your life, serving as his heavenly leaven. His Spirit is his seal of his ownership of you and qualifies you to inherit all that is his. In the place that Jesus prepared for you, you find a place of absolute inclusion and refuge.

Reflect on ways that the death and resurrection of Jesus has changed your daily life. Thank him for the changes that he has already brought in your life so that you experience greater freedom in him, and invite him to have his way in things where you desire greater unity with him.

Father, thank you for baptizing me into Jesus and the cleansing, forgiveness, and change that it initiates. I pray that I will remain in union with your Spirit and welcome your transformation as you work through every aspect of my being and my life. Thank you for remaining with me and surrounding and submerging me in your presence, provision, protection, and character. I present myself to you to submerge and saturate me in Jesus more fully.

In Context:
Or don't you know that all of us who were baptized into Christ Jesus were baptized into his death? We were therefore buried with him through baptism into death in order that, just as Christ was raised from the dead through the glory of the Father, we too may live a new life. For if we have been united with him in a death like his, we will certainly also be united with him in a resurrection like his (Romans 6:3–5).

> **You have been crucified with Christ.** — Galatians 2:20

By faith, you personally accept Christ's sacrifice. By your dependence on him, you identify with him. Many scriptures use the phrase "in Christ" or its equivalent. You identify with him and by doing so, you are brought into life in him and with him. He is in you, and you are in him (John 14:20). Because God is not bound by the constraints of time, you were crucified with Christ. He was aware of you in him and took all your sin, guilt, and shame into himself as he sacrificially hung on the cross.

Living by faith is choosing continually to be aware that he dwells in you and leads you in love. This means abiding in him, trusting him, and resting in him and his ability. It can give you power to overcome temptation, anxiety, or feeling the need to fend for yourself. Believing in Jesus and choosing to allow the "old you" to be crucified allows you to manifest his character and his Spirit dwelling in you.

Crucifixion leads to death. You have been crucified with Christ. Therefore, the "old" you, prior to coming into relationship with the Lord is dead. With God's Spirit dwelling in you, you are a new creation and can live a new life. Along with your sin being crucified and put to death with Jesus, everything of you that is not of him also went to the cross in him and died. Truly, the old you no longer lives. You are free to live by faith, trust, and rest in the Son of God. Depending on Jesus as the way brings you into his place of absolute inclusion and refuge.

Meditate on ways that the crucifixion of Jesus has freed you from your need to make sacrifices to atone for your sins. Consider whether there are things in your life where you need to receive the provision of Jesus' sacrifice on your behalf. Prayerfully invite his Spirit to minister his provision into those areas.

Jesus, thank you for your sacrifice in my place. Thank you that it fully accomplished all that was necessary for me to be forgiven for past, present, and future sins. Thank you that you reconcile my life by substituting your righteousness for my unrighteousness, that you made the way for me to be in relationship with my heavenly Father, and that your Spirit has come to take up residence in me. I pray that I will not make choices to resurrect the sinful, lost, or dead patterns of my old life. I pray that I will depend on your presence and your provision as I go through each day. I ask that my awareness of your presence in me, who I am in you, and your great love for me would continue to increase. I choose to trust in you and what your scriptures say about who I am in you. Thank you for including me in you as you went to the cross in my place.

In Context:
I have been crucified with Christ and I no longer live, but Christ lives in me. The life I now live in the body, I live by faith in the Son of God, who loved me and gave himself for me (Galatians 2:20).

> **I died, and my life is now hidden with Christ, in God.**
> **— Colossians 3:3**

Scripture often addresses matters of life and death. It talks about life in the kingdom, death to sin, eternal life, death and resurrection of the body, life as a child of God, and death to the old self, behaviors, and thoughts.

You are part of the body of Christ. Your life is hidden in Christ, overshadowed and contained in him. When God looks at you, he sees you in Christ or through Christ so he loves you with the same love which with he loves Jesus (John 17:23). To be hidden with Christ makes you completely sheltered and safe in God. Christ is in the Father and you are in Christ, and he is in you (John 14:20). All of your life is hidden, both the good (God gets the glory — Christ in you the hope of glory), and your sin and failures. Your sins are fully expunged from your record as you confess them (1 John 1:9). His righteousness is substituted for your life choices.

The things that matter are that you are in Christ, a child of the Father, and living according to the leadings of the Spirit of God. All else is just details. Scripture tells us to set our minds on things above. I don't think that means to speculate about how the food will be in heaven, and whether we can eat as much we want without gaining weight or whether there will be mosquitoes in heaven and whether they will bite and cause itching. I think it means focusing on your relationship with Jesus, the Father, and the Holy Spirit. I think it means choosing to keep the door closed to orphan-hearted self-care, self-recognition, glory seeking, or life choices that don't honor God.

Being hidden with Christ involves an awareness of walking with him in the garden in every conscious moment. It is trying to live in a way that mirrors what my heavenly Father says and does. It is dying to self and living with and for him. It is not relying on and resurrecting the self apart from Christ, Father, and Spirit. It is being who he created me to be — uniquely expressing him throughout all the days he ordained for me before the beginning of time.

If you were playing hide and seek and ducked under a blanket, but your arm was sticking out, you would not be fully covered. Ask the Lord to show you if you have fully submitted all parts of your life to his covering. Invite his character to completely overshadow all of you. Contemplate how being hidden in Christ is the safest and most wonderful place to be — a place of absolute inclusion and refuge.

Father, thank you that my life is hidden with Christ. Thank you for the absolute security of being in you. Thank you for the eternal refuge, safety, love, and intimacy that you share with me. I pray that I would continue to be hidden with Christ. I pray that his character in and through my life would increase and that my old sinful patterns of life would decrease and disappear. God, I pray that those I interact with would recognize your character in and through me. I choose to remain hidden with Christ in God.

In Context:
Your crucifixion with Christ has severed the tie to this life, and now your true life is hidden away in God in Christ (Colossians 3:3).

You died with Christ to the basic principles of this world. — Colossians 2:20

Placing your life in Jesus by trusting in his perfect life and sacrifice on your behalf set you free from the old, law-based covenant. It is for freedom that Christ set you free (Galatians 1:5.). In Christ, you are a citizen of heaven (Philippians 3:20). You are part of the household of God (Ephesians 2:12). You are a child of God (1 John 3:2) and his heir (Romans 8:17).

The closest I can come to understanding the basic principles of the world is that it represents human rules, false humility, and worldly wisdom, which is not really wisdom at all (for instance, "look out for number one"). Many people are quick to impose lifestyle restrictions and weigh in with conflicting judgments about right ways to live. However, apart from the commands of Christ, the law of his Spirit has set us free from the law of sin and death (Romans 8:2). Being dead to the basic principles of this world does not mean that you do not follow the clear decrees of scripture or that the law of gravity does not apply to you. It means that you are free from the traditions of man and empty rules of religion. It means it is not necessary to adhere to the opinions of the masses or even "informed sages." Instead, adhere to the clear teachings of scripture, follow the Spirit, and be free in Christ.

We are living in a fallen world. But we do not need to magnify that by subjecting ourselves to the judgments and fallen nature of people and cultures. Be free from false humility and restrictions that place you in bondage to the rules of men. Scripture teaches that the doctrines of men and corrupt customs are worthless to help you spiritually. Of course, submit to legitimate authority, honor others, show love, and live life to the full. Besides that, obey God's clear commands. Otherwise, be free! God's commands bring life. Man's bring bondage and death.

One of the most basic principles of the world, according to anthropologists, is the "law" of reciprocity. We died to reciprocity with God when we accepted Christ's sacrifice for us. The reality is that there is nothing that we can do that would adequately reciprocate God's sacrifice on our behalf. Another basic principle of the world is fueled by orphan-spirited thinking — fending for self and attempting self-improvement (the root of "looking out for number one"). In John 14:18, Jesus declared to his followers, most of whom had living parents, that he would not leave them as orphans. Being left "as an orphan," without a loving parent to care for us, requires self-care and self-dependence. Recognizing that we have the Spirit that calls out "Abba, Father!" should decrease self-striving or put it to death.

Dying to the basic principles of the world brings death to the "old man," sin nature, orphan-hearted thinking, and the obligation to follow human rules that permeate the world. Religious values of men trap us into submission because they seem wise, and following them gives us the appearance of a serious commitment; but that commitment is to rules and religion, not relationship with the living God. It takes our focus from relationship to a rule structure. Doing well in that scenario entails obedience, and any infraction makes it feel like we are not loved or not a "good witness." Being a child of God is rooted and grounded in love, which puts that thinking to rest and gives us the power to obey the commands of God.

The Message translates Colossians 2:20–23 this way: "So, then, if with Christ you've put all that puffed-up and childish religion behind you, why do you let yourselves be bullied by it? "Don't touch this! Don't taste that! Don't go near this!" Do you think things that are here today and gone tomorrow are worth that kind of attention? Such things sound impressive if said in a deep enough voice. They even give the illusion of being pious and humble and austere. But they're just another way of showing off, making yourselves look important."

Meditate on the truth that your faith in Jesus frees you from the basic principles of this world. Be thankful for the place of absolute inclusion and refuge that Jesus has prepared for you. Invite the Holy Spirit to show you areas of your life where you frequently experience pressure, or lack of freedom from the principles of this world and ask for grace to move forward in the freedom of Christ.

Lord, thank you that in Jesus, I died to the basic principles of this world. Thank you for freeing me from the law of sin and death, from the need to follow the empty rules of manmade religion, and from the need to fend for myself. Thank you that as your follower and beloved child, your Spirit dwells in me and cares for me continually. Thank you that I can depend on you for the big things in life as well as the details and small stuff. I pray that you will help me to live in the freedom that you intend for me. I pray that in pursuing freedom in you that you would keep me from rebellion to the clear principles of your kingdom. Help me to walk closely with you in the joy of a full life as your beloved child.

> **In Context:**
> Since you died with Christ to the elemental spiritual forces of this world, why, as though you still belonged to the world, do you submit to its rules: "Do not handle! Do not taste! Do not touch!"? These rules, which have to do with things that are all destined to perish with use, are based on merely human commands and teachings. Such regulations indeed have an appearance of wisdom, with their self-imposed worship, their false humility, and their harsh treatment of the body, but they lack any value in restraining sensual indulgence (Colossians 2:20–23).
>
> Since, then, you have been raised with Christ, set your hearts on things above, where Christ is, seated at the right hand of God. Set your minds on things above, not on earthly things. For you died, and your life is now hidden with Christ in God. When Christ, who is your life, appears, then you also will appear with him in glory (Colossians 3:1–4).

You were buried with Christ in baptism. — Romans 6:4

Your acceptance of and identity with Jesus has you share in his death and burial and resurrection. Dead is dead. Buried is buried. Risen is risen.

When you identified with his death, it completely snuffed out your sinful nature. Dead is dead. In the Spirit, it no longer has any life. This applies to all old ways. Your old nature is dead, buried, gone. You are now a new creation (2 Corinthians 5:17). You are a child of the living God (John 1:12), and the triune God is living in you in union. The old you is hidden in Christ, covered over, buried with him. Your sin and shame are forgotten, removed as far as the east is from the west.

When you chose baptism, you identified with and received the benefits of Jesus' crucifixion, death, and burial. The power of the Father resurrected Christ. As you depend on him and his incomparable power, you choose to remain dead to your old nature of sin and orphan-hearted self-care; you remain hidden in Christ, receiving his cleansing, resurrection to new life, love of the Father, and his inheritance. When you are buried, you are immersed in whatever you are buried in. As his follower, you are buried in Jesus!

Returning to the old ways of the orphan spirit puts us at all kinds of risk. It is essentially equivalent to crawling off the altar of being a living sacrifice to walk in our own ways instead of depending on God to care for us. It is a rebellious, defiant statement that we believe that we are more trustworthy than God. The most life-giving thing that we can do is to choose to remain dead to self-sufficiency and dependent on Jesus and the love and power of God in our lives. That is the most secure and life-giving place and posture in the universe. It is choosing to remain in a place of absolute inclusion and refuge.

Meditate on being buried with Christ. Consider what that means for dying to life choices that distance you from God. Ask the Holy Spirit to give you specific examples and to show you ways to trust God more fully in your daily life. Invite him to transform your thinking about the challenges you face and to see them from his perspective.

Thank you, Lord, that when I chose to trust in Jesus, you buried me with him and in him. Thank you for attributing the benefits of his sinless life of unity with you to me. Thank you for including me and not requiring me to reach perfection or to suffer the punishment that my choices and behavior truly deserve. I pray that I will choose to depend on your love and acceptance and to remain hidden in Jesus. I pray that you will help me to see when I am striving in my own strength to earn favor or acceptance with you — things that are already mine by your grace and great love for me. God, I choose to quiet my soul and to rest in the perfection of who you are.

> **In Context:**
> Or don't you know that all of us who were baptized into Christ Jesus were baptized into his death? We were therefore buried with him through baptism into death in order that, just as Christ was raised from the dead through the glory of the Father, we too may live a new life. For if we have been united with him in a death like his, we will certainly also be united with him in a resurrection like his (Romans 6:3–5).

You have been raised in Christ through faith in the power of God, who raised Christ from the dead. — Colossians 2:12

Your faith must be in God, not yourself. It is his power that raised Christ from the dead. His power gives life. His power makes new. His power and his presence in you make you a new creation, just as seeds fall to the ground and come to life in a new form and bring a new harvest. Again, it is your identification with Christ and maintaining the attitude of a child dependent on the Father that raises you up and gives you life to the full.

This is not a one-time event. You must continue to trust in the power of God rather than trusting in yourself and your ability to do anything in your own strength. Life in the Spirit is different from life in the flesh. In Christ, you have been given every spiritual blessing. Believing that, trusting that, receiving that, and depending on that changes everything.

Note that it is your faith in the power of God that causes you to be raised in Christ. You are raised to a life seated in the heavenly realm at the right hand of the Father. Raised to life and free from sin and death. Raised to be a new creation. Raised to be truly free. It is for freedom that Christ set you free (Galatians 5:1). Free from your futile ways to strive and try to make yourself pleasing to God. Free to remain in his love, care, and presence. Truly free. Meditate on the truth that you have been raised in Christ, into a place of absolute inclusion and refuge. Ask the Holy Spirit to reveal to you ways to practically trust in being raised in Christ as you go through this day.

God, thank you for your great power. Thank you that it is and always will be the greatest power in the universe. Thank you that your power is manifested in love. Thank you for your continual love for me. Thank you for raising me from my sinful separation and spiritual death into relationship with you in Jesus. I pray that I will experientially know your power in my life, that I will be aware of being raised up in Jesus and seated with him by your side. I pray that I will not make choices that resurrect the things to which I died when I accepted Jesus' sacrifice on my behalf. Father, I choose to remain in Jesus and with you as I go through this day.

> **In Context:**
> …having been buried with him in baptism, in which you were also raised with him through your faith in the working of God, who raised him from the dead. When you were dead in your sins and in the uncircumcision of your flesh, God made you alive with Christ. He forgave us all our sins, having canceled the charge of our legal indebtedness, which stood against us and condemned us; he has taken it away, nailing it to the cross (Colossians 2:12–14).

God raised you up with Christ and seated you in the heavenly realms in Christ Jesus. — Ephesians 2:6

It is the Father's love, power, and grace that has given you all of this: everything necessary to cleanse you so that you could be reunited in relationship with him; abundantly more than you could imagine or hope; the ability to boldly enter his presence because of the sacrifice of Jesus; the privilege of being seated with him in the heavenly realms.

Your acceptance of Jesus as your Lord and Savior affords you identity, esteem, protection, provision, health, and access to the Father. You have been given authority to declare his victory over the enemies and circumstances of your life. You are currently seated with him in the heavenly realms, providing you with every spiritual blessing in Jesus: rest, peace, authority, ultimate victory, eternal life. You have the best seat in the house if you can authentically say, "I'm with him."

This seat is an awesome seat. Jesus is at the right hand of the Father, and spiritually, you are right there with him now. A mercy seat. A seat of honor. A place of rest. A place of ultimate and eternal refuge. A place to remain and stay seated. A place to bask in his presence and to enjoy God himself. The Passion Translation declares that you are co-seated with Christ.

Pause and meditate on that reality, and what it means for how you go through this day. Consider its implications for a place of absolute inclusion and refuge.

God, thank you for raising me up and including me in Jesus. Thank you for seating me with him, associating me with all the goodness, honor, and glory that is his. Thank you for your generous grace and love, bestowing these unfathomable gifts on me independent of what I have or have not done. Thank you that my acceptance of Jesus' sacrifice on my behalf places me in your family and gives me choice seating and all the benefits associated with being your child. I pray that the reality of your grace and favor would continue to register and grow in my experiential understanding of your love for me. I pray that I would trust in you and lean into all that you have so freely given to me because of your love. I pray that your peace that surpasses understanding would let me rest in you and your kindness.

> **In Context:**
> But because of his great love for us, God, who is rich in mercy, made us alive with Christ even when we were dead in transgressions — it is by grace you have been saved. And God raised us up with Christ and seated us with him in the heavenly realms in Christ Jesus, in order that in the coming ages he might show the incomparable riches of his grace, expressed in his kindness to us in Christ Jesus. For it is by grace you have been saved, through faith — and this is not from yourselves, it is the gift of God — not by works, so that no one can boast (Ephesians 2:4–9).

A Place of Absolute Inclusion and Refuge: Summary and Application

You are called to one hope, to one faith, to one baptism, and to one God and Father of all (Ephesians 4:4–6). You have been baptized into Christ Jesus, baptized into his death (Romans 6:3). You have been crucified with Christ (Galatians 2:20). You died, and your life is now hidden with Christ, in God (Colossians 3:3). You died with Christ to the basic principles of this world (Colossians 2:20). You were buried with Christ in baptism (Romans 6:4). You have been raised in Christ through faith in the power of God, who raised Christ from the dead (Colossians 2:12). God raised you up with Christ and seated you in the heavenly realms in Christ Jesus (Ephesians 2:6).

Ephesians 1:13 says, "And you were also included in Christ when you heard the message of truth, the gospel of salvation. When you believed, you were marked in him with a seal, the promised Holy Spirit." Your inclusion in Christ was a "come as you are" call. Ephesians 2:1–6 says, "As for you, you were dead in your transgressions and sins, in which you used to live when you followed the ways of this world and of the ruler of the kingdom of the air, the spirit who is now at work in those who are disobedient. All of us also lived among them at one time, gratifying the cravings of our flesh and following its desires and thoughts. Like the rest, we were by nature deserving of wrath. But because of his great love for us, God, who is rich in mercy, made us alive with Christ even when we were dead in transgressions — it is by grace you have been saved. And God raised us up with Christ and seated us with him in the heavenly realms in Christ Jesus."

Our calling and inclusion brought us into union with the living God. Although we were called exactly as we were, experiencing his great love, mercy, and grace leads us to change. To remain hidden in him. To keep our old, sinful nature dead and buried. To live a life worthy of our calling (Ephesians 4:1). To remain in him in the place of absolute inclusion and refuge. To remain a refugee in him rather than demanding our own ways and things.

> **Ask the Holy Spirit to bring the truth of these scriptures into your inmost being and to transform your life to live in consistency with what they say about who you are in Christ.**

> I am called to one hope, to one faith, to one baptism, and to one God and Father of all.

- I have been baptized into Christ Jesus, baptized into his death.
- I have been crucified with Christ. I died, and my life is now hidden with Christ, in God.
- I died with Christ to the basic principles of this world.
- I was buried with Christ in baptism.
- I have been raised in Christ through my faith in the power of God, who raised Christ from the dead.
- God raised me up with Christ and seated me in the heavenly realms in Christ Jesus.
- In Christ, I am in a place of absolute inclusion and refuge.

Notes

Notes

CHAPTER 14

A Place of Continual Relationship with God

You are clothed in Christ (Galatians 3:27) and included in Christ (Ephesians 1:13). You are united with the Lord (1 Corinthians 6:17). You no longer live, but Christ lives in you (Galatians 2:20). In Jesus, you are being built together to become a dwelling in which God lives by his Spirit (Ephesians 2:22). You yourself are God's temple (1 Corinthians 6:19).

> **You are clothed in Christ.** — Galatians 3:27

Your clothing is seen and noticed early in interactions with others. How you are clothed changes the way you look, feel, and are received by others. Being clothed saves your body from the scrutiny of others, the embarrassment of nakedness. Being clothed in Christ is the greatest "performance wear" available. His performance as the sinless Son of God covers you, protects you, and allows you to be comfortable in any circumstance. When the Father sees you, he sees you clothed in Christ. Just as he provided animal skins for Adam and Eve after the fall, the first clothing in all of history, he provided the ultimate covering for you: the Lamb of God, who takes away the sins of the world.

Just like you wouldn't go to an important event, like a wedding or a business meeting, without dressing for it, you can choose to put on Jesus — to come under his covering as you go into every circumstance of every day. Getting dressed is an intentional act. You do it every day with the events and contexts of the day in mind. You may even need to change clothing several times in a single day. You choose different clothing for work, social interactions, being at home, dirty or dangerous jobs, exercise, and bed. Paul tells us to put on the full armor of God. This is an intentional act. Clothing yourself in Jesus is an intentional act as well. Being clothed in Christ goes with anything and prepares you for any circumstances.

Clothing does not obscure who you are. No matter what you are wearing, it's still you. Being clothed in Christ outfits us for whatever is to come. It makes us beautiful to others. Truly, you look your best to others when you are clothed in

Jesus. It makes him desirable to those who see his character on you. Being aware of being clothed in Jesus keeps you in tune with seeking him first, deferring to him, and interacting with others in a way that honors God.

Meditate on ways that you can more regularly be aware of clothing yourself in Jesus by remaining in a place of continual relationship with God. Perhaps regularly praying Proverbs 3:5 (trusting in the Lord with all of your heart and not leaning on your own understanding, acknowledging him in all of your ways ...) or mindfully putting on each component of the full armor of God each day (Ephesians 6:10–18) would facilitate clothing yourself in Jesus. Invite the Lord to show you a tangible way to remain clothed in him.

Father, thank you that you have provided Jesus as the perfect covering for me and for my sins. Thank you that I do not need to strive to cover myself from you with mere fig leaves or any other shield. Thank you that you already know everything about me and that you love and accept me. Thank you that in Jesus, I am forgiven and acceptable to you. Even more, thank you that you see me clothed in Jesus and you love me with the same love that you love him with. I pray that you will increase my awareness of being clothed in Jesus and that when I become aware of having stepped out of his covering, that I would confess my sin and errors to you quickly, receive your forgiveness in Jesus, and return to being clothed in him. I pray that I would be conscious of choosing to clothe myself in Jesus in every circumstance and in every interaction with others. Thank you for the wonderful blessing of clothing me in Jesus!

In Context:
... for all of you who were baptized into Christ have clothed yourselves with Christ (Galatians 3:27).

You are included in Christ. — Ephesians 1:13

Think of a time you were excluded, overlooked, forgotten, passed by, or denied. That is never your situation in Jesus. You are included, wanted, invited, desired, sought out, and brought in by God himself!

The love of God and his desire for relationship with you is what caused you to be planned for and created in the first place. His passion for you means that you were included in his plans for the universe. So, of course, you are also included in Christ, God's plan for our redemption so you can live as his lavishly loved child. Wow, the generosity of God! Even more than being included, your redemption, forgiveness, and salvation is the whole reason Christ came from the Father to the earth to live as a human and to offer himself as the once-and-for-all, perfect and complete sacrifice for your sins. You are included in all that God planned, wanted from the beginning, and set in motion at creation. By responding to the word of truth with acceptance and receiving the gift of Christ's sacrifice for you, you are included in God's family as well as his plan, desire, and purpose.

Independent of your own striving, you are included. You are included by hearing and believing the good (great!) news of your salvation. The Message translates Ephesians 1:13–14 in this manner: "It's in Christ that you, once you heard the truth and believed it (this message of your salvation), found yourselves home free — signed, sealed, and delivered by the Holy Spirit. This down payment from God is the first installment on what's coming, a reminder that we'll get everything God has planned for us, a praising and glorious life."

Included. Selah.

Included in the likeness of the Father. Included in his line, lineage, and family. Included in his inheritance. Included in his love that is flowing toward you and into you, even right now. The place Jesus prepared for you is a place of continual relationship with God.

Reflect on how it feels to be included by God. Consider if there are areas in your life where you need to experience more of the feeling of being included in Jesus and ask the Holy Spirit to apply the love of God to those places in your thoughts and feelings.

Jesus, thank you so much for including me. For including me in your thoughts, plans, and desires. Thank you for including me and thinking of me when you sacrificed your life on the cross. Thank you for including me in your kingdom, your household, and your family. Thank you for loving me this much. I pray that I will come to experientially know more and more of the depth of your love for me, and all that it includes. I pray that between now and when I see you face-to-face, I would live in greater awareness of who I am in you.

> **In Context:**
> And you also were included in Christ when you heard the message of truth, the gospel of your salvation. When you believed, you were marked in him with a seal, the promised Holy Spirit (Ephesians 1:13).

You are united with the Lord. — 1 Corinthians 6:17

Searching the word united in various dictionaries yields entries such as: to act in accordance with. Harmonious. Acting as a single entity. Made one. Combined. A united family.

As his child, you truly represent the Father. The love of God coming to and through you permeates what you do and say. His love changes who you are, so it changes how you are in all circumstances. Some translations indicate that because you have joined yourself to the Lord, you are mingled into one spirit with him.

Of course, you always have a choice; this is the gift of free will as part of who you are as God's creation. But choosing to exercise that choice apart from him is what breaks union with his Spirit. Staying aware of the indwelling presence of the Holy Spirit and choosing to remain in or to abide in Jesus keeps you in the unity of relationship and intimacy that God desired from the beginning. That is what brings fullness of life.

Being united also infers that there is no substantive division in the union. As we have considered in previous parts of this book, when God looks at you, he sees you in Christ, so there is no division.

Quietly consider whether there are places in your life or identity where you do not feel that unity. Ask the Holy Spirit to draw you into more full union with God in all aspects of your life. Invite him to bring you more fully into the experience of continual relationship with God.

Thank you, Lord, for desiring to be united with me in close relationship and for doing everything necessary for that to be possible. I choose to walk in the fullness and closeness of relationship with you, remaining in union with your Spirit. I pray for increased awareness of your presence, your leading, your love flowing into me, and your joy in relating to me. I pray that I will remain attuned to you and that I will make choices that bring glory to you in the ways that I represent you and your character through all of my interactions and decisions this day.

In Context:
But whoever is united with the Lord is one with him in spirit (1 Corinthians 6:17).

You no longer live, but Christ lives in you. — Galatians 2:20

When you put your faith in Christ, he indwells you. His crucifixion, death, burial, and resurrection are applied to you. His Spirit, living in you, cleanses you and gives you all that you need to live as a child of the living God.

As the Amplified translation states, you live in faith by adhering to, relying on, and completely trusting in the Son of God. When you choose to do things your way, or depend on self for direction and strength to go through your day, you are essentially ignoring or nullifying the generous gift of God's grace, his amazing, unmerited favor. Jonah 2:8 tells us that those who depend on worthless idols forfeit the grace that could be theirs.

There is a stark contrast between what my life looks and feels like on my own power in comparison to relying on Jesus. It can be frustrating to find myself again recognizing that I have wandered into the orphan-hearted habit of trying to do things on my own steam as opposed to trusting God. Jesus stated it clearly in John 15:5, "Apart from me you can do nothing." Psalm 16:2 reminds us that apart from God we have no good thing.

The Passion Translation renders Galatians 2:20–21 in this manner: "My old identity has been co-crucified with Christ and no longer lives. And now the essence of this new life is no longer mine, for the Anointed One lives his life through me — we live in union as one! My new life is empowered by the faith of the Son of God who loves me so much that he gave himself for me, dispensing his life into mine! So that is why I don't view God's grace as something peripheral."

Viewing God's grace as precious to the inmost part of your being and then living out of that reality in every circumstance, relationship, and challenge of life is how you no longer live, but allow Christ to live in you and through you, bringing change to everything. Depending on him to fill you to overflowing and to pour out into the atmosphere around you brings his kingdom to and through your life.

Quietly meditate and ask the Holy Spirit to bring to mind the places in your life where you can invite more of him and less of you. Ask the Holy Spirit to empower you to live more fully from a place of continual relationship with God.

Jesus, thank you that just as you came to earth in the dirt and humble circumstances of a stable, you have come into my own dirt and humble circumstances. I welcome you! I choose to nurture your presence and invite you to live in and through me more fully. I choose to decrease as you and your Spirit increase in me. I pray that you would permeate every aspect of my inmost being — my thoughts, feelings, behavior, and character. I pray that you would overflow me as a spring of living water and flow out into every relationship and circumstance of my life. Thank you that you live in me! I welcome you as you manifest more fully your character, love, and power for life through me.

> **In Context:**
> I have been crucified with Christ and I no longer live, but Christ lives in me. The life I now live in the body, I live by faith in the Son of God, who loved me and gave himself for me. I do not set aside the grace of God, for if righteousness could be gained through the law, Christ died for nothing" (Galatians 2:20–21).

In Jesus, you are being built together to become a dwelling in which God lives by his Spirit. — Ephesians 2:22

In him, you are being built together. Your life has many parts, and God is a master designer and assembly expert. He is bringing all aspects of your life into an integrated whole and actively working all things together for your good (Romans 8:28). In Jesus, you are not torn apart, set aside, or cast away. You are being lovingly formed and joined by the carpenter — the master builder who himself is the chief cornerstone. Part of his architectural plan from the beginning was to make a unique place, fit perfectly for you, and reserved for you, a place prepared. You are being placed by him, having been created for this. As you give yourself to him as fully as you know how to, you can trust that you are walking in accordance with his plans and purposes for you, which are coming to pass. There is really nothing better than being shaped and fitted by the Spirit of God. What a delightful and honorable purpose, to become part of a holy temple in the Lord. You are a part of the crowning object of his creation: the Body of Christ, a bride for his son. It is his Spirit doing the building, bringing the unity, fitting you and joining you to him and all your brothers and sisters who are also his dearly loved children. The result is a dwelling in which God lives by his Spirit.

The dwelling where I live is called home. I am being built together into God's home, by God himself. I do not need to strive to find my place or to make myself fit or to cling to the structure. I am being shaped (matured, transformed), placed, and secured in him. He will not lose me, harm me, abandon me. It will bring him joy to fit me into the building — a perfectly designed piece, rightly fit into my unique place and purpose for which I was created. We are each a living stone in his dwelling. Meditate on this delightful and wonderous truth and specifically consider how you experience being a home for the Spirit of God. How does your awareness of being a dwelling in which God lives shape the way you see your current circumstances?

Lord, thank you for including me and building me into your home. Thank you that you have selected me, paid the cost to make me yours, cleaned me, shaped me, and fit me into the perfect place in your home. I pray that I will trust you in every step of this building process and that I would delight in your loving craftsmanship in each step of the process. Lord, I am delighted to give myself into your hands and to live in the ongoing experiences and anticipation of your full indwelling.

> **In Context:**
> … built on the foundation of the apostles and prophets, with Christ Jesus himself as the chief cornerstone. In him the whole building is joined together and rises to become a holy temple in the Lord. And in him you too are being built together to become a dwelling in which God lives by his Spirit (Ephesians 2:20–22).

You yourself are God's temple. — **1 Corinthians 6:19**

Recognition that you are God's temple speaks to the care that you should take of your body out of respect for our Lord and his continual presence in you. But you are much more than a physical body. Being his temple has implications for every aspect of your being: thoughts, feelings, and behaviors. Being his temple means that you need to practice keeping your thoughts and awareness on him.

Rather than creating your own set of legalistic shoulds and should nots, the important aspects of temple-keeping come into line when you simply focus on loving him with all your heart, soul, mind, and strength (Mark 12:30). The first and most important commandment according to Jesus aligns you to host God's Spirit.

Think about how we prepare our homes, yards, and even vehicles for guests we value or love. If you thought about God coming over to spend the day in all aspects of your life, how would it change your plans or how you present yourself?

Offering myself as a living sacrifice to God (Romans 12:1) entails living intentionally to welcome and nurture the presence of God himself. He is my "roommate" in my body, mind, emotions, circumstances, and the one with me everywhere I go. The one! The one who pours his love into my heart through his Spirit (Romans 5:5). The one who reminds me of all Jesus said and teaches me all things (John 14:26). The one who gives me gifts of love, joy, peace, patience, and kindness (Galatians 5:22). That one.

Meditate on the glorious truth that the Holy Spirit dwells in you, that you are his temple. Ask him to help you remain in a place of continual relationship with God and whether there are things to do in your life to welcome him into his home, you yourself. Plan to follow through on at least one thing he shows you as you consider this.

God, thank you that you have promised to never leave or forsake me. Thank you that your Spirit dwells in me. I pray for greater awareness of your continual presence in me and with me. I pray that the things that I choose to do and say will reflect your image and infuse those around me with an awareness of your love. I pray that you will continue to show me things about my life, words, behavior, and thoughts that need to change to be more consistent with your presence in my life. I pray that as I walk in the freedom that you give to me as your child, I would do it in a manner that is a conduit of your love to those in my life. Please increase my awareness of your continual presence in my life.

In Context:
Do you not know that your bodies are temples of the Holy Spirit, who is in you, whom you have received from God? You are not your own; you were bought at a price. Therefore honor God with your bodies (1 Corinthians 6:19–20).

A Place of Continual Relationship with God:
Summary and Application

You are clothed in Christ (Galatians 3:27) and included in Christ (Ephesians 1:13). You are united with the Lord (1 Corinthians 6:17). You no longer live, but Christ lives in you (Galatians 2:20). In Jesus, you are being built together to become a dwelling in which God lives by his Spirit (Ephesians 2:22). You yourself are God's temple (1 Corinthians 6:19).

When Jesus went to prepare a place for us, it was not his plan B or a side job. He came to earth as the way. The way to his Father. The way into continual relationship with God. The way that allows me access, inclusion, unity. My identification with Jesus and my inclusion in him clothes me in him, makes me a living host of the Spirit of God, and brings him into my life, where he can dwell in me as his temple. Meditate on the immensity of these truths, the eternally transformative implications.

> **Prayerfully invite the Holy Spirit to seal these truths in your inmost being as you contemplate them and declare them about yourself.**

- I am clothed in Christ and included in Christ.
- I am united with the Lord.
- I no longer live, but Christ lives in me.
- In Jesus, I am being built together to become a dwelling in which God lives by his Spirit.
- I myself am God's temple.
- In Jesus, I am in a place of continual relationship with God.

Notes

CHAPTER 15

A Place of Unshakable Union with God

God's Spirit, whom you received from God, is in you (1 Corinthians 6:19). You are one with God in Spirit (1 Corinthians 6:17). Jesus is in his Father, and you are in Christ, and he is in you (John 14:20). You are marked with a seal (Ephesians 1:13). By the deposit of the Holy Spirit, your inheritance is guaranteed (Ephesians 1:14). The anointing you received from him remains in you and teaches you about all things (1 John 2:27).

> **God's Spirit, whom you received from God, is in you.**
> **— 1 Corinthians 6:19**

The God of creation and of the universe has done everything necessary for you to come into fullness of relationship with him as you walk on his earth. He has made himself known to you and given you his holy scriptures so that you can grow in trusting the promises in his word to be true — not just true for all people, but true for you personally. At Jesus' request on your behalf, the Father sent his Holy Spirit to come to you and to dwell in you. The Spirit of the living God was sent to you personally to bring you comfort, to remind you of the words of Jesus, and to teach you all things (see John, chapters 14 and 16).

You can choose to nurture and develop your awareness of his presence, to follow his promptings, and to welcome his comfort. He is gentle as a dove.

I live in an area that has a mix of open fields and mature hardwood forests, and I enjoy feeding birds in my yard. After seeing doves at my feeder on rare occasion, I decided to look into how to attract and host more doves. I learned that they prefer platform feeders and particular grains for food. I modified a feeding station and the food I made available, and doves started to come more often and to stay longer at each visit. I also learned to walk more quietly and slowly down my back steps to avoid frightening them. As a result of these changes, we have more doves lingering in the yard.

This experience helped me to think about being aware of my body and my life being the temple for "the dove." Recall that when Jesus was baptized by John, the

Holy Spirit, in the form of a dove, descended and remained on him. How delicately you would have to move, live, and behave to have a dove remain on you! This is a metaphor for how aware we need to be regarding grieving the Holy Spirit, which the Apostle Paul describes in Ephesians 4:30.

As his bountifully loved child, God's Spirit is in you. You are his temple. You can increase your awareness of his presence in your life and choose to live in a manner that "hosts the dove." Meditate on ways that you can be more aware of welcoming the Holy Spirit's presence in your life. Ask God to show you how to remain in a place of unshakable union with him and to continually host the dove.

God, thank you for the presence of your Holy Spirit in my life. Thank you for all that you do within me. I pray that I will be more continually aware of your presence in me, your still small voice, and the things you are prompting me to do and not to do. I pray that you will help me to bring all aspects of my life into alignment with the presence of your Holy Spirit, and to be more aware of continually hosting you as a cherished and honored resident in all aspects of my life.

> **In Context:**
> Do you not know that your bodies are temples of the Holy Spirit, who is in you, whom you have received from God? You are not your own; you were bought at a price. Therefore honor God with your bodies (1 Corinthians 6:19–20).

You are one with God in Spirit. — 1 Corinthians 6:17

The Holy Spirit is described as Counselor, Helper, Comforter, and gentle as a dove. The Spirit of God is God and does not contradict him. This same Holy Spirit is in you. You are united with him. He permeates you. You are "walking in the Spirit," "led" by the Spirit, anointed by the Spirit, and filled by the Spirit. The unity of the Trinity dwells in you, and you are being transformed. You were made in God's image in the first place, and now you are indwelt by his Spirit, who reminds you of all that Jesus said and teaches you all things (John 14:26). As the gift of his Spirit increases in your life, more of his character manifests in your life, changing people and circumstances and atmospheres around you. The kingdom of God increases through you as his Spirit in you transforms who you are and flows through you.

Just as God and his Spirit are in unity, as you cultivate sensitivity to his Spirit and walk in agreement with him, submitting your character and decisions and behavior to him, you are transformed. Each time you decide to follow the promptings of the Holy Spirit, you become a little more like your Father and Jesus. This living fellowship with God is the reason you were created. God himself desired close relationship with you and gave you free choice so that your decisions to follow his ways and to draw near to him are meaningful. You are not a robot preprogrammed for submission to God's Spirit; the choice is all yours. When you yield to his Spirit, you are choosing to experience closeness to God and to come into unity with his ways. It brings you into life to the full.

It is the Spirit of God who gently whispers the still small voice of God into your awareness — the very thoughts of God toward you. It is the Spirit of God who pours the love of God into your heart (Romans 5:5). It is the Spirit of God who deposits the fruit of the Spirit into your life (Galatians 5:22). It is the Spirit of God who gives you spiritual gifts.

When the Holy Spirit descended on Jesus at his baptism, he appeared as a dove and remained on him. Thinking about the Holy Spirit as a dove lighting on you helps you to understand how easily his presence can be grieved or quenched (Isaiah 61:3, Ephesians 4:30; 1 Thessalonians 5:19). Thinking about hosting the dove makes you aware of his presence and his leading. Tuning into the Spirit of God brings your life, thoughts, behaviors, and emotions into convergence with God and his goodness, love, mercy, generosity, kindness, and gentleness. As you experience those traits of his Spirit in the way he consistently relates to you, it transforms you. You are drawn to be more like him as you experience the quality of his character and love. His presence and the outpouring of his love into you heals the wounds of this life and gives you glimpses of a higher, better, more perfect way to live. It calls you upward, matures you, and makes the old ways dull and unfulfilling. Being in unity with his Spirit brings hope and calls you forward to the most excellent way. The way of love. Jesus declared that he was the way — the way to the Father. The way of God himself, the one who is love.

The Spirit of love living in you pours out the love of God into your heart, bringing you into union with love himself. Let these truths settle in your spirit today as you experience the presence of God in your life.

God, thank you that you have made me one with you through Jesus and the indwelling of your Holy Spirit. Thank you for your presence in my inmost being. I pray that I will be ever more vigilant and aware of hosting your Spirit. Help me to make choices and live in a manner that invites and maintains the presence and preeminence of your Spirit over me. I pray that I will walk in the love and gentleness of your Spirit with your presence being honored through all aspects of my life. Rest on me, Holy Spirit, as I rest in you.

In Context:
But whoever is united with the Lord is one with him in spirit (1 Corinthians 6:17).

> **Jesus is in his Father, and you are in Christ, and he is in you.** — John 14:20

These are the words of Jesus recorded in John chapter 14. "Because I live." On that day you will realize... the position (can you envision it?) ... "that I am in my Father, and you are in me, and I am in you." The utter safety. Protection. Inclusion. Fullness. He is in you... the Spirit of the Son. With God in closeness. Permeated by him. The place prepared is in Christ, in the Father and filled by the Spirit.

How would things be different if you approached life with the understanding that God is in you and you are in him? What if you walked into the room, your day, or any circumstance in full awareness of your position in Jesus, in the Father, and filled by his Spirit? It would change everything, including your confidence, approach, hope, and sense of dependence. It would bring substantial change to your circumstances and surroundings.

As his beloved child, you are continually in the midst of a God sandwich! Realizing our position and inclusion changes our understanding of the presence of God and our access to him.

When you read the story of Jesus walking on the water after feeding the 5,000, you notice that when Jesus came into the boat, it changed everything. The disciples went from straining against the oars (Mark 6:48) to arriving immediately at their destination (John 6:21). Jesus in the boat is one thing, but his Spirit in you, you in him, and him in the Father is another! This implies much greater relationship, permeability, access, and intimacy than we stay aware of on a daily basis.

It is because Jesus is in the Father and he remained there throughout his days on earth as a human, that everything he said and did was a representation of the Father's words and actions. Because you are in Jesus, when the Father sees you, he looks through Jesus to see you. There is no greater filter available! That's why you're blameless, spotless, holy, without wrinkle or blemish. The Holy Spirit in you pours out and reveals the love of God into your heart (Romans 5:5), settling your need for belonging and giving you reason for your existence. He reminds you of what Jesus said and teaches you all things (John 14:26). The Spirit in you is ministering God's love, words, and wisdom into your core.

Meditate on the secure position you occupy in Jesus, in the Father, with Jesus in us. Picture yourself, wherever you are right now, as being in Jesus, who is in the Father, and with you being filled with his Spirit. That is the place he prepared for you, surrounded and filled. Thank God for bringing you into this place prepared for you, a place of unshakable union with God.

God, Father, Son, and Spirit, thank you for coming close to me, holding me, allowing me in you, and inviting me to remain in you. There is nowhere else I would rather be. Thank you for your incredible openness, generosity, and love for me. I pray that I will remain aware of my position in you and your presence in me as I go through every moment and circumstance. You in me is truly my hope of glory. Me in you is a place of safety, wholeness, and fullness of life. Thank you, God! Help me to live my life to the fullness that you desire for me.

> **In Context:**
> I will not leave you as orphans; I will come to you. Before long, the world will not see me anymore, but you will see me. Because I live, you also will live. On that day you will realize that I am in my Father, and you are in me, and I am in you (John 14:18–20).

You are marked with a seal. — Ephesians 1:13

The seal that you are marked with is the seal of a monarch. God himself, the Holy Spirit, is the seal of your belonging with and to the King of Kings and Lord of Lords.

You are marked in Christ. This is significantly different than being branded as part of a herd. The Holy Spirit is a living seal. The seal is responsive, sensitive, and completely good. Because he is the Spirit of God, he has no darkness or shifting shadow. He is an all-powerful seal. You are marked as belonging with and to God. As a result of believing in Jesus and his sacrifice and applying it to you personally, the price was already paid. There is no question of the buyer being approved. Being sealed connotes that the transaction is fully completed. It's a done deal!

From the cross, Jesus declared, "tetelestai" (John 19:30). Literally translated, the word tetelestai means, "It is finished." It's a single Greek word but rich in meaning, completeness, and perfection. Preceptaustin.org summarizes multiple resources to provide a wealth of information on multifaceted nuances of the Greek and its usage in the time of Jesus' crucifixion. Teteslestai is not a dying man's cry of desperation or defeat, but a living, life-giving redeemer's cry of triumph. It is a divine proclamation that the work of redemption had been fully, finally, and forever accomplished. The word tetelestai means to bring something to a successful end or to its intended or destined goal. It does not mean to merely complete a task but to carry it out fully, to bring it to the finish or to perfection. Tetelestai is in the perfect tense, which conveys that it is finished, it remains as finished, and it always will be finished!

In New Testament times, the word was commonly used across a wide range of daily contexts. When a servant had finished an assigned task or completed a day's work, they would report to their master, "tetelestai," meaning, "I have fully completed the work assigned to me." Every year on the day of atonement, the high priest would make a special sacrifice for the sins of the people of Israel. After the priest had killed an animal without blemish, he would emerge from the temple and announce to the waiting crowd, "It is finished." When Jesus said the same words, he was declaring that there was no need for repeated sacrifices because his completed sacrifice brought total fulfillment to what the temple sacrificial system had foreshadowed. One of the most common uses of tetelestai was in the context of debt collecting. When a person fully paid off a debt, they received a receipt, sealed with the word "tetelestai," which certified that their debt was paid in full. The receipt could be shown as legal verification that they no longer held any responsibility for their debt. Scripture makes it clear that our sin created a debt to God, one that we could never pay back on our own. When Jesus died, he paid off our debt of sin once and for all. We owed a debt we could never pay, and Jesus paid a debt he did not owe! His righteousness has been credited to our account.

We are marked with a seal; his Spirit in us certifies that it is finished, it remains finished, and it will always be finished. Jesus has brought us into the place he prepared for us, a place of unshakable union with God. Meditate on this truth and how you experience it in your daily life.

Jesus, thank you for doing everything necessary, once and for all, to completely pay my debt and to mark me personally as forgiven and included in you. Thank you for the seal of the Holy Spirit in my life. I pray that I will continually be aware of the presence of your Spirit and of being included in you. I pray that I will trust the completeness of your sacrifice on my behalf to bring full, complete, and permanent forgiveness for every sin I confess to you. Thank you for the freedom you have established for me at such a cost to you. I choose to live in obedience to your commands and to remain in relationship with you all the days of my life.

In Context:
And you also were included in Christ when you heard the message of truth, the gospel of your salvation. When you believed, you were marked in him with a seal, the promised Holy Spirit (Ephesians 1:13).

By the deposit of the Holy Spirit, your inheritance is guaranteed. — Ephesians 1:14

Though I don't often think of him in this way, the scriptures declare that the Holy Spirit is a deposit. He is a wonderful, living, portion of what we will inherit. He is a down payment, like earnest money, guaranteeing the full inheritance. We have already seen and experienced many aspects of God's kingdom, yet the kingdom is also still coming. Until the return of Jesus, the King of Kings, his kingdom on earth is not yet as full as it will be. Nevertheless, we are given a foretaste of the fullness of relationship ahead.

Think about a house under contract with a significant deposit. Though there is a contractual understanding of both parties in the sale, it is not a done deal until the closing, when the full execution of the contract is completed. Though there are many steps in the sale of a home — from showings all the way to a contract — ownership doesn't change until the closing. After that comes full habitation by the new owner. The deposit is the guarantee until closing. While buyers wait for the closing, they may have plans and dreams for remodeling, improvements, moving in, and placing their belongings into particular arrangements and places. While under contract, nothing can be done by the current owner to deface the property or to void the contract. The owner can only make changes to the property that are approved by the depositor.

Right now, we have the indwelling of the Holy Spirit as the guarantee of our full inheritance. Now, we only see in a mirror dimly. At the completion of the ages, after the return of Jesus, then we will fully know — we will see him face to face. Before that we hold hope, excitement, and consideration of possibility. Anticipation of the greatest owner in the universe.

The current indwelling of the Holy Spirit is but a foretaste of face-to-face relationship with Father, Son, and Spirit. He is a living, active, indwelling presence of God himself, a wonderful counseling, comforting, leading, prompting manifestation of God himself, residing in us. As we attune our sensitivity to his leadings, we recognize that he reminds us of the words of Jesus, which were words the Father was speaking. When we see God face-to-face, we will be completely transformed to be like him. Now, with the deposit of the Holy Spirit indwelling us, we are nudged by his still, small voice to become more like him. Being fully in his presence, we will be undone and fully transformed into the new creation that God desired us to be before the beginning of time.

God is continuously acquiring new territory. His kingdom is expanding as the gospel spreads and people trust the sacrifice of Jesus to bring them back into right standing and relationship with God. The Father then places a deposit, the Holy Spirit, into each believer to guarantee full transfer into the kingdom and full rights of ownership when Christ returns to establish the new heaven and the new earth.

People write and execute wills to pass inheritance from one to another. The legal transfer is guaranteed by a document recorded with the registrar of wills carried out by executors and approved by legislated authority. This is a mere shadow of God's kingdom truth. His inheritance for us — relationship with him for eternity as sons and daughters, with full rights to access every spiritual blessing in Christ — is of inestimable value. The same inheritance that Jesus earned through his sacrifice is for us. In fact, Ephesians 1:3 declares that we already have it (in deposit form). That deposit is the Holy Spirit, and his indwelling seals, certifies, and guarantees the remainder of our coming inheritance at the completion of the age.

An inheritance is something that you did not strive to earn. It is given to you, independent of your merit, because of a legal transfer that you can access after that person's death. When the document of the will is fully executed, you come into full possession of all that is recorded and sealed for you. The Holy Spirit is your guarantee of getting your full inheritance in Christ as a child of the living God. An heir, a joint heir with Christ.

Meditate on the wonder of what you already have, experience, and possess and consider what is yet to come at the end of the age. Invite God to show the inheritance that you already possess and ways to more fully trust in the coming inheritance that he has qualified you for.

Father, thank you for the indwelling deposit of your Holy Spirit. Thank you that his presence is your guarantee of my full inheritance as your child. I pray that I will be continually aware of his presence and his leading in my life — that everything I do will be in accordance with his approval, manifesting more and more of your love and character. Thank you for the unmerited and exceedingly generous gift of the inheritance you have set aside for me as your child. I pray that I will live now in a manner that represents your generosity in my life.

In Context:
And you also were included in Christ when you heard the message of truth, the gospel of your salvation. When you believed, you were marked in him with a seal, the promised Holy Spirit, who is a deposit guaranteeing our inheritance until the redemption of those who are God's possession — to the praise of his glory (Ephesians 1:13–14).

> **The anointing you received from him remains in you and teaches you about all things. — 1 John 2:27**

In John 16:15, Jesus declared, "All that belongs to the Father is mine. That is why I said the Spirit will receive from me what he will make known to you."

The Father sent Jesus to the earth to reveal himself to us. As the Son of God, Jesus did all that was necessary to reveal him. He showed his love, taught about him and his kingdom, and declared the truth to set us free. Jesus gave his life for us and sacrificially fulfilled all that was needed to cleanse us of our sins so that we could be restored in relationship to the Father. It was the Father who brought Jesus back to life and raised him up to be seated at his right hand. But God with us, Emmanuel, did not leave us. He sent the Spirit in the name of the Son to teach and remind us of everything that Jesus said and to make it known to us.

This is all about relationship — astounding love, generosity, and goodness — all of it from God, pursuing us across eternity to restore us into relationship with our Father. Think about the father running (Luke 15:20). The running Father who would invest and pour out all he had to gain us back and invite us into his house of feasting and love and unity. This is not just a one-time celebration. It's a life of dwelling with him and walking through each day with him.

We can shift our thinking from seeing Jesus as our divine buffer from God's wrath to understanding him as the exact representation of his Father's love and the glue that binds and seals us as a child of the loving Father, who is so loving that he is love itself. He does not offer a touch or a dash or a feeling of love; love is not a facet of him. He is full-on, constant, all-in, never-ending love. God is loving us right now. Who else could possibly represent and reveal the love of God to a human other than God himself?

The heart of the Father is for you without reservation. Some people say that we were born with a "God-shaped hole" in our hearts, perhaps. But God certainly has a "you-shaped hole" in his boundless heart. He shaped space in his heart for you! And me! Eventually, we will all be fit together as living stones. That is what the Spirit of God himself, dwelling in our inmost being, pours into our hearts — a place of unshakable union with God.

Quietly consider the depth, the height, the length and the width of God's love for you. Thank him for ways that you have recently experienced this place prepared and the fullness of life that you experience as a result. Ask God to show you a way that you personally can experience more of his boundless love for you and reflectively sit in that experience.

Father, thank you for your boundless, constant love for me. Thank you for pursuing me to make yourself known to me. Thank you for sending Jesus to be the sacrifice for my sin and rebellion and to restore me into relationship with you. Thank you for sending your Spirit to indwell me to remind me of Jesus' words and to teach me and allow me to experience knowing you. I choose to remain in you. I pray that your love that continually flows to me would "stick." I pray that I would be more fully aware of your presence and your love in my life, that I would experientially grow in knowing you, and that my experience of your great love for me would transform me to be more like you.

In Context:
As for you, the anointing you received from him remains in you, and you do not need anyone to teach you. But as his anointing teaches you about all things and as that anointing is real, not counterfeit — just as it has taught you, remain in him (1 John 2:27).

Notes

A Place of Unshakable Union with God: *Summary and Application*

God's Spirit, whom you received from God, is in you (1 Corinthians 6:19). You are one with God in Spirit (1 Corinthians 6:17). Jesus is in his Father, and you are in Christ, and he is in you (John 14:20). You are marked with a seal (Ephesians 1:13). By the deposit of the Holy Spirit, your inheritance is guaranteed (Ephesians 1:14). The anointing you received from him remains in you and teaches you about all things (1 John 2:27).

When you consider the richness of the descriptions and the frequency of their appearing in different portions of scripture, it becomes clear that Jesus has prepared a place of unshakable union with God for each one of us. God's Spirit is so fully and so constantly in you that you are one with God in Spirit. You have been accepted by and included in Jesus. Jesus is in His Father. I cannot fathom a more complete picture of unity. He goes ahead of us, he is behind us, he is around us. His Spirit is in us. We are centered in the height, depth, breadth, and width of his love. Nothing can separate us from the love of God that is in Jesus (Romans 8:39).

> **Ask the Holy Spirit to convey to you an experiential sense of the complete, engulfing, saturating, never-ending love of God. Ask him to write the truth of each of these statements in your inmost being:**

- God's Spirit, whom I received from God, is in me.
- I am one with God in Spirit.
- Jesus is in his Father, and I am in Christ, and he is in me.
- I am marked with a seal.
- By the deposit of the Holy Spirit, my inheritance is guaranteed.
- The anointing I received from him remains in me and teaches me about all things.
- Jesus prepared a place of unshakable union with God for me.

* * Additional note space located on page 215 * *

CHAPTER 16

A Place of *Oneness in Love*

You love because God first loved you, and love comes from God (1 John 4:10, 7). You are strengthened with power through the Spirit in your inmost being (Ephesians 3:16). Like living stones, you are being built into a spiritual house (1 Peter 2:5). You are a part of the body of Christ (1 Corinthians 12:27).

> **You love because God first loved you, and love comes from God.** — 1 John 4:19, 7

As we have considered previously, in love, you were chosen by God before the beginning of the world (Ephesians 1:4). You are lavished in God's love (1 John 3:1). You are a deeply loved child of God (Ephesians 5:1). You are rooted and established in love (Ephesians 3:17). Nothing in all of creation is able to separate you from the love of God that is in Christ Jesus, our Lord (Romans 8:37–39).

God is love (1 John 4:16). His core nature has always been and will always be love. He never acts in a way that is outside of loving. He is loving you right now. You can receive his love right now. God has poured out his love into your heart by the Holy Spirit, whom he has given us (Romans 5:5). His love changes you, transforms you to be more like him. His love fills and fulfills your belonging needs. He accepts you in love (Romans 15:7). His love, changing you, brings you to the place where you can love others with his love. You love because he first loved you, and love comes from God, who is love.

Much of the rest of the passage in 1 John 4 that these key verses come from makes it clear that if we truly know God (that is, know him experientially and relationally, not simply knowing about him), then we will love one another. In speaking to his disciples, Jesus said, "By this everyone will know that you are my disciples, if you love one another" (John 13:35). When asked by an expert in the law which is the greatest commandment (Matthew 22:37–40), Jesus replied, "'Love the Lord your God with all your heart and with all your soul and with all your mind.' This is the first and greatest commandment. And the second is like it: 'Love your neighbor as yourself.' All the Law and the Prophets hang on these two commandments."

Love for one another derives from our love for God, comes from God because he first loved us, and transforms our relationships with one another. Love should be so pervasive in our lives that everyone will know that we are followers of Jesus because of it. Knowing that our love for others originates in God frees us from needing to manufacture or force it. As we receive God's love for us, there is more than enough for others. Freely we receive, so freely we can give.

Throughout my life, as I have felt that I have not had enough patience or kindness or gentleness, I have prayed for more of those characteristics to be established in me by God. Recently, I have come to understand that patience, kindness, and gentleness are characteristics of love (1 Corinthians 13:4–8). Now, when I become aware of lacking ability to treat others with greater patience, I simply pray for God to make me more receptive of the love that he is already pouring into my heart. Receiving more love brings more patience.

Meditate on places in your life where you desire to be more aware of God's boundless love for you so that you can more effectively give it to others.

Father, thank you for your love — for its height, depth, breadth, and width. Thank you that I am never outside of your love, and that nothing can separate me from your love in Jesus. Thank you that your love continuously flows toward me and into me. I pray that as your Spirit pours your love into my inmost being that I will sense it, know it, receive it with joy, and be encouraged and comforted. I pray that I would be moved to freely share your love with others. Thank you that your love is the most transformative force in the universe. I choose to receive your love.

> **In Context:**
> Dear friends, let us love one another, for love comes from God. Everyone who loves has been born of God and knows God. Whoever does not love does not know God, because God is love … And so we know and rely on the love God has for us. God is love. Whoever lives in love lives in God, and God in them … We love because he first loved us (1 John 4:7–8, 16, 19).

You are strengthened with power through the Spirit in your inmost being. — Ephesians 3:16

This is a part of Paul's powerfully rich prayer for the Ephesian believers. To see many subtle components of how God's Spirit strengthens us with his power, I recommend that you read and meditate on the whole prayer (Ephesians 3:14–20).

First, this strengthening is based on the glorious riches of God, which he lavishes on us in his love (1 John 3:1). It is his nature flowing toward and into us.

Second, it is not necessarily directly observable on the outside; it is an inner strength that overflows to observable characteristics.

Third, it is a glorious treasure of God that roots and establishes us in love, which is his most distinguishing trait. This is being continuously poured into our inmost being by the indwelling Holy Spirit. That which can be poured is a liquid, which is capable of covering and permeating every low point, crack, nook, hole, and fault. It saturates. It makes dry and broken things pliable as it is absorbed, engorging them until they reach overflowing. Gentle soaking rain is vastly different from torrents of water, which violently rush, clearing everything in its path and bringing destruction. No, the love of God is continuously distributed so that it can be absorbed, bringing life.

Fourth, it takes God's power for us to grasp the enormity of our trinitarian God's love, which surpasses knowledge. But I have experienced many things I do not understand. For example, I often sit on a chair and science tell us that chairs are made up of countless particles that rapidly spin. The chair only "feels" solid; the reality is that it is made up of more open space between the particles than solid surface. I have sat on so many chairs that it really does not take faith for me to experience this regularly. Though I know this is true about the particles, I still do not understand it. I just experientially know that I can securely sit on vast empty spaces. Clearly, I do not need to fully comprehend things I can rest on.

Fifth, God's supply of love is unending, because he is infinite and he is love. He is pouring an abundance of love into our hearts right now, both to soak and nurture us and to rearrange the landscape of our inmost being. The water always wins! It always levels everything. It moves the otherwise unmovable and breaks the seemingly unbreakable. I have seen thirty-inch diameter trees snapped after floodwaters have receded. The flow of God's love, like water in nature, is the basis of life and the great transformer of the landscape of our inmost being. It is power, indeed — power for life and power for change. In developed areas, we focus on stormwater management, drought control, sea level change, and many other aspects of stewarding water. We are dependent on water for life. We are dependent on God's love for life. The best stewardship of his love that I know is to freely receive it so that I can freely give it.

Sixth, we do have the capacity to receive God's love, and to be filled to the measure of fullness of God. He designed us in that manner, and he is the one who measures our measure of fullness. Is that to be as fully loving as he is? Or is it to keep receiving until he says, "There, complete, mature, perfect"? Either way, he is continually pouring his love into our hearts to bring us closer to the measure of his fullness — not yours or anyone else's. The fullness of God.

Seventh, the strengthening of our inmost being is his love being received. We may not be able to fully comprehend our role in this, but we can choose to receive the love of God. Amazing love. A place of oneness in love.

Meditate on ways that God's love is transforming you and giving you the ability to share his love with others. Invite his love to permeate every aspect of your life and relationships more fully.

Father, thank you for your love and for your Spirit in my inmost being. I pray that I will be aware of your presence in my life today as you pour more of your love into my heart by your Spirit. I pray that your love will transform the landscape of my heart, mind, and life to reflect your workmanship more fully.

In Context:
I pray that out of his glorious riches he may strengthen you with power through his Spirit in your inner being (Ephesians 3:16).

Like living stones, you are being built into a spiritual house. — 1 Peter 2:5

Jesus is the living stone, the cornerstone (1 Peter 2:5) and the capstone (1 Peter 2:7). We, too, are precious and chosen by him (Ephesians 1:4).

We are being built into a spiritual house — by God, not by our effort. The spiritual house is a family of the children of God, a holy priesthood (1 Peter 2:9). Like any builder, the master builder selects each stone. He purchases it. He cleans it. He shapes it. He fits it. He places it in juxtaposition to the other stones. He mortars it into place, supported and surrounded by others, resting on the cornerstone and covered by the capstone. We both give support to other stones and receive support from them. Together, built in orientation to the cornerstone, we are stronger. We can securely rest on him. Each one of us is placed, integrated, and needed to complete the structure. Each living stone has purpose, function, beauty, and unique characteristics. We are each part of a bigger building — masterfully planned, built, and maintained by the master builder of all. A missing stone would mean the building has a hole.

We are not inanimate stones, we are living stones, living in relationship with the Spirit of God indwelling us, and interacting together. We are created by God, being built by God into a spiritual house, resting on God, selected by God, purchased by God, cleaned by God, placed by God, and stuck by his mortar to other living stones and to him. We were created and chosen and placed for a purpose. A living stone, with life, in concert with other living stones in the building. Indwelt and filled by God himself.

The cornerstone sets the height and the direction of the building. It is the first stone laid. All others are laid in reference to the cornerstone. Often the cornerstone marks history or remembrance. It can declare ownership or design and can be used for inscription and preservation. A capstone is another name for a keystone, which is a capping or covering for a wall that holds all things together and provides covering. A capstone protects the structure from rain and snow soaking into the joints and creating weaknesses through freezing and thawing. Jesus declared himself to be the Alpha and the Omega, the first and the last, the beginning and the end (Revelation 22:13) — both the cornerstone and the capstone.

We are surrounded by and filled by Christ. Our life as a living stone is all about him.

What are spiritual sacrifices? Presenting our bodies as living sacrifices (Romans 12:1). Sacrifices of faith (Philippians 2:17). Sacrifices of praise (Hebrews 13:15). Sacrifices of doing good (Hebrews 13:16; Romans 12:13; James 1:27). Sacrifices of material assistance (Philippians 4:18). These are all part of the living stone part of priesthood. These bear his fruit when we do them as God prompts us to do them, not out of obligation, but in the love that comes from him.

Meditate on ways that you have benefitted from leaning on other stones in your spiritual household. Consider ways that you can provide steady support for other stones you are in contact with. Prayerfully select something to do today to demonstrate loving support to someone whom God puts on your heart. Ask God to ground that person in love today by partnering with you to demonstrate his loving support for them.

Jesus, thank you for being our cornerstone and capstone. Thank you that I can rest on you and come under your covering. Thank you for placing me where you want me and at just the right time to bring completion to your building of the kingdom. I pray that you will remind me to rest on you and to stay under your covering as I go through each day. I pray that you will help me to both give and receive support from those you have placed in my life today. I pray that your Spirit will prompt me to do the things that you have prepared in advance for me to do this day, and that as I do, your love would permeate all that I do and say. I thank you for the opportunity to be a part of your spiritual building and to offer spiritual sacrifices as a part of your family.

> **In Context:**
> As you come to him, the living Stone — rejected by humans but chosen by God and precious to him — you also, like living stones, are being built into a spiritual house to be a holy priesthood, offering spiritual sacrifices acceptable to God through Jesus Christ (1 Peter 2:4–5).

You are a part of the body of Christ. — 1 Corinthians 12:27

1 Corinthians 12:18–20 says, "But in fact God has placed the parts in the body, every one of them, just as he wanted them to be. If they were all one part, where would the body be? As it is, there are many parts, but one body." Each part of the

body has different and necessary functions. God arranged me just as he wanted me to be, creating me with my unique gifts, talents, characteristics, and ways of relating to others. As I reflect on this, I become thankful for who I am in Christ — how he has shaped, formed, gifted, and placed me. I am fearfully and wonderfully made (Psalm 139:14). Every day of my life was ordained and written in his book before one of them came to be (Psalm 139:14). I am literally in Christ (John 14:20), united with him (1 Corinthians 6:17), and included in him (Ephesians 1:13). I am a dwelling in which Christ lives (Ephesians 2:22); I am his temple (1 Corinthians 6:19). I am growing up into him (Ephesians 4:15).

It is also true that we are a part of the body of believers, the church, with at least one spiritual gift. 1 Corinthians 12:7 says that to each one the manifestation of the Spirit is given for the common good. There is great diversity in the gifts of the Spirit, "and he distributes them to each one, just as he determines": wisdom, messages of knowledge, healing, miraculous powers, prophecy, distinguishing between Spirits, speaking in different kinds of tongues, and interpretation of tongues. Nowhere does it say that this list is exhaustive, but it is, at the least, representative of manifestations of the Holy Spirit of God working through his children. It also does not imply that each of his children gets one and only one gift (see 1 Corinthians 12:11,10).

Christ's Spirit in us makes us a part of his body. His manifestation through us gives us needed function within his body as we work and live in concert with other "parts" of his body, who also have needed functions to bring it to wholeness. When all parts are functioning to their capacity in their intended purpose, it brings life to the full (John 10:10). Part of our life to the full is to be placed in a functioning body, where the other parts are doing their part by manifesting Christ's Spirit through their giftings.

The different parts of our physical bodies do their part when needed, but all parts of the body are not fully active all the time. Rest, regulation, feeding, recuperation, and regeneration is needed between active times of service. The physical body functions best when it is in the unity of each part contributing its full function at the right time.

The body itself has purpose and effects, just as each part does. Christ is the head of the body (Ephesians 5:23). He is the source, director, and integrator. If a person experiences whole-brain death, they are physically dead and are not able to be resuscitated. Life is coordinated in and directed from the head. Christ, the head of his body, is alive eternally and will never die again! Because our head is eternal, we are eternal, and every part of his body is eternal.

It is good to be a part of the body of Christ. It is good to have a function in a place of oneness in love. Consider your function in the body of Christ and pray for ways to effectively use the spiritual gifts that you have been entrusted with. Trust the Lord to give you eyes to see ways and places to use the spiritual gifts that he has given you to share as a part of his body.

Jesus, thank you for including me as a part of your body. Thank you that you have chosen me, cleaned me, and placed me among other parts to do the things you created me to do. Thank you for your indwelling Holy Spirit and the spiritual gifts that his presence brings. I pray that I will be faithful to enact my full functions in your larger body at the right times. I pray for your leading to teach me when to exercise the gifts you have placed in me and when to rest, allowing other parts of your body to exercise their full function. Thank you that you are the eternal head of this body, and that I can rest in the joy of life to the full under your headship.

In Context:
Now you are the body of Christ, and each one of you is a part of it (1 Corinthians 12:27).

A Place of Oneness in Love:
Summary and Application

You love because God first loved you, and love comes from God (1 John 4:10, 7). You are strengthened with power through the Spirit in your inmost being (Ephesians 3:16). Like living stones, you are being built into a spiritual house (1 Peter 2:5). You are a part of the body of Christ (1 Corinthians 12:27).

The place that Jesus prepared for you is a part of the kingdom of God. As you live from that place, he leads you in unity with your brothers and sisters in Christ. Your place aligns with theirs to form a living home, a tapestry of God's giftings, callings, and character, to transform this world and to minister to both those who have and those who have not yet entered his kingdom.

As his living stones, God's kids always fit together. Instead of looking for differences, things change when you look for intersections, edges that go together. Differences in his children are merely extensions of his kingdom that offer or manifest aspects of his kingdom that you do not have or have not been assigned to bring. It is important not to despise or envy others, or to strive to have the giftings and callings of others. Be yourself, in Christ, and let him keep you in your place and others in theirs. In him, all things hold together.

Each of us is in the shepherd's flock, experiencing the care of the good shepherd. While many others share the experience of being cared for by the good shepherd, his relationship with you is unique. He is the one who would leave the ninety-nine to go out and find the one who strayed. The protection, unity, and support of others can help you understand his care.

While his followers are unique and many, we are part of one body, with functions that fit together with those of every other child of God. As much as it is up to you, live at peace with all people (Romans 12:8). Forgive as the Lord forgave you (Colossians 3:13) — completely, frequently, and without regret. Treat others as you would want to be treated, which sums up the Law and the Prophets (Matthew 7:12). Ask God's Spirit to speak to you regarding the place he prepared for you in his body, a place of oneness in love.

> **Choose in your heart to value the place that he has prepared for you in his body.**

- I love because God first loved me, and love comes from God.
- I am strengthened with power through the Spirit in my inmost being.
- Like living stones, I am being built into a spiritual house.
- I am a part of the body of Christ.
- In Jesus, I am in a place of oneness in love.

Notes

CHAPTER 17

A Place of *Power for Life*

Grace has been given to you as Christ apportioned it (Ephesians 4:7). His grace is enough for you (2 Corinthians 2:19). In your weakness he is your strength (2 Corinthians 2:19). You can do all things through him who gives you strength (Philippians 4:13).

> **Grace has been given to you as Christ apportioned it.**
> **— Ephesians 4:7**

Our own weakness, inability, and dependency on God does not defeat us. No! In fact, Those things bring us into the place where we experience more of his power in our lives. Our own weakness and awareness of our limitation is the place where we know, experientially, that he accomplishes things on our behalf and through us that we could never achieve on our own. He meets us in our inability and our weakness, and his love, power, and provision come through to manifest his character in our lives and circumstances.

Much of western contemporary culture places a focus and a premium on independence, self-sufficiency, and being your own person. We are raised to champion these traits and we celebrate them as marks of great accomplishment. In truth, they represent the false beliefs that we must take care of ourselves and put ourselves first. The serpent used these deceptions to bring Adam and Eve to question the goodness of God and to take their destinies into their own hands. This is the heart of orphan-spirited thinking: "I cannot trust God and depend on him; I can only trust my own efforts." When Jesus talked with his disciples in his last few days on earth, telling them that he was going to prepare a place for them, he said that he would not leave them as orphans (John 14:18). Our inclusion in God's family means that we do not need to engage in self-centered striving for the care that he abundantly gives us.

Jesus stated that apart from him we can do nothing (John 15:5). Psalm 16:2 declares that apart from the Lord, we have no good thing. Recognizing and embracing our dependence on God brings the perfection of his power and provision. He apportions (Ephesians 4:7) and gives us sufficient grace (2 Corinthians 12:9) for all circumstances. The gospels show us that everywhere Jesus went he provided an abundance of what was needed. Wine from water. Feeding thousands from a few fish and loaves. Power to calm storms. Love for those crucifying him. Grace is given to us as Jesus apportions it. We do not need to worry that there will be a shortage of grace for whatever the circumstances require. The Apostle Paul wrote that the secret of being content in any and every situation is to recognize that we can do all things through Christ who gives us strength (Philippians 4:12–13). Through Jesus, who gives us strength and apportions grace to us, we are in a place of power for life.

Ask the Holy Spirit to show you places in your life where you frequently depend on your own strength or ability before inviting Jesus to bring the grace that he has apportioned for you. Consider ways to seek him first more regularly in those areas of life. Ask him for grace to receive his counsel and accept his direction in a path forward.

Father, I acknowledge that I have many flaws and areas of weakness. I know that I cannot overcome them in my own ability, power, or strength. I choose to trust in you, your love, your power, and your goodness to work in my life and in all my circumstances. I pray that I would choose to do everything through you instead of trying to fend for myself. Thank you for your presence, the provision of grace to me, and for fully knowing my weaknesses and needs. I trust you to be the source of all that I need for this day and all that it brings to me. I choose to experience it through you and not apart from you.

In Context:
But to each one of us grace has been given as Christ apportioned it (Ephesians 4:7).

His grace is enough for you, for in your weakness, he is your strength. — 2 Corinthians 12:9

God's grace is apportioned to me by Christ. It is enough for all situations of every day. It transforms and matures me as I depend on him and his grace. It brings me into a fuller representation of him and into closer relationship with him — walking in sonship. Life to the full.

When Jesus apportions grace to me, it is not like he is feeding chickens or throwing a bale of hay to a herd of cattle. The grace he apportions is personally designed and administered/delivered for me and to me by his indwelling Spirit. In his time of walking the earth as a human, Jesus demonstrated time and again that he knew when to show up — and his timing was impeccable. God, who is love, never fails. His grace (the Father's, Son's, and Spirit's) is available to me if I depend on him instead of my own solution, ability, "power" or strength. There is something about my weakness that displays God's perfect power. His power is made perfect when I am weak.

When I acknowledge the inferiority of my solutions, abilities and efforts — when I depend on him to bring his solutions to me and through me — not just orphan-heartedly striving in self-effort or self-determination, then his grace is made mature in me, sufficient in him, and I reflect his glory as his power is made perfect in me. Truly depending on Papa to supply all of my needs is what he intends and has intended from the beginning.

The Apostle Paul learned that his lineage, education, experience, position, and own effort led to nothing of lasting value. In fact, he stated that he learned to boast in things that showed his weaknesses (2 Corinthians 11:30). This is because he had experienced that in his weakness God's faithfulness, power, and character were demonstrated. Jeremiah 9:23–24 says, "This is what the Lord says: "Let not the wise boast of their wisdom or the strong boast of their strength or the rich boast of their riches, but let the one who boasts boast about this: that they have the understanding to know me, that I am the Lord, who exercises kindness, justice and righteousness on earth, for in these I delight," declares the Lord."

This is about learning the secret (see Philippians 2:12) of Christ's presence and provision in all circumstances. This is about experientially knowing the Lord. Psalm 73:26 says, "My flesh and my heart may fail, but God is the strength of my heart and my portion forever."

Invite the Holy Spirit to teach you patience and gentleness and self-control in trusting God for his all-sufficient grace and strength for every situation. Meditate on the truth that in Christ, you have access to the fullness of grace needed for anything and everything you are facing today.

Father, thank you for giving me every spiritual blessing in Jesus, including all of the grace you have apportioned to him and through him. Let it flow into me and give me grace to wait for you to fill me with your presence so that I can go through this day filled with your presence and love. I choose to rely on you to fill me and flow through me rather than trying to fend for myself. Thank you, Father.

> **In Context:**
> But he said to me, "My grace is sufficient for you, for my power is made perfect in weakness." Therefore I will boast all the more gladly about my weaknesses, so that Christ's power may rest on me. That is why, for Christ's sake, I delight in weaknesses, in insults, in hardships, in persecutions, in difficulties. For when I am weak, then I am strong (2 Corinthians 12:9–10).

> **You can do all things through him who gives you strength.**
> — Philippians 4:13

God himself is with you and for you. You do have the ability to choose to remain in him and receive his love, grace, wisdom, strength, provision, perspective, and power. You can decide which things to do in him, and when to ignore the grace that could be yours by trusting in your own orphan-hearted, self-striving solutions (Jonah 8:32). Saying that you can do all things in him does not mean that you can lift two thousand pounds; it means that you can choose to face your circumstances in dependency on him instead of independently choosing to go it on your own. You can choose to experience life through him, in the place he prepared for you, instead of on your own.

The larger context of this verse has to do with facing circumstances of need or plenty in him and choosing to be content in every circumstance. The Message renders the passage in this way: "I've learned by now to be quite content whatever my circumstances. I'm just as happy with little as with much, with much as with little. I've found the recipe for being happy whether full or hungry, hands full or hands empty. Whatever I have, wherever I am, I can make it through anything in the One who makes me who I am."

The emphasis is on choosing to depend on God for contentment and deep peace in every circumstance. The emphasis is not on how you can individually strive to overcome things or to stubbornly power through impossible circumstances. Depending on your relationship to him for his love and inner power to come through to you and then through you to affect you, affect you in the circumstances, and to affect the circumstances through you. Even Jesus stated that apart from the Father, he could do nothing. In the same way that Jesus recognized and expressed his total reliance on God, you can posture yourself as a little child, waiting for your father to care for whatever is necessary.

You can do all things through him who gives you strength. You can choose to remain in a place of power that Jesus provided for you to experience your life in Christ. Meditate on ways that you can be more trusting of God working in and through you than you currently are. Pray for his grace to allow you to live more dependently on him.

Father, right now I choose to rely on your grace for all that I am facing in my life — for the places where I perceive plenty and the places where I perceive lack. I thank you that you are with me and for me. I thank you for your presence in my life, in my inmost being, and for your love and every spiritual blessing flowing toward me right now. Thank you that Jesus overcame the world and that I am free from the elementary principles of the world. I choose to rely on you and your strength in my inmost being to make me a victorious overcomer of the world. I pray for your peace, contentment, and love to flow to me and through me to bring your kingdom into the circumstances and to the people around me.

In Context:
I know what it is to be in need, and I know what it is to have plenty. I have learned the secret of being content in any and every situation, whether well fed or hungry, whether living in plenty or in want. I can do all this through him who gives me strength (Philippians 4:12–13).

A Place of Power for Life:

Summary and Application

Grace has been given to you as Christ apportioned it (Ephesians 4:7). His grace is enough for you (2 Corinthians 2:19). In your weakness he is your strength (2 Corinthians 2:19). You can do all things through him who gives you strength (Philippians 4:13).

> **Wherever you find yourself, there are valuable questions to consider. Take the time to check in and ask the Lord at least one of the following questions:**

- What are you doing in this place?
- What kind of place do you desire this to be?
- What is this a place of? (What is the function or character of the place?)
- What aspect of your character do you want you to manifest or deposit here?
- How can I submit to you and let you flow through me as the conduit of your Spirit in this place?

The verses you have just considered establish that Jesus himself apportions grace to you. There is enough of his love and power for you to depend on to get through anything you are facing.

In Jesus, all things hold together (Colossians 1:17). It is not your job, responsibility, or ability (and certainly not your paygrade!) to hold everything together. In him. Your weakness is his strength.

When his disciples were sent back across the lake after Jesus fed the five thousand, a fierce wind kept the professional fishermen from making headway. They were straining at the oars. In the middle of the night, Jesus came walking on the water near them. When he entered their boat, they immediately arrived at their destination. You can decide to stop straining at the oars flailing in the storms of life, trying on your own to navigate the obstacles. You can invite Jesus into your boat. He is more than able to bring you to the destination that he has designated for you. With him. In his presence.

This beautiful illustration of expert boatmen in the storm unable to proceed occurred before the indwelling of his spirit. Now we are in a different time, place, reality. His Spirit is always with us because he indwells us. This far surpasses him sitting beside you in a boat. This is how you can do even greater things. Christ in you is your hope of glory. Jesus has prepared for you a place of power for life.

> **Ask the indwelling Spirit of God to show you how to rest in the truth of these verses as you navigate the storms of your life:**

- Grace has been given to me as Christ apportioned it.
- His grace is enough for me.
- In my weakness he is my strength.
- I can do all things through him who gives me strength.
- In Jesus, I am in a place of power for life.

Notes

CHAPTER 18

A Place of *Life to the Full*

God has made known to you the path of life, he fills you with joy in his presence, with eternal pleasures at his right hand (Psalm 16:11). The joy of the Lord is your strength (Nehemiah 8:10). Jesus came so that you may live a new life (Romans 6:4) and have life to the full (John 10:10).

> **God has made known to you the path of life. — Psalm 16:11**

The path of life — life to the full — is living as a deeply loved child in relationship with your heavenly Father, your Papa. Jesus is the only way to the Father — a narrow gate. The narrow road is walking the pathway of Jesus, loving the Father, listening to his voice and seeing and doing what he is doing. This involves trusting in his word to be a lamp to your feet, deferring to him in all matters, loving him with all of your heart, mind, soul, and strength.

Matthew 7:13–14 says, "Enter through the narrow gate. For wide is the gate and broad is the road that leads to destruction, and many enter through it. But small is the gate and narrow the road that leads to life, and only a few find it."

Deuteronomy 30:19–20 says, "This day I call the heavens and the earth as witnesses against you that I have set before you life and death, blessings and curses. Now choose life, so that you and your children may live and that you may love the Lord your God, listen to his voice, and hold fast to him. For the Lord is your life, and he will give you many years in the land he swore to give to your fathers, Abraham, Isaac and Jacob."

There are many decisions in life that are not directly addressed in scripture. Some of them are life-changing: should I keep my current job or change employment? Is this the place where you want me to live in this season of my life? Though deadlines and other contingencies often require us to make decisions before we have fully settled our minds, I have experienced that the Lord will lead you as you seek him and submit your ways to him. Decades of trusting him and viewing life retrospectively have convinced me that even through life's trials and uncertainties, he works all things together for good (Romans 8:28) because of his goodness flowing toward me continually. This has been true for me even when his goodness is not readily apparent in the present while traversing challenges or losses. Looking back over time, I can always find his superior perspective, wisdom, and care. Thank you, Jesus, that in you, I am in a place of life to the full.

Review past turning points in your life and consider the ways you tried to defer to God's direction. Meditate on ways that God has brought good into your life even through things that have been difficult to experience. Ask him to help you to trust him to continue to work in your life for good.

God, thank you for leading me on the path of life. Thank you for this life, for life in you, for your Spirit in me teaching and leading me, and for the hope of eternal relationship with you. Thank you for making all things work together for my good. Thank you for your love. I pray that I will continue to make choices that are consistent with your word and your leading. I pray that I will be attuned to and enjoy your presence and all that being with you brings to life.

In Context:
You make known to me the path of life; you will fill me with joy in your presence, with eternal pleasures at your right hand (Psalm 16:11).

> **He fills you with joy in his presence, with eternal pleasures at his right hand. — Psalm 16:11**

The second half of Psalm 16:11 elaborates on the path of life. "You will fill me with joy in your presence, with eternal pleasures at your right hand." That is the best path for life.

Being in the presence of God — love, life, healing, wholeness, belonging, joy — is what we were created for. All of creation — even in the best of places and conditions — is under the curse and authority (which is limited, both in time and in scope) of the "prince of the air." He has no dominion over God and nothing in common with God's character and presence.

God's presence brings the fullness of life (John 10:10) that you were designed to enjoy. As you sense his presence, it brings love and peace and joy. His presence brings the fruit of his Spirit.

Notice, he fills you with joy in his presence. First, it is his continual, deep, and unchangeable goodness that flows to you and into you. Second, it does not come occasionally, rarely, or in diminutive amounts. It is not insufficient; it doesn't partially fill you. It is not a mere sniff or a taste. He fills you with joy. When you are full of joy, it displaces all worry, fear, and neediness. Every little thing is all right. There is nothing better for you to do but to receive and soak up his goodness and relate to him as his offspring. Third, the joy is related to being in his presence. This is what you were made for. You cannot go outside of his presence and get genuine joy and pleasures. Outside of him are counterfeits that bring death and separation and thinking grounded in the tree of the fruit of the knowledge of good and evil. In his garden, his presence, you are filled with joy and sit in the flow of eternal pleasures. What a contrasting difference from fear of judgment, wrath, and punishment.

Enter his gates with thanksgiving and his courts with praise (Psalm 100:4). Enter now. He is loving you right now. His goodness is flowing to you and all around you right now. His presence is available to you right now. Enter now and receive. Heaven, the new earth, and eternal life are all about being in his presence. But all of this is available to us the moment we hear the good news of Jesus' sacrifice for us and accept him and his incomparable gift. He was and is the way to the Father and his presence. In Jesus, you are in a place of life to the full.

Meditate on the presence of God with you right now. How does recognizing his nearness change the way that you are thinking about today or tomorrow, or even difficulties from the past?

Father, thank you for the joy of being in your presence. Thank you for creating me for fullness of relationship with you and for providing Jesus and his sacrifice for me as the way back into your presence. Thank you for your invitation to enter your presence and to remain with you. Thank you that your desire for relationship with me is so great that you are making me over into an eternal dwelling where we can remain together. I pray that I will experience the joy of remaining in your presence today, that I will hold awareness of your presence in my thoughts, and that I will sense the joy of being your child, secure in your love for me.

In Context:
You make known to me the path of life; you will fill me with joy in your presence, with eternal pleasures at your right hand (Psalm 16:11).

The joy of the Lord is your strength. — Nehemiah 8:10

Note that this is the joy of the Lord, not your joy in him. This is his joy. It does not give you strength, it is your strength. Let this register in your spirit: God's joy is your strength.

Zephaniah 3:17 declares: "The Lord your God is with you, the Mighty Warrior who saves. He will take great delight in you; in his love he will no longer rebuke you, but will rejoice over you with singing."

Jeremiah 40:38–41 provides yet another window into God's heart for you as his child: "They will be my people, and I will be their God. I will give them singleness of heart and action, so that they will always fear me and that all will then go well for them and for their children after them. I will make an everlasting covenant with them: I will never stop doing good to them, and I will inspire them to fear me, so that they will never turn away from me. I will rejoice in doing them good and will assuredly plant them in this land with all my heart and soul."

Your strength — what keeps you going — is completely trustworthy, steadfast, and everlasting. God delights over you and he will never stop doing good to you. This is the steadfast goodness of God. He delights to do good for you and to you. He uses all things for good in your life (Romans 8:28). He is delighting in you and singing over you right now. He is loving you right now.

Meditate on these truths. It is his joy that is your strength. In Jesus, you are in a place of life to the full.

Father, thank you for your steadfast love for me that causes you to joyously sing over me and delight in me. Thank you that your great love for me causes you to work all things for good in my life. Lord, I pray that I will depend on your joy to be my strength.

> **In Context:**
> Nehemiah said, "Go and enjoy choice food and sweet drinks, and send some to those who have nothing prepared. This day is holy to our Lord. Do not grieve, for the joy of the Lord is your strength" (Nehemiah 8:10).

Jesus came so that you may live a new life. — Romans 6:4

Jesus taught many revolutionary things. For example, he declared that he was and is the way, the truth, and the life, and that no one comes to the Father, except through him (John 14:6–7). Further, Jesus said that if we know him, then we know the Father as well (John 8:19). And this is eternal life, that we may know the only true God, and Jesus Christ (John 17:3). The Apostle Paul proclaimed that just as Christ was raised from the dead through the glory of the Father, we too may live a new life (Romans 6:4). A new life in comparison to what?

Knowing God and living in relationship to him sets us on a course that is quite different than our past life course. As we have previously considered, God has rescued us from the dominion of darkness and brought us into the kingdom of the Son he loves (Colossians 1:13). We have become members of God's own household (Ephesians 2:12), his children through faith in Jesus (Galatians 3:26), with access to the Father (Ephesians 2:18). These attributes truly represent a new life. It is not simply an "upgrade" of our old life; it is a qualitatively new life. In Christ, we are new creations (2 Corinthians 5:17), not refurbished or retrofitted. New.

Living a new life in Christ and growing into the fullness of maturity in life entails awareness of our identity in Christ — who the scriptures declare us to be and living accordingly by his grace. Living as a new creation gives ever-increasing rise to life as a son or daughter of God. This is more than just knowing about him; this is experiencing him relationally through awareness of his presence through all our days. In Jesus, the Way, Father God accepts us, joyously welcomes us, sings over us, and pours his love into our hearts through the indwelling of his Spirit.

"The steadfast love of the Lord never ceases; his mercies never come to an end; they are new every morning; great is your faithfulness" (Lamentations 3:22–23, ESV). Meditate on ways that you have recently experienced the steadfast love of the Lord, and ways that his mercies have made it possible for you to live a new life. Consider a challenge that you are facing right now and invite him to shower his mercies on you so that you can experience and testify of his faithfulness.

Jesus, thank you for coming to live among us so that we could be given a new life, freed from our sin and shame and free to live in fullness of relationship to God because you provided the way. Thank you for the truth of your scriptures that declare your love for me, your purposes in coming to rescue me, the sacrifices that you made on my behalf, and the freedom and inheritance that all of this brings to me. I choose to believe in you, including your life, death, and resurrection, and all the freedom that you give to me. I choose to live a new life in you — life as a child of God. Transferred from the domain of darkness into the kingdom of the Son. Forgiven and cleansed, with the Holy Spirit indwelling me and leading me. Thank you, thank you, thank you!

In Context:
Or don't you know that all of us who were baptized into Christ Jesus were baptized into his death? We were therefore buried with him through baptism into death in order that, just as Christ was raised from the dead through the glory of the Father, we too may live a new life (Romans 6:3–4).

> **Jesus came so that you could have life to the full.**
> **— John 10:10**

In Jesus, we have a heavenly calling (Hebrews 3:1), rescued from the present evil age (Galatians 1:4), with God's power working in us (3:20). Being God's workmanship (Ephesians 2:10), receiving the full rights of a child of God (Galatians 4:4–5) and being blessed with every spiritual blessing in Christ (Ephesians 1:3) brings many aspects of life to the full. This is our reality for the here and now. Many Christians think that these verses refer to the afterlife, living in relationship with God after the coming return of Jesus. If we meditate on these scriptures with an open heart, we can see that while they certainly pertain to our relationship to God throughout eternity, there is nothing that explicitly states these attributes do not apply to us in this life. As presented in John 14:2–3, Jesus said that he was preparing a place for us so that we could be where he is. His words recorded in John 20:19–20 are,

"Because I live, you also will live. On that day you will realize that I am in my Father, and you are in me, and I am in you." He is alive right now, so at this time we are both filled by him and in him. Accepting his sacrifice for us personally allows us to enter that place that he prepared now. Living this life from the place that he prepared for us brings life to the full.

In John 8:31–32, Jesus speaks many things that help us glimpse what life to the full entails. "If you hold to my teaching, you are really my disciples. Then you will know the truth, and the truth will set you free." Holding to his teaching can refer not only to following his commands, but to embracing what he taught about the Father's love for us and the place he has prepared for us to enter. He continued, "whoever belongs to God hears what God says" (John 8:47), and in many passages in the gospels, Jesus declared that he only said what the Father was saying. Jesus was living fullness of life by listening to what the Spirit residing in him said. The same Holy Spirit dwells in our inmost being and teaches us all things and reminds us of what Jesus said (John 14:26). In his discourse with his followers, Jesus further elaborated, "But when he, the Spirit of truth, comes, he will guide you into all the truth. He will not speak on his own; he will speak only what he hears, and he will tell you what is yet to come. He will glorify me because it is from me that he will receive what he will make known to you. All that belongs to the Father is mine. That is why I said the Spirit will receive from me what he will make known to you" (John 16:13–15).

Life to the full is characterized by living in the fullness of relationship with God as we traverse all aspects of our life, walking in the counsel of the indwelling Holy Spirit while simultaneously remaining mindful of the things we are engaged in in daily life. God's continual presence is how Jesus walked through each day of his earthly life. Succinctly stated, life to the full entails mindfully straddling this life while fully embracing our spiritual inheritance, both now and to come.

Meditate on the words of Jesus that he shared with his followers regarding life to the full. Ask the Holy Spirit to bring to mind things you can do to more consistently experience the fullness of life that Jesus desires for you.

God, thank you that I am not stuck in the destructive patterns of life apart from you, a self-directed life that steals, kills, and destroys the fullness of life for which I was created. I pray that I would wholly trust in you to be my way to living a new life, a life of continual awareness of your presence. I pray that you would increase my sensitivity to the still, small voice of your Holy Spirit. Thank you for coming so that I can have life to the full.

> **In Context:**
> I am the gate; whoever enters through me will be saved. They will come in and go out, and find pasture. The thief comes only to steal and kill and destroy; I have come that they may have life, and have it to the full (John 10:9–10).

A Place of Life to the Full: Summary and Application

God has made known to you the path of life, he fills you with joy in his presence, with eternal pleasures at his right hand (Psalm 16:11). The joy of the Lord is your strength (Nehemiah 8:10). Jesus came so that you may live a new life (Romans 6:4) and have life to the full (John 10:10).

No matter where we are, because God is there with us and for us, each place is perfectly designed to build us up in relationship with him and to bring the manifestation of his presence into it. Because of his Spirit coming through us, atmospheres shift. His fragrance, character, seeds, and fruit fill the earth through his people. He is always willing to do things through us if we remain in him and submit our will to his.

Sometimes we experience difficult times and circumstances that do not show signs of yielding to what we believe God would desire. Even in those times and places, God is God, and he is still on his throne. When we face circumstances that persist despite our prayers and giving our best attempts to do what we believe God would have us do, it is important to not lose faith in him and his goodness. We are called to persevere, to remain in him through the severe conditions we face. Keep on sowing prayers and doing what we know to do in the Spirit. That perseverance and dependency on God sows seeds. In Mark 4:26–29, Jesus shares the following parable: "He said, 'This is what the kingdom of God is like. A man scatters seed on the ground. Night and day, whether he sleeps or gets up, the seed sprouts and grows, though he does not know how. All by itself the soil produces grain — first the stalk, then the head, then the full kernel in the head. As soon as the grain is ripe, he puts the sickle to it, because the harvest has come.'"

Even on hard ground where there are rocks and weeds, seeds still sprout and create small fissures that are more receptive of future seeds. Rocks get broken down by seasons of seeds that sprout and fail to mature to harvest. Eventually, one or more seeds live and grow to maturity. The surface is no longer impenetrable. Ask the Lord of the harvest to show you where and how and when to sow the seeds he has given you. Ask him to guide you to a fruitful place to sow.

Know that wherever you are, in Jesus, you are in a place of life to the full. Ask him to show you what he is doing in various places in your life right now as you meditate on the truths of these verses. Ask him to direct your path, your decisions, and your words and actions as you walk with him. Trust him to show you that in every aspect of your life, you are in a place of life to the full.

Trust him to lead you where to sow seeds as well as when and how to sow them. Acknowledge him as Lord of the harvest.

- God has made known to me the path of life.
- He fills me with joy in his presence, with eternal pleasures at his right hand.
- The joy of the Lord is my strength.
- Jesus came so that I may live a new life and have life to the full.
- In Jesus, I am in a place of life to the full.

Notes

CHAPTER 19

A Place of Transformation *And Increasing Maturity*

God is pleased to reveal his Son in you (Galatians 1:16). In Christ, you are a new creation, the old is gone and the new has come (2 Corinthians 5:17). You are created to be like God in true righteousness and holiness (Ephesians 4:24). In all things, you are growing up into him who is the head, Christ (Ephesians 4:15).

> **God is pleased to reveal his Son in you.** — Galatians 1:16

This verse comes in the context of the Apostle Paul describing his encounter with Jesus and his call to preach the gospel to the Gentiles. God does not show partiality (Romans 2:11). The Amplified version of this verse reads, "For God shows no partiality [no arbitrary favoritism; with Him one person is not more important than another]." Though I would never compare my life with that of Paul, the scriptures clearly indicate that God reveals himself through the life and character of his children. It gives God pleasure to reveal his Son in you. Part of his delighting in you (Zephaniah 3:17) is that he is revealing his Son in you.

Romans 8:29 says, "For those he foreknew, he also predestined to become conformed to the image of his Son, that he might be the firstborn among many brothers and sisters." Not only does God reveal his son to you, but in you and through you. The indwelling Christ (Galatians 2:20, Ephesians 3:17), who lives in your heart by faith, does not remain hidden there. His life and love for the Father and the love of God himself conforms you to the image of his Son. You are influenced by and become like those you spend considerable time with. Living in unity with the Spirit of God and deciding to align your life with the principles of his scriptures brings transformation. God's indwelling Spirit changes you and reveals Christ-like character in you. The fruit of his Spirit (Galatians 5:22) appears in your life in increasing measure. The fruit of his Spirit reflects the character of God himself. As you increase in the fruit of his Spirit, you reflect more of God's character.

It pleases God to reveal his Son in you, just as Jesus reveals the Father to you. In John 17:26, as he concludes his prayer to his Father soon before his crucifixion, Jesus says, "I have made you known to them, and will continue to make you known in order that the love you have for me may be in them and that I myself may be in them."

Clearly, the Father loves Jesus. He loves you with the same love as he has for Jesus (John 17:23), and Jesus reveals the Father to you, in you, and through you. It delights your heavenly Father to reveal his Son in you. It's a wonderful thing when others begin to see Jesus' character in you. It is not your goodness. Apart from him, you can do nothing (John 15:5). You have no righteousness on your own. In Jesus, you are in a place of transformation and increasing maturity.

Reflect on ways that you sense God revealing his character through you. What can you do to appropriately acknowledge the things he is doing in and through you while practicing humility?

Father, thank you for indwelling me and for changing me to be more like you. I pray that you will continue to increase in me and that my ungodly ways will continue to decrease. I invite you to transform me more fully from my inmost being and in every detail of my life. I trust in you and your incomparable power to overcome my weaknesses and to flow through me into my relationships and circumstances. Father, as your Son has revealed you to me, I invite you to reveal more of your Son through me.

> **In Context:**
> But when God, who set me apart from my mother's womb and called me by his grace, was pleased to reveal his Son in me so that I might preach him among the Gentiles, my immediate response was not to consult any human being (Galatians 1:15–16).

In Christ, you are a new creation, the old is gone and the new has come. — 2 Corinthians 5:17

As one who has accepted Christ as your savior, you are forgiven for all your sins — past, present, and future. That makes you righteous. There is no longer any condemnation or legal judgment against you. You are reconciled, holy, blameless, and free from accusation (Colossians 1:22). You are washed, sanctified, and justified (1 Corinthians 6:11; Galatians 3:8, 3:24). You are God's child (Galatians 3:26) with Christ dwelling in your heart (Ephesians 3:17) and his Spirit in you (1 Corinthians 6:19) making you one with God in Spirit (1 Corinthians 6:17). Through Christ Jesus, the law of the Spirit who gives life has set you free from the law of sin and death (Romans 8:2).

There is no doubt that you are a new creation. It is like being a new species because in Christ, you are dead to the basic principles of the world (Colossians 2:20). Christ has brought you into his family and household, transforming you from your old sinful nature to a new reality. All of this makes you into a human that contains God within you. If that is not a new creature, nothing is! You are a new creation because your sinful nature was put to death. In its place, you have the Spirit of God dwelling in you. Your nature is transformed. You are a temple of the Holy Spirit, a dwelling of living stones (1 Peter 2:5). You are an eternal being now — not one who will die and perish in the grave. You are one who will rise and dwell with God forever. Your destiny has always been to be in relationship with God and to dwell in his presence forever. You were a on a different path, but now you are on the path of life — joy in his presence and eternal pleasures at his right hand (Psalm 16:11). In Christ, you are a new creation. In Jesus, you are in a place of transformation and increasing maturity.

Reflect on the new things that you sense God doing in your life and consider ways to yield to his leading. Consider whether there are things that you can do to lean into the transformation that he is bringing to you.

God, thank you for making me anew. Thank you for freeing me from my old patterns, habits, and traits. Thank you for changing everything about the path I was on. Thank you for restoring me to the destiny you have planned for me. I pray that I will continue to grow in relationship with you and to depend on you to lead me through each day, to walk with me and to have your Spirit flow through me. Thank you that in Christ, the reality of my new life is so transformative that I am truly a new creation. I pray for grace to stay in awareness of that through this day and to walk in the fullness of life that you intend for me.

In Context:
So from now on we regard no one from a worldly point of view. Though we once regarded Christ in this way, we do so no longer. Therefore, if anyone is in Christ, the new creation has come: The old has gone, the new is here! All this is from God, who reconciled us to himself through Christ and gave us the ministry of reconciliation (2 Corinthians 5:16–18).

You are created to be like God in true righteousness and holiness. — Ephesians 4:24

Righteousness entails right standing. Holiness means set apart. Truth comes from the truth, Jesus. In Christ, you can experience true righteousness and holiness. This was God's intention for you from before the beginning of creation.

True righteousness does not come from me or my efforts or my behavior. It is imparted to me on my behalf in Christ. His righteousness is attributed to me. I was set apart to receive it before the beginning of time. Receiving what he has finished on my behalf fulfills my destiny — making me righteous and holy — as God intended. It restores me to relationship. That is true righteousness and holiness.

Trying to create my own righteousness through doing good is orphan-hearted thinking, futile striving, and idolatry. It leads to weakness and continuous failure. The accuser of the brethren often reminds me of my own failures. That has nothing to do with me being truly righteous and holy. Christ, the unblemished lamb of God, serves as my one and only atoning sacrifice that justifies me and strikes down every accusation of my guilt.

His righteousness and holiness. It is finished. His victory is ours — victory over sin and death. Being on "team Jesus" makes us victorious overcomers because his team has won! Because we have been accepted by him, our champion's victory and rewards are ours too. Christ in us is our hope of glory. His intimacy with his Abba tore the veil in two from top to bottom so that we can boldly enter the presence of God. We are created to be like God in true righteousness and holiness. In Jesus, you are in a place of transformation and increasing maturity. Meditate on the mileposts in your life that God has brought you beyond and trust him to continue to draw you into closer relationship with him. Thank him for the good that he continually does in your life. Be specific in your gratitude.

Father, thank you for your love for me and for sending Jesus to earth to be my way into relationship with you as your child, bringing me into true righteousness and holiness. I choose to put off my old self and my own striving to be good. I choose to depend on Jesus and accept the gift of his sacrifice on my behalf. Thank you that in Christ, I am holy, spotless, and blameless. Thank you that you are transforming me to grow up into your character and to share your love and the hope of life in and with you.

In Context:
That, however, is not the way of life you learned when you heard about Christ and were taught in him in accordance with the truth that is in Jesus. You were taught, with regard to your former way of life, to put off your old self, which is being corrupted by its deceitful desires; to be made new in the attitude of your minds; and to put on the new self, created to be like God in true righteousness and holiness (Ephesians 4:20–24).

In all things, you are growing up into him who is the head, Christ. — Ephesians 4:15

Growing up takes time. Development takes time. But there are things we can do to facilitate positive outcomes in development, including making good decisions and following through. Isaiah 32:8 says, "But the noble makes noble plans and by noble deeds they stand." Our acceptance of Christ brings immediate changes in many things. We are born again as a child of God and become a member of his family. We become citizens of heaven and have access to the Father and the indwelling of his Spirit. Newborn human infants are alive months in the womb before birth, but after they are born, they still have much growing to do — biologically, psychologically, socially, and spiritually.

All of lifespan development is about growing up into who we have the potential to become. Each of our experiences, decisions, and investments in education, nutrition, exercise, and relationships change our developmental trajectories. There are things we can do to maximize or facilitate our development. Perhaps the most significant things we can do as Christians parallel some basic human development principles in key areas of growing up.

Becoming an adult entails developing a healthy and realistic identity, a sense of who we are (and who we are not). Mature identity entails a close match between how we see ourselves and how we are seen by those who know us. God, who knows us better than we know ourselves, has great love for us and greatly desires us to relate to him. As we come to know and meditate on what the scriptures state about us (as reflected in these one hundred statements about who we are in Christ), it transforms our understanding of who we were created to be, who we are, who we are to God, and who we are becoming. Our sense of who we are can mature toward seeing ourselves as God sees us. The meditations in this book centrally address our identity in Christ, but also our identity in the Father and in the Spirit. Knowing who we really are requires experientially knowing who the scriptures declare us to be in relation to our trinitarian God.

Another hallmark of mature adulthood is intimacy — a true, emotionally open, caring relationship with a well-functioning other. This means sharing our true self — what we feel, think, long for, like, dislike, care about, and so forth. God, who does nothing out of selfish ambition or his own need, invites us into full, open, intimate relationship with him.

Development of trust is another critical component of human development that results from emotional attachment and regular, ongoing relationship with a trustworthy other who consistently provides well-timed reciprocal relationship with our well-being in mind. Ideally, it begins between an infant and his or her caregivers and continues through life in other meaningful, close relationships. Positive social relationships are characterized by consistency, honesty, and rooted and grounded in love and benevolent, reciprocal care. As we spend time with loving, wise, caring, patient others, it brings a solid foundation for positive adjustment in every domain of life, yielding good outcomes in identity, intimacy, and the ability to trust and care for others. Things really are not much different in our Christian development. The obvious distinction is that God is flawlessly consistent and loving toward us. No parent or partner could ever compare.

Development takes time. It is enhanced by receiving love and direction from God through sensitivity to his indwelling Holy Spirit. Praying, trusting, worshipping, reading his word, keeping our hearts open and tender toward God, and focusing on things above are all a part of our spiritual development. Renewing our mind (including the way we think about ourselves) by living in a manner consistent with these scriptural truths also matures us.

Reflect on the ways that God is maturing you right now. Consider whether there are ways that you know of to give yourself more fully to his processes.

God, thank you that you are maturing me in my faith in you and the life that faith brings. I pray that I will continue to grow in my experiential knowledge of who you are and your continual goodness in my life. I pray that I will mature in my identity in you as your child and that I will be securely grounded in your love for me. I pray for increasing sensitivity to your Spirit and closer obedience to your word and your promptings. I choose to place my trust in you, not only to save me and to transform me, but to complete the good work that you have begun in me. I trust you that in your time and way you will mature me.

In Context:
Then we will no longer be infants, tossed back and forth
by the waves, and blown here and there by every wind
of teaching and by the cunning and craftiness of people
in their deceitful scheming. Instead, speaking the truth
in love, we will grow to become in every respect the
mature body of him who is the head, that is, Christ.
From him the whole body, joined and held together
by every supporting ligament, grows and builds itself
up in love, as each part does its work (Ephesians 4:14–16).

A Place of Transformation and Increasing Maturity: Summary and Application

God is pleased to reveal his Son in you (Galatians 1:16). In Christ, you are a new creation, the old is gone and the new has come (2 Corinthians 5:17). You are created to be like God in true righteousness and holiness (Ephesians 4:24). In all things, you are growing up into him who is the head, Christ (Ephesians 4:15).

Scripture is full of accounts of everyday people who do extraordinary things as they encounter the presence of God, walk with him, and allow him to move or manifest through them. Jesus, of course, has the highest percentage of doing it well — 100 percent. While on earth as a person, he was fully human, walking through life and living from the place his Father prepared for him. His disciples less fully manifested God's presence and transforming power. A major difference was that at Jesus' baptism, the Holy Spirit descended in the form of a dove and remained on him. Until his resurrection, the Holy Spirit was not given to people to permanently reside in them. Once Jesus' followers had received the indwelling presence of God himself, they began to extend the kingdom of God with much greater consistency and effectiveness.

As followers of Jesus, we have the indwelling Spirit of God in us. Because he lives, we realize that Jesus is in the Father, and we are in him, and he is in us (John 14:20). We inhabit the place prepared for us. Living from that place changes everything.

The place prepared for us is dynamic yet also familiar because it is grounded in God's character and presence. It is experienced as a function of the quality of our relationship with God, like attachment is. As we receive more of his substance, we get healed and set free from old wounds, whether they are the result of unjust treatment or self-inflicted through sinful or poor choices. He pours the balm of his presence and character into us. He anoints us. His presence and character saturate us and overflows.

God himself created us with our unique characteristics. He gave us our lives, placing us in this time in history, and remains with us everywhere we go. He is fully invested in seeing us through to maturity in relationship with him.

> **God is continually at work in our lives to use all things for good. In Jesus, we are in a place of transformation and increasing maturity.**

- God is pleased to reveal his Son in me.
- In Christ, I am a new creation, the old is gone and the new has come.
- I am created to be like God in true righteousness and holiness.
- In all things, I am growing up into him who is the head, Christ.
- In Jesus, I am in a place of transformation and increasing maturity.

Notes

CHAPTER 20

A Place of *Divine Destiny*

You are destined for glory. When Christ, who is your life, appears you will appear with him in glory (Colossians 3:4). Christ in you is the hope of glory (Colossians 1:27). God gives you the victory through your Lord Jesus Christ (1 Corinthians 15:57). In all these things, you are more than a conqueror through him who loved you (Romans 8:37).

> **You are destined for glory. When Christ, who is your life, appears you will appear with him in glory.** — Colossians 3:4

In everyday life, creations — whether they are works of art, gourmet food, woodworking projects, or excellent performances in music, theater, dance, athletics — bring praise and glory to their creators. The glory of the one who created, planned, or accomplished it is displayed by what you have experienced or appreciated.

You are God's workmanship (Ephesians 2:10). Apart from him you can do nothing (John 15:5). But you can do all things through him who gives you strength (Ephesians 4:13). In him, you are a new creation (2 Corinthians 5:17) and a part of his body (1 Corinthians 12:27).

I cannot begin to imagine the magnitude of the glory of God that will be manifested when he brings all things together under Christ, in whom all things hold together (Colossians 1:17). In eternity, you will have time to see how the good works he prepared in advance for you to do are a part of his plan (Ephesians 2:10) and the advancement of his glorious kingdom. You will have a fuller recognition of how he miraculously worked all things together for your good in your life and in the lives of your loved ones and friends (Romans 8:28).

If all that Jesus did was recorded, the books would fill the entire world (John 21:25). There is more than enough material to fill a full-length book (or series of books) about what Jesus did in your life and about what he did in the life of every individual ever created (Psalm 139:16). There could be books about how Jesus worked our lives together, and that's true for all relationships across eternity across all generations. There could be books about how the prayers of great grandparents manifested in the lives of their offspring and their spouses and their offspring. Books could be written on his answers to prayer for bringing rain and making crops grow and providing for us and protecting us and transforming us and maturing us. We are largely oblivious to much of this now. But someday we will more fully see the tapestry of his goodness, love, perfection, and masterful workmanship in our lives.

I will see how you reflect his glory, and you will see how I reflect his glory, and we will all see how he built us together as living stones into a spiritual house (1 Peter 2:5) to be a part of his body (1 Corinthians 12:27), his bride for eternity.

You are destined for glory because he is glorious, and his glory includes you and you are part of his glorious story. The musician, Michael W. Smith wrote, "If the word of God is any indication, I am doing even better than I know." How profoundly true. In Jesus, you are in a place of divine destiny.

Meditate on the glorious nature of God and the way he works in all of creation. Consider the glorious things he has done in your life and the hope he has given you for the future.

God, thank you for the beauty of your creation, your plans for all of creation, and for your work in my life. Your work is truly glorious. Thank you for making me a part of your glorious work. I pray that I would be quick to give you glory for all that is good in my life and in the world around me. I pray that I would trust you to continue to work all things together for good in my life and that I would be a clear reflection of your glory.

> **In Context:**
> When Christ, who is your life, appears, then you also will appear with him in glory (Colossians 3:4).

Christ in you is the hope of glory. — Colossians 1:27

Christ in you is your hope of glory. Salvation, forgiveness, cleansing, entering the presence of God himself, the indwelling of his Spirit, the giftings that his Spirit brings, resurrection, and eternal life all begin with and depend on Christ in you. In him you live and move and have your being (Acts 17:28).

When you walk with Christ, you fulfill his plan for your life. When you follow his Spirit's indwelling leadings and do the things prepared in advance for you to do, then that brings him glory (Colossians 3:4). Christ in you truly is the hope of glory. Apart from God's will, purposes, and plans being achieved, there is no true glory.

Webster's Dictionary defines glory as "praise, honor, or distinction extended by common consent: renown. Worshipful praise, honor, and thanksgiving. Giving glory to God. Great beauty and splendor." It defines hope as "to cherish or desire with anticipation: to want something to happen or to be true. Trust. To expect with confidence. A desire accompanied by expectation of or belief in fulfillment. Someone or something on which our hopes are centered. An only hope for victory."

It is that sense in which Christ in you is the hope of glory. Without his presence there is no hope. He is the hope. The only hope. No one can come to the Father except through him (John 14:6). He is the way (John 14:6). The hope of glory. In him, through him, by him, it is finished. He is our only hope. Apart from him, there is no hope at all, but in Jesus, you are in a place of divine destiny.

Meditate on the place that God has prepared for you and the ways that you have experienced his glorious presence in your life. Thank him for the ways he has shown himself to be faithful in your life.

Jesus, thank you that you are my only hope and that your presence in my life brings glory to our Father, to you, and to your Holy Spirit. Thank you that I can trust and expect with confidence that you have finished everything needed to accomplish this. I pray that I will joyously anticipate the fulfillment of your desires in every aspect of my life. I pray that I will trust that your life in and through me will bring you glory. Help me not to strive to do what only you can do. Jesus, I pray for greater ability to trust in your all-sufficiency and to rest from my own striving. Thank you for being my hope.

In Context:
To them God has chosen to make known among the Gentiles the glorious riches of this mystery, which is Christ in you, the hope of glory (Colossians 1:27).

> **God gives you the victory through our Lord Jesus Christ.**
> **— 1 Corinthians 15:57**

This verse comes in the context of the Apostle Paul telling us about our eternal resurrection bodies. In 1 Corinthians 15:53 he states, "For the perishable must clothe itself with the imperishable, and the mortal with immortality." You are clothed with Christ (Galatians 3:27). You are included in Christ (Ephesians 1:13). His resurrection victory is credited to you through your faith in him and our dependence on him. Because you have clothed yourself in Christ, when God looks at you and your life, he sees Jesus and his sinless, victorious life in place of yours. In Christ, there is no condemnation because through Christ Jesus, the law of the Spirit of Life set us free from the law of sin and death (Romans 8:1–2).

It is God, the referee, the judge, the ultimate authority, and ruler — the one who planned and created our existence and who has given and sustained our life all along. He is the one who gives us the victory. It is finished. In Christ, our victory is secure, our inheritance and our eternity established and settled, freely given, not earned. In Jesus, we are in a place of divine destiny.

When we consider our position from a scriptural perspective, it stands in stark contrast to the things we often feel and focus on in this world. The place that Jesus has prepared for us is experienced by faith. Experiencing the bounty of his love and grace gives us perspective that transforms our perception of challenges and circumstances we face in our lives.

Meditate on the victory that God has graciously given to you. Consider aspects of your perspective that require adjustment given the certainty of your place in Jesus.

God, thank you that you have given me victory. Thank you that the outcomes of my life are determined by being included in Jesus. Thank you for giving me victory over sin, over death, and over the challenges of life. I choose to receive your unfathomable love, generosity, and grace. I choose to apply the victory of Jesus to my failures and to remain in him. I choose to live all the days of my life in step with him.

In Context:
I declare to you, brothers and sisters, that flesh and blood cannot inherit the kingdom of God, nor does the perishable inherit the imperishable. Listen, I tell you a mystery: We will not all sleep, but we will all be changed — in a flash, in the twinkling of an eye, at the last trumpet. For the trumpet will sound, the dead will be raised imperishable, and we will be changed. For the perishable must clothe itself with the imperishable, and the mortal with immortality. When the perishable has been clothed with the imperishable, and the mortal with immortality, then the saying that is written will come true: "Death has been swallowed up in victory." "Where, O death, is your victory? Where, O death, is your sting?"

The sting of death is sin, and the power of sin is the law. But thanks be to God! He gives us the victory through our Lord Jesus Christ. Therefore, my dear brothers and sisters, stand firm. Let nothing move you. Always give yourselves fully to the work of the Lord because you know that your labor in the Lord is not in vain (1 Corinthians 15:50–58).

> **In all these things, you are more than a conqueror through him who loved you. — Romans 8:37**

Keep in mind everything the scriptures declare concerning who we are in Jesus. A child of God. A member of his body. A citizen of heaven. A temple of his Spirit. A likeness of Jesus. A sibling to all other children of God. Justified. Glorified. This is all from him, through him, in him. Jesus is the Way. Our victory comes through him, not through our effort. It is God's provision, protection, grace, and love that gives us victory. This is a gift, not earned.

If we focus on our shortcomings or listen to the voice of the accuser instead of believing what God's word says, we will find it difficult to believe that we are more than a conqueror. But through Christ, we are. That is the truth of God's word. In Christ all things hold together (Colossians 1:17). By God's grace and in his love, the victory and perfection of Jesus' life is applied to us and our account.

Of course, doubts and fears do come to our minds. Jesus knew that they would. In Luke 24:38, Jesus asked his disciples a question that we should all hear him asking us: "Why are you troubled, and why do doubts rise in your minds?" When we are troubled in our circumstances, it is often the result of doubts that first appear in our minds. They come as fleeting thoughts, but then we dwell on them and magnify them. We ponder troubles and worst-case scenarios. Circumstances change constantly, and feelings are fleeting. That is why it is essential to believe what God's eternal word says and to take all of our thoughts captive and make them obedient to him (2 Corinthians 10:5), which transforms us by renewing our minds (Romans 12:2). By focusing on what God's word declares as true, we can quell many of our doubts. We can choose to focus on "whatever is true, whatever is noble, whatever is right, whatever is pure, whatever is lovely, whatever is admirable — if anything is excellent or praiseworthy" and think about such things (Philippians 4:8).

I am certain that there is much more potential for me to experientially apply the victory of Christ to my life and its circumstances. In the same way that I can choose to accept and receive Jesus' atoning sacrifice for my sins, I can accept and receive his victory in many aspects of life. My salvation is dependent on hearing and believing and confessing with my mouth. I believe that the same is true of my victorious overcomer status. I need to hear about my traits as an overcomer, believe God's word about them in my life, and receive them into my daily walk by applying them spiritually to my life and circumstances. No, I cannot create or manufacture them. Jesus was and is all-sufficient in all that he did on my behalf. But, as I depend on his provision on my behalf, as I receive it and feed my spirit, mind, and soul on it, it transforms me and gives me victory beyond my natural ability. In my weakness, he is my strength. His grace, which he apportions to me, having lived on earth as a human and experiencing every hardship I am facing (and more) is sufficient for me. Through him, I can do all things. I can abide in him through my days and that makes me more than a conqueror. Because of my faith, I am a victorious overcomer of the world. So, in him and through him, I am a chosen, set apart, called, blameless, holy, dearly loved child of God.

In Jesus, you are in a place of divine destiny. Quietly reflect on areas of your life where doubts tend to rise and then magnify in your mind. Invite God to show you how to take the doubtful thoughts captive in him, and to bring you appropriate peace and trust in him. Ask him to clearly show you your part and where to rest in him.

Jesus, thank you for giving me all that I need to be victorious in all that I face this day. I choose to depend on you, your presence, your leading, your protection, your provision, and your love to bring me through all my circumstances in the victorious overcomer status that is yours. I pray that I will trust you to be with me and to go ahead of me in all that I experience today. Help me to trust you to use all things in my life for good. I pray for discernment to know where I need to act and where I need to depend on you to work on my behalf. I choose to depend on and rest in you today.

In Context:
No, in all these things we are more than conquerors through him who loved us. For I am convinced that neither death nor life, neither angels nor demons, neither the present nor the future, nor any powers, neither height nor depth, nor anything else in all creation, will be able to separate us from the love of God that is in Christ Jesus our Lord (Romans 8:37–38).

A Place of Divine Destiny:

Summary and Application

You are destined for glory. When Christ, who is your life, appears, you will appear with him in glory (Colossians 3:4). Christ in you is the hope of glory (Colossians 1:27). God gives you the victory through your Lord Jesus Christ (1 Corinthians 15:57). In all these things, you are more than a conqueror through him who loved you (Romans 8:37).

The Word of God is active and alive. It is a lamp to your feet. It leads you through the darkness to see obstacles and the path through them. No promise of his word has ever failed. As you feed on his word, including what it says about you and who you are in Jesus, you continue to mature in relationship with God. You begin to manifest more of his Spirit and his character. This is all a part of your divine destiny. You are becoming transformed to conform to his image more fully and to experience the fullness of life that he desires for you. In Jesus, you are in a place of divine destiny.

Encountering God, living the adventure, seeing lives transformed, and experiencing community are all outcomes of entering, remaining in, and exploring the place that Jesus has prepared for you. With God in you, you are a new creation. Because the King indwells you, you have the potential to bring his kingdom into the atmosphere wherever you go. That is how Jesus walked among us during his time on earth as a man. That is how he allows us to walk as well. In Jesus, you are in a place of divine destiny.

Ask the Holy Spirit to quicken to you the ways that he wants to bring these truths into manifestation through you:

- I am destined for glory.
- When Christ, who is my life, appears, I will appear with him in glory.
- Christ in me is the hope of glory.
- God gives me the victory through my Lord Jesus Christ.
- In all these things, I am more than a conqueror through him who loved me.
- In Jesus, I am in a place of divine destiny.

Notes

Notes

CHAPTER 21

A Place of Absolute Security

Nothing in all creation will be able to separate you from the love of God that is in Christ Jesus, our Lord (Romans 8:38–39). God is for you, who can be against you? (Romans 8:31). He provides you with plenty and fills your heart with joy (Acts 14:17). God richly provides you with everything for your enjoyment (1 Timothy 6:17). Apart from God, you have no good thing (Psalm 16:2). God has assigned you your portion and your cup (Psalm 16:5). He has made your lot secure (Psalm 16:5). The boundary lines have fallen for you in pleasant places (Psalm 16:6).

> **Nothing in all creation will be able to separate us from the love of God that is in Christ Jesus, our Lord. — Romans 8:38-39**

Love wins. Jesus wins. God is love.

Though in this fallen world we face many challenges and we fail in many ways, God's love for us personally is indelibly and historically recorded and validated in the life, death, and resurrection of Jesus of Nazareth. Nothing is stronger or more perfect than God's love for us. Nothing. No thing in all of creation. Let's not forget that God, love itself, created all things and has dominion over them. His kingdom and his rule are not temporary, limited, endangered, or frail. No. He is the all-powerful creator and eternal ruler of the universe.

The one who is love sent his Son for us. From the beginning of creation, God's love was the reason for the universe. God's love is the reason for our lives in his creation and at this time in history. His love is flowing toward us and into us right now. We can receive it and experience it right now and in any moment for all of eternity because in this constantly changing and shifting world, God and his love are the sole constant. He does not change yesterday, today, or tomorrow (James 1:17). He has always been love and will always be loving. As we grow in experiencing his love, we come to trust this more and more.

There are many perplexing things in the world and in our lives every day. But if we can stop questioning God's love for us and his full commitment to pouring it out for us, sending it to us, and ministering it into us by his Spirit, it changes our experience of everything. Jesus experienced every concern people have and faced every challenge of life. He was a man of sorrows. This is the God of all comfort and love who can transform our experience of life's difficulties and challenges.

We are carved on the palm of his hand — the hand that formed us now has the scar from wounds that restored us. His side has the scar from being pierced as his heart literally flowed out, in love, for us. Jesus invited Thomas to thrust his hand into his side — to experience his heart. The reality of his outpouring. When suffering comes our way, we can remember how Jesus suffered and know that he is present with us in our grief.

His love for us is our beginning. His love for us has been the constant of our lives through all time and circumstances. Nothing can or does change that, and nothing ever will. Love wins. And nothing can separate us from his love. In Jesus, we are in place of absolute security.

Reflect on things that have recently caused concern in your life circumstances. How does focusing on the inseparability of God's love bring greater peace to you?

God, love, thank you for who you are. Thank you for your boundless love for me. Thank you for all you have done to bring me into your love. Thank you for the awareness of your great love for me growing in my heart, mind, and spirit. Thank you that nothing can ever separate me from your love in Jesus. I pray that today I would know more of your love, receive more of your love into my experience, and that all that I do and say would reflect your love to those around me.

In Context:
No, in all these things we are more than conquerors through him who loved us. For I am convinced that neither death nor life, neither angels nor demons, neither the present nor the future, nor any powers, neither height nor depth, nor anything else in all creation, will be able to separate us from the love of God that is in Christ Jesus our Lord (Romans 8:37–38).

God is for you, who can be against you? — Romans 8:31

This is stated as a rhetorical question. It comes in the context of Romans 8:28–30 which describes God working all things for our good. The question is sandwiched between that truth and another observation linked to a second rhetorical question: "He who did not spare his own Son, but gave him up for us all — how will he not also, along with him, graciously give us all things?" (Romans 8:32). By now, we have meditated on a sampling of biblical statements that make it abundantly clear that God is for us.

Even seeing as in a mirror, dimly (1 Corinthians 13:12) — seeing a mere fraction of the strength, breadth, depth, height, and width of his love — I am filled with great encouragement, faith, and hope. If I have any faith whatsoever regarding the supremacy of God, then I know the security of his being for me. I know that ultimately nothing else matters because his love toward me and his goodness toward me will prevail. Nothing can separate me from his love (Romans 8:38–39). Ultimately, it does not matter who is or who has been against me. The plans, intentions, words, and actions against me will be overcome by the most high God and his love and advocacy on my behalf.

In the story in John, the disciples, who were professional fishermen, strained against the oars of their boat in a storm and got only a few miles for their relentless effort. Jesus walked out to them and as soon as he entered their boat, they immediately reached the shore where they were heading (John 6:21). I have decided to quit straining against the oars. Jesus is in my boat because I invited him. The storms of my fears must succumb to his will and his plans and love for me.

No person, no storm, of life and no spirit can prevail against me when Jesus is in my boat. No accusation, even when warranted (John 8:1–11), or condemnation (Romans 8:1) can win. Nothing in all of creation can stand against the creator, who is for me. It is much more than Jesus being for me or in my boat. I am in him, and he is in the Father, and he is in me (John 14:20). There is no greater place of security. This is part of the place that Jesus has prepared for me (and you).

Meditate on the truth that God is for you and not against you. How does this truth change the way that you are feeling about today's challenges? Are there "oars" that you have been straining against that you can invite Jesus to take so that you can arrive at the intended destination?

Father, Son, and Spirit, thank you for being for me. Thank you that you have always been for me and will always be for me. Thank you that there is nothing that can separate me from your love and nothing can prevail against your desire to bring me into fullness of relationship with you. God, as I go through this day, I pray that I will stay aware of your presence in my life and that I will trust in you being for me, not against me. I pray that I would trust you to overcome the obstacles that stand against me in following you and achieving your best. I pray that I will remain attuned to your Spirit pouring your love into my inmost being, and giving me comfort, strength, wisdom, and direction. I pray that today I will choose to do all things through you.

In Context:
What, then, shall we say in response to these things? If God is for us, who can be against us? He who did not spare his own Son, but gave him up for us all — how will he not also, along with him, graciously give us all things? (Romans 8:31–32).

> **He provides you with plenty and fills your heart with joy.**
> — Acts 14:17

God's generous provision supplies all your needs. Every good and perfect gift is from above, coming down from the Father of the heavenly lights, who does not change like shifting shadows (James 1:17).

Experientially knowing this, Jesus told his followers, "Therefore I tell you, do not worry about your life, what you will eat or drink; or about your body, what you will wear. Is not life more than food, and the body more than clothes? Look at the birds of the air; they do not sow or reap or store away in barns, and yet your heavenly Father feeds them. Are you not much more valuable than they? Can any one of you by worrying add a single hour to your life?" (Matthew 6:25–27).

The joy in your heart is not from the plenty that you have but in his care for you and the pouring of his love into your heart by the power of his Holy Spirit (Romans 5:5). Yes, your joy includes his provision of plenty in the material realm, but it is grounded in so much more.

By including you in Jesus, the Father has given you every spiritual blessing in Christ (Ephesians 1:3). Joy comes through experientially knowing that he has made you holy and blameless in Jesus, that you are included among his children and sealed with his Holy Spirit. Trusting that he provides all that is needed for life and godliness allows you to joyously rest in him. In Jesus, you are in a place of absolute security.

Reflect on the many ways that God provides good and perfect gifts in your life. Consider listing five specific ways that you have experienced his plenty in the recent past. Thank God for the things he has brought to mind and ask him to help you to mindfully practice gratitude on a regular basis.

Thank you, Father, for your care and provision. Thank you that you abundantly give me everything I need for life, life to the full. I pray that I will continuously see your hand in my life and its circumstances and give you glory and thanks for all that you so generously give to me. I pray that I will be filled with joy as I come to know you more fully and trust you more deeply. I pray that my joy would be rooted in you and not in the things that you give to me. Thank you for your good and perfect gifts in my life.

In Context:
We too are only human, like you. We are bringing you good news, telling you to turn from these worthless things to the living God, who made the heavens and the earth and the sea and everything in them. In the past, he let all nations go their own way. Yet he has not left himself without testimony: He has shown kindness by giving you rain from heaven and crops

in their seasons; he provides you with plenty of food and fills your hearts with joy (Acts 14:15b–17).

> **God richly provides you with everything for your enjoyment.** — 1 Timothy 6:17

Some trust in chariots and some in horses, but we trust in the name of the Lord our God (Psalm 20:7).

We should not trust in what we have, but in our Heavenly Father, who provides us richly with everything — life, food, air to breathe, health, family, friends, the body of Christ, daily provisions.

He does this out of his great love for us; he does this for our enjoyment. How easy is it to be fooled into taking credit or pride in "our" achievements that result in material goods or retirement plans and investments. It is not our skill, ability, investment advisors, hard work, good fortune, luck, or even inheritance from ancestors that provides for us. It is God, our Heavenly Father, who richly provides us with everything, including those jobs, skills, opportunities, advisors, and benefactors. Yes, all of it takes our management, but without his provision of our daily bread, and of all things, there would be nothing to manage. What he has provided is more than sufficient.

There is enough to enjoy. Can we shift our thinking and enjoy sharing so that the plenty that he provides is distributed to those who have not enjoyed the same opportunities because of evil systems of people — because of race, class, gender, and age discrimination? We can choose to monitor our heart attitudes to prevent greed or pride from preventing us from being generous. We can also choose to be grateful to God for giving us things to enjoy instead of thinking about the next bigger or better thing that we "need." Godliness with contentment is great gain (1 Timothy 6:6). It is the key to knowing that we always have enough.

Doing good includes being rich in good deeds. This is sharing our time and abilities with kindness and joy. "Love is patient, love is kind. It does not envy, it does not boast, it is not proud. It does not dishonor others, it is not self-seeking, it is not easily angered, it keeps no record of wrongs. Love does not delight in evil but rejoices with the truth. It always protects, always trusts, always hopes, always perseveres. Love never fails" (1 Corinthians 13:4–8).

Meditate on these attributes of love listed in 1 Corinthians 13, what it is and what it is not. Instead of praying for more generosity or more godly attitudes, focus instead on praying to receive and experience more of the love that God is already pouring into our hearts. It changes everything. When we experience his love, we are transformed to be more like him, making us more capable of enjoying everything he richly provides to share with his other children.

This is experiencing life to the full. This is living from the place Jesus prepared for us, a place of absolute security.

God, thank you that your heart is to provide me with everything and to provide it for my enjoyment. Thank you that every good and perfect gift comes from you. I pray that today you will make me more aware of the love that you are pouring into my inmost being. I pray that awareness will transform me and give me gratitude and contentment with all that you have provided to me. I pray that I would not live from a place of greed or striving or obligation but that your love would be the foundation for choices I make in generously sharing the provisions you have given to me. I pray that this would be true for material possessions and spiritual and relational possessions as well.

> **In Context:**
> Command those who are rich in this present world not to be arrogant nor to put their hope in wealth, which is so uncertain, but to put their hope in God, who richly provides us with everything for our enjoyment. Command them to do good, to be rich in good deeds, and to be generous and willing to share. In this way they will lay up treasure for themselves as a firm foundation for the coming age, so that they may take hold of the life that is truly life
> (1 Timothy 6:17–19).

Apart from God, you have no good thing — Psalm 16:2

Because every good and perfect gift comes from him (James 1:17) and because he provides all things for your enjoyment (1 Timothy 6:17), apart from him, you have no good thing.

Outside of what he provides, there is no joy. Outside of what he graciously provides is the place of your scratching and clawing and striving to meet your own desires — "orphan-hearted striving" instead of childlike receiving of the perfect, custom-designed, and divinely timed thing that he has given to you and that you can benefit from.

In the Bible, Jesus healed people in different ways: some were touched, one had mud made with spit applied to his eyes, to some he simply spoke their healing, and some were healed by methods unspecified in the gospels. Each person was living with a different condition, and they approached Jesus differently. Jesus, doing what the Father was doing, brought uniquely designed perfection to each one in his time and in his way. Some of them had tried for many years through many means to receive their healing.

In the contemporary church, we have the term "secret sin." In reality, there is no such thing, but it is the epitome of pursuing something apart from God. In his presence, in awareness of his presence, where Jesus lived the totality of his life, there is no sin. In his presence is all good. It is only apart from him that evil exists. Life, light, wisdom, peace, all fruit of the Spirit originate in God and flow from him to us. In John 15, Jesus instructed his disciples to remain in him, to abide. Cultivate practicing his presence, or more accurately, your awareness of his presence and continually remaining aware of his Spirit in you always. In John 14:20, Jesus declared that after his resurrection, you "will realize that I am in my Father, and you are in me, and I am in you."

In Christ, everything that you need is richly supplied, freely given to you for your enjoyment. Godliness with contentment is great gain (1 Timothy 6:6). In context, Paul is instructing Timothy on sound teaching — the teaching of Jesus. About people who do not agree to the sound teaching of Jesus, he says, "They are conceited and understand nothing. They have an unhealthy interest in controversies and quarrels about words that result in envy, strife, malicious talk, evil suspicions and constant friction between people of corrupt mind, who have been robbed of the truth and who think that godliness is a means to financial gain" (1 Timothy 6:4–5).

Paul goes on to say (verses 6–8): "But godliness with contentment is great gain. For we brought nothing into the world, and we can take nothing out of it. But if we have food and clothing, we will be content with that." Later in his letter (verses 20–21), he says to Timothy, "Turn away from godless chatter and the opposing ideas of what is falsely called knowledge, which some have professed and in so doing have departed from the faith." He also says, "But you, man of God, flee from all this, and pursue righteousness, godliness, faith, love, endurance and gentleness. Fight the good fight of the faith. Take hold of the eternal life to which you were called when you made your good confession in the presence of many witnesses" (verses 11–12).

Apart from God, you have no good thing. Pursue God, maintain awareness of his presence and his provision, and cultivate the fruit of his Spirit. Determine in your heart and mind to cultivate contentment. Do not let your heart be troubled. In Jesus, you are in a place of absolute security.

Meditate on the goodness that you have experienced in your relationship with God. Ask him to increase contentment in you. Give God full permission to govern the desires of your heart.

God, thank you for all the good that you provide to me and for working all things together in my life for good. Thank you for your heart of love, compassion, and goodness toward me. I choose to receive the good things you have for me and to cultivate contentment in my life. I pray that your Holy Spirit will show me where I am striving for things that are outside of your love and provision. I pray that I will stop pursuing things that are not of you and live in enjoyment of what you provide for me.

In Context:
I say to the Lord, "You are my Lord; apart from you I have no good thing" (Psalm 16:2).

> **God has assigned you your portion and your cup, he has made your lot secure. — Psalm 16:5**

God has given you this day your daily bread — manna. This is not merely food, it's life sustenance. When God was leading the children of Israel through the desert, they needed to gather the manna that he provided daily, except for the sabbath. This is a foreshadowing of life to the full under the new covenant. Scriptures we have already meditated on tell us that grace is apportioned to you by Jesus. God prepared good works in advance for you to do. Every day of your life was written before you were born. God has plans for your good. His personal attention is on you and your life. His many thoughts toward you are too many to be numbered, like the grains of sand on the seashore. Jesus encouraged his followers to pray for the Father's daily bread. Each of these aspects of life in Christ speak to the importance of attending to what God has provided to you for now. He has assigned you your portion and your cup.

Webster's Dictionary defines portion as: "1) an individual's part or share of something, like a share received by gift or inheritance. Enough food especially of one kind to serve one person at one meal" (today, we say a serving size). "2) an individual's lot, fate, or fortune. One's share of good and evil. 3) a part of a whole." The dictionary defines cup as "an open usually bowl-shaped drinking vessel and its contents. The consecrated wine of the communion. Something that falls to one's lot."

Making your lot secure can refer to your land, the place where you dwell. God is your security. He has clearly given you "a lot," and he is the giver and the protector of all he gave. He is the guarantor. His presence is supreme. When God is for you, who can be against you?

Lot is a word not well understood in contemporary language. It connotes so much more than a building lot. Webster's Dictionary defines lot as "an object used as a counter in determining by chance (e.g., casting lots). The resulting choice. Something that comes to someone upon whom the lot has fallen, share. One's way of life or worldly fate: fortune. The lot of man. A portion of land. A measured parcel of land having fixed boundaries and designated on a plot or survey. A number of units of an article offered as one item (as in an auction or a sale). Lot 45 is a dining room set. A considerable quantity or extent. A lot of money, lots of friends."

No matter which of these meanings you consider, the scripture simply declares that God has made your lot secure. God has made your fortune, destiny, and fate secure. He has made your chance secure, giving you the opportunities of life. He has made all that he has given to you secure. He has made your portion of land, your measured physical space, your parcel secure. He has made all of the elements of your life secure. He has given you a considerable quantity and extent of life — life to the full — and made the whole lot secure. Apart from him, you have no good thing (Psalm 16:2). In Jesus, you are in place of absolute security.

Your portion and your cup and your lot are all metaphors for the same thing. These images serve to remind you that every good and perfect gift comes from God, and he makes it secure. We are reminded that his provision comes daily, or even continually.

Meditate on the fact that everything you need for life to the full is apportioned and provided for you by God. Reflect on different things that you know God has provided in your life. Thank him for securing your lot. In Jesus, you are in place of absolute security.

Father, thank you for your loving attention to my needs for life, and for your generous provision so that I can experience life to the full. Thank you that I do not need to depend on my own ability or creativity to get what I need on my own. I pray that I will choose to trust you for all that I need to go through this day in step with what you have planned for me. Thank you for the good works that you planned for me in advance, and for all aspects of my daily bread. I pray that I will have your grace to gather all that you have designed for me this day and not to strive for more. God, thank you for securing my lot. Thank you that you wrote all the days of my life into your book before one of them came to exist. Thank you for being the giver and guarantor of all that I have that is good. I pray that I will continue to trust in you for your provision, protection, and all aspects of my life. Thank you for your loving care.

In Context:
Lord, you alone are my portion and my cup; you make my lot secure. The boundary lines have fallen for me in pleasant places; surely I have a delightful inheritance (Psalm 16:5–6).

> **The boundary lines have fallen for you in pleasant places.**
> **— Psalm 16:6**

Because of Jesus, you are a dearly loved child of God (1 John 4:3), you have access to the Father (Ephesians 2:18), and you can freely and boldly enter the presence of the Almighty. You are a citizen of his kingdom (Philippians 3:20), and a member of his household (Ephesians 2:12). The boundary lines have fallen for you in pleasant places, not against you. You have a choice. You are invited to choose life, life to the full, and to abide in his presence.

Boundaries are fixed, secured, protected, and legally binding. Webster's Dictionary defines boundary as "something that indicates or fixes a limit or extent."

Boundaries mark what is out as well as what is in. God's love has established the boundaries. Trust him instead of pushing the boundaries to include things that are not intended for you or good for you. The love of God for you is what established the boundaries. Instead of railing against his boundaries, we can choose to appreciate them and see the care, providence, and wisdom of them. The boundaries are set for us and are wonderful and pleasant, because they are a constant testimony of the presence and care of God in our lives.

Our lot — our fate, life, portion, and cup — is pleasant. It is pleasing to go anywhere within our secured lot. Lots of pleasing places and experiences and things. There is great joy in resting in different places within our boundaries. There is much to cultivate, care for, do, and share.

After the fall, God banished Adam and Eve from the garden (he set a boundary line) and placed a cherub with a flaming sword to protect the tree of life. He provided a protected border to prevent them from entering eternity in a fallen state.

In everyday experience, attentive, loving parents set boundaries. They monitor their young children to give them just the right balance between freedom to explore the world with wonder and joy and allowing them to do things that are harmful or dangerous to self or others. In the same way, God sets pleasant boundaries for you. They include more than enough of things to do, experience, and enjoy.

The boundaries will change as your life unfolds. They are developmentally appropriate for you. When parents first teach children to cross the street, they might carry them across. Later, they walk hand in hand and discuss the necessity of looking both ways. Later, parents will give permission for a child to cross the street on their own. God teaches you in similar ways, reflecting his care and investment in lovingly watching over you.

Your boundaries are pleasant for you. Mine are pleasant for me. I should not try to live within yours, nor you within mine. The boundary lines are tied to my delightful inheritance (Psalm 16:6). Staying within those boundaries keeps you on his path of life, and it keeps you aware of his presence (Psalm 16:11). In Jesus, you are in place of absolute security.

Meditate on the pleasantness of the boundary lines that God has lovingly placed for you. Ask him to draw your attention to the many good things he has set within your boundaries. Ask him to show you if there are things beyond his pleasant boundaries that you have been wrongfully striving for. Invite and trust God to give you appreciation for his pleasant boundaries for you.

Thank you, Lord, for placing boundary lines for me. Thank you for all that you provide for me to experience and enjoy within the boundaries that you have specifically designed for me. I pray that I will remain within the boundaries that you have set for me. I pray for contentment within the boundaries that you have lovingly placed. I trust you to lead me and to help me stay within the pleasant boundaries you have set for me.

In Context:
Lord, you alone are my portion and my cup; you make my lot secure. The boundary lines have fallen for me in pleasant places; surely I have a delightful inheritance (Psalm 16:5–6).

A Place of Absolute Security: Summary and Application

Nothing in all creation will be able to separate you from the love of God that is in Christ Jesus our Lord (Romans 8:38–39). God is for you, who can be against you? (Romans 8:31). He provides you with plenty and fills your heart with joy (Acts 14:17). God richly provides you with everything for your enjoyment (1 Timothy 6:17). Apart from God, you have no good thing (Psalm 16:2). God has assigned you your portion and your cup (Psalm 16:5). He has made your lot secure (Psalm 16:5). The boundary lines have fallen for you in pleasant places (Psalm 16:6).

The treasure of God is in you, in jars of clay, to show that this all-surpassing power is from God and not from you (2 Corinthians 4:7). Jars of clay originate in the hands of the potter. It is where you should commit to remain. His hands squeeze you to shape you into what you are designed for. You can trust him to keep you secure within the boundary lines that he lovingly designs and maintains for you. Psalm 91:1–2 says, "Whoever dwells in the shelter of the Most High will rest in the shadow of the Almighty. I will say of the Lord, 'He is my refuge and my fortress, my God, in whom I trust.'" In Jesus, you are in a place of absolute security.

Proclaim the following truths over your life:

- Nothing in all creation will be able to separate me from the love of God that is in Christ Jesus, my Lord.
- God is for me, who can be against me?
- He provides me with plenty and fills my heart with joy.
- God richly provides me with everything for my enjoyment.
- Apart from God, I have no good thing.

- God has assigned me my portion and my cup.
- He has made my lot secure.
- The boundary lines have fallen for me in pleasant places.
- In Jesus, I am in place of absolute security.

Notes

CHAPTER 22

A Place of Experientially Knowing
God's Constant Goodness

God has plans to prosper you, not to harm you, plans to give you hope and a future (Jeremiah 29:11). You will be like him, for you shall see him as he is (1 John 3:2). I will see the goodness of the Lord in the land of the living (Psalm 27:13). You will see the goodness of God in the land of the land of the living (Psalm 27:13). I am confident that he who began a good work in you will carry it on to completion until the day of Christ Jesus (Philippians 1:6).

> **God has plans to prosper you, not to harm you, plans to give you hope and a future.** — Jeremiah 29:11

This is a well-known and often quoted passage of scripture. After reading and meditating on so many statements form his word, can you see in your heart that this is true for you? God has plans to prosper you in every dimension of your life, to pour his love on you in never-ending cascades, to relate to you for eternity, to give you life to the full. God has guaranteed everything necessary to accomplish that in your life on your behalf.

This offers great hope — hope that in no way depends on your ability, your circumstances, or your goodness. All of it rests on God's character and his desire to prosper you, to do what is best for you, and to see it through to completion (Philippians 1:6). That is what sustains: All things hold together in Christ (Colossians 1:17). May this offer you ultimate hope for today and tomorrow and every day ahead into the future, because all the days are filled with his dominion, power, care, and providence. His goodness and his love are never waning or wavering. They are the reason for your existence to begin with. You do not need to depend on others. God's plans for you are personal, and they are yours.

He uses all things for good in your life (Romans 8:28). Even things others meant for evil or harm. He does not harm you in any way at any time. His perfect love casts out fear (1 John 4:18). God is completely, fully, totally trustworthy — true to his promises. Every one of them either has already been fulfilled or is in the process of being fulfilled in the future. Not a single stroke of his word will fall; it accomplishes its purpose. He cannot forget you, for he has his love for you carved on the palms of his hands.

The best is yet to come. This is not mere wishful thinking or a trite slogan. Your future, planned and unfolding in the presence of God is being established in your life moment by moment. He does not change. God changes the fruit of hurtful events in your life for your good. That is prospering you. That is both a hope and a future, and it all leads to conversing with him (prayers that are heard) and finding him. Nothing else in all of life or eternity can compare to finding him and being with him — walking in the garden he has created for you, walking with him not only in the cool of the evening, but continually. That was his intent from before the beginning of time. He is restoring it, overcoming sin, rebellion, death, disease, and all of the curses of the fall to restore unrestrained unity and peace and wholeness. Making life to the full available to you.

When you seek and find him (and he is not hiding), you prosper. It is in his presence that all good exists. Apart from him, you have no good thing. You can do all things in Christ. In all things you are more than a conqueror. In Jesus, you are in a place of experientially knowing God's constant goodness toward you.

Quietly think back over the scriptures that we have been considering regarding the place that Jesus has prepared for you. Ask him to bring to your mind those that most directly relate to his good plans for you in your current season of life. Rest in the encouragement that his plans for you are to prosper you.

Father, Abba, thank you for your good plans for me, for my life on earth and for all of eternity. Thank you that you have done, and that you continue to do, things to prosper me in body, mind, soul, spirit, and strength. Thank you that in your presence all is well. Thank you that you are with me and that I am with you in Jesus. We are inseparable for eternity. Thank you for your goodness that I have already seen in the land of the living and for the hope of eternity in your presence.

> **In Context:**
> "For I know the plans I have for you," declares the Lord," plans to prosper you and not to harm you, plans to give you hope and a future. Then you will call on me and come and pray to me, and I will listen to you. You will seek me and find me when you seek me with all your heart. I will be found by you," declares the Lord" (Jeremiah 29:11–14).

You will see the goodness of God in the land of the land of the living. — Psalm 27:13

Most bible scholars believe that David wrote Psalm 27 when King Saul was pursuing him to kill him. While there is some controversy regarding the events he was experiencing at the time of his writing, there is widespread agreement that it was composed prior to David ascending the throne of Israel, and during times of significant troubles in his life. While there are many themes in the psalm, it highlights the place of praise and hope in the midst of difficulties.

Perhaps David's confidence rested in his experiences of the goodness of God when he faced opposition in the past such as facing literal giants and lions and bears. His experiences indelibly convinced him of God's presence and goodness in his life. They gave him confidence to trust God in later challenges.

Though few of us have likely faced literal giants and lions and bears, you have all encountered circumstances in your lives that have tested your faith. When you look at the obstacles confronting you, do you have confidence that God's goodness will prevail? Are there times that you know from personal experience that God's goodness is what brought you through past difficulties?

Meditate on prior experiences in challenging times and how you can now see God's goodness operating on your behalf. Though things may have been painful to experience and to go through, in retrospect, you can see God using all things together for good in your life (Romans 8:28). Specifically focus on times when you know, beyond doubt, that God's goodness prevailed on your behalf. Perhaps it was through his provision, protection, leading, or timing. How does reflecting on God's goodness in your past change the way you currently feel about the difficulties you may be facing now?

God, thank you for allowing us to see your goodness in our lives. Thank you for reminding us of your closeness in times of trouble and the ways that your presence gives hope. Thank you that we do not have to wait for the afterlife to experience your goodness. I pray that you will give me confidence to trust in your goodness and the wisdom to wait for you to reveal your goodness in the circumstances of my life.

In Context:
I remain confident of this: I will see the goodness of the Lord in the land of the Living. Wait for the Lord; be strong and take heart and wait for the Lord (Psalm 27:13–14).

You will be like him, for you shall see him as he is.
— 1 John 3:2

Seeing the resurrected, fully triumphant King of Kings when his kingdom is fully established and has displaced all sin and revoked Satan's temporary authority as "prince of the air" will change you to be like him. Glory! When you are fully united with him face to face, you will fulfill your destiny by reaching your potential in him. He will be so attractive to you that you will desire with all your being to be just like him. There will no longer be any sin or shame or other hinderance to prevent you from being changed. His voice and his touch will be fully tangible, accessible to you. You will not be limited to glimpses, as now, through dim mirrors, briefly. Then your view will not be from afar and filtered by the enemy's guilt, condemnation, doubt, fear, or deception. You will see him as he is. That will be enough!

Though you will not experience the fullness of this freedom and relationship that Jesus accomplished for you until you see him face to face, you can get deeper experiential understanding of the truth of his word and the security of your position in Jesus through revelation by his Holy Spirit. My prayer is that as you meditate on the truth of these one hundred scripturally based truths that you will experience an infusion of trust in God's love, character, and devotion to you for your good. Unquestionably, it is God's love that compelled Jesus to leave the side of the Father and come to earth, live in the world as a human, and do all things necessary to bring you into glorious relationship and union with God himself.

I pray that you will experientially know that what Jesus declared as finished while still on the cross places you in him and him in you (John 14:20). Although all that he finished is still coming to full manifestation, nothing in all of creation can separate you from the love of God in Christ (Romans 8:39) — not now and not ever. Experiencing the truth of these scriptures as you meditate on them fixes your identity as a dearly loved child of God and empowers you to walk more fully in your destiny until that day when you become like him because you see him as he is. In Jesus, you are in a place of experientially knowing God's constant goodness toward you.

Consider whether there are things that you can do to know God more fully and to be more continually aware of his presence in your life. Ask him to lead you into continuously deeper relationship with him.

Thank you, Lord, that you have known the end from before the beginning and that your plans, desires, and will for me will prevail. Thank you for your steadfast love and your presence in my life. I pray that you will give me wisdom and power to believe your scriptures and to not be discouraged by others' perspectives. Lord, I pray that your Spirit will open the eyes of my heart to see the height and depth and width and length of your great love for me. Even now, let your Holy Spirit pour Father's love into my heart, experientially. Thank you that you are loving me now, Abba. I receive your love.

> **In Context:**
> See what great love the Father has lavished on us, that we should be called children of God! And that is what we are! The reason the world does not know us is that it did not know him. Dear friends, now we are children of God, and what we will be has not yet been made known. But we know that when Christ appears, we shall be like him, for we shall see him as he is. All who have this hope in him purify themselves, just as he is pure (1 John 3:1–3).

> I am confident that he who began a good work in you
> will carry it on to completion until the day of Christ Jesus.
> — Philippians 1:6

In Christ, all that is needed for your maturation into completion is finished, but you are still growing up into him (Ephesians 4:15). He has made your lot secure (Psalm 16:5). He will do immeasurably more than you can ask or imagine (Ephesians 3:20). Your experience in this life is characterized by elements of kingdom now and kingdom come. No promise of God has ever failed. The soles of the Israelites' shoes did not wear out in the desert during their forty-year transition to the promised land. God provided daily manna. He led them as a cloud by day and a pillar of fire by night, walking with and before his people through every hardship.

We are living in the tension between being a lavishly loved child of God and living in a fallen world. Each one of us is in transition toward our maturity, completion, and fullness.

In the end, in Jesus, nothing will be stolen, killed, or destroyed (John 10:10). In Jesus we are filled, living, and restored. We experience his presence and provision in good measure, pressed down, and overflowing. The unchanging, unbounded, generous love of God, Father, Son and Spirit is ours. He is continually leading and speaking to us. He is thinking countless thoughts, like grains of sand, toward us. We are receiving much more care than the lilies of the fields or the birds of the air.

Freely we have received, so freely we can give.

Springs of living water are permeating us and flowing to others as we choose to pour out our lives as a drink offering to his children. When we finally see him — and we will — we will be like him. Our knees will bow and our tongues will confess that he is our Lord. In the twinkling of an eye all will change and be made new. I am confident that God, who began this good work in us will carry it on to completion. In Jesus, we are in a place of experientially knowing God's constant goodness toward us.

Meditate on the character of God that we have explored through these hundred biblical statements. Consider how they have applied to your life personally. Thank God for his father's heart toward you and the ways that he showers his love on you. Consider how all of this works together to bring you confidence that God will complete the good work he has begun in you.

God, thank you for giving me life, for making yourself known to me, for sending Jesus to make a way into the fullness of relationship that you desire for me. I pray that your Holy Spirit would continually remind me of these scriptural truths about who I am in you. Thank you that I am your child. Give me increasing ability to receive and reflect your love in my interactions with all whom I meet. Thank you for your constant presence in my life. Continue to transform me to be more like you.

In Context:
… being confident of this, that he who began a good work in you will carry it on to completion until the day of Christ Jesus (Philippians 1:6).

A Place of Experientially Knowing God's Constant Goodness:

Summary and Application

God has plans to prosper you, not to harm you, plans to give you hope and a future (Jeremiah 29:11). You will see the goodness of the Lord in the land of the Living (Psalm 27:13). You will be like him, for you shall see him as he is (1 John 3:2). I am confident that he who began a good work in you will carry it on to completion until the day of Christ Jesus (Philippians 1:6).

As you face the challenges of life and confront your doubts, choose to lift your eyes to the hills and consider where your help comes from. It comes from the Lord (Psalm 121:1). The character of God is unchanging. He is the same yesterday, today, and tomorrow. Yet his creative expression — how he does things and what he does — is infinite. Praise him for the goodness that he has already shown in your life and expect that his goodness will continue to prevail through all of your days. As you come to experience his character, you will be transformed to bear his image more closely. Come to him. Converse with him. Then offer yourself to submit to him and co-participate with him as you walk through every phase of your day.

> **As you remain in the place that Jesus has prepared for you, hold to the truth that in Jesus you are in a place of experientially knowing God's constant goodness toward you:**

- God has plans to prosper me, not to harm me, plans to give me hope and a future.

- I will see the goodness of God in the land of the living.

- I will be like him, for I shall see him as he is.

- I am confident that he who began a good work in me will carry it on to completion until the day of Christ Jesus.

- In Jesus, I am in a place of experientially knowing God's constant goodness toward me.

** Additional note space located on page 215 **

CHAPTER 23

A Place Prepared: *Living from the Place Prepared*

I have written, re-written, edited, and re-edited this manuscript many times. Each time has brought me great life, joy, and fullness. Each time I read the scripture, meditated on it, prayed about it and asked God to minister it to my heart, it brought greater closeness in relationship with my God. Each time, when I thought that I had completed my task, I have seen that there is more. In the many processes of writing, I have come to see that I have only started to plumb the depths of the place that Jesus has prepared for me. In fact, there is no end, because our God, who had no beginning and will have no end, is infinitely loving toward us and continues to do good in our lives for eternity. As one who felt an assignment from God to lay out, meditate on, and narrate my thoughts on the place prepared by Jesus, it's been my experience that each time through the scriptures, the meditations, and the thoughts, I have come to a deeper place of experientially knowing the place prepared. Revisiting these verses, meditations and prayers regularly will likely continue to produce maturity and new fruit in your relationship with the Lord. God's word is active and alive, and if the Holy Spirit draws you to revisit a chapter or a verse, it is because he has greater life, love, freedom, and relationship to draw you into.

I expect that as you more fully encounter the place prepared for you, God will bring healing to you in every area where you need it. He will more fully establish your understanding of who you are as his extravagantly loved child and deepen your relationship with him. In many ways, exploring the place he has prepared for you is simply and humbly accepting the generosity of the invitation to draw near to God and he will draw near to you.

Our relationship with God is often called a walk of faith. Learning to walk entails hundreds of falls and getting up again. It entails learning to traverse different terrains using the same basic skills, adapted for where you are at the moment. As we walk, we move from one place to another. Everywhere we are, we experience it through what we have learned from the places we have already been.

As I explore trails in the greenspaces around my home, I greatly enjoy the experience of connecting my world. When a newly traversed trail brings me to a place I am familiar with from past explorations, the pieces of my world fit together in a larger and more fully elaborated cognitive map. In the Father's house are many rooms. The tapestry of his love and goodness indeed has many places with many functions in each of our lives. The many places are interconnected by the master architect of creation to construct a great and complete home for his whole family — a home where we are welcomed as members of God's own household and where we can truly experience life to the full.

I am confident that as we open ourselves to the leading of the Holy Spirit and have faith in his love and care for us, God himself will meet us in the place that he has prepared for each one of us personally. That's who he is and that's what he does!

Please understand that this is not a prosperity gospel. I am not saying, "If you just get this, everything will be great!" Jesus said we would have troubles in this world, but he also said that we should take heart because he overcame the world and that he was leaving his peace for us. In Philippians 4:7, the peace of Christ is described as peace that passes understanding. Jesus was dearly loved by his Father. Still, it is a dramatic understatement to say that he went through many challenging times in his life. The truths of the scriptures we have considered don't mean we won't face challenges or suffer. But they do mean that we can face those things from the place that God has prepared for us. We can remain with him as we go through whatever we have to face.

Our place in God does not guarantee "easy street." But is it a place where all our needs are fully and abundantly met, beyond what we can hope or imagine. That provision does not always line up with our expectation of what we believe we should have or what God "should do." His ways are not our ways, his thoughts are not our thoughts. His ways are far beyond ours. Trusting in him with all of our hearts, not leaning on our own understanding, and acknowledging him in all of our ways (including circumstances, challenges, and failures) positions us in Christ. Remaining in him, allows us to do all things through him as more than conquerors.

Experiential knowledge and intimate relationship with God does not fix everything we experience in this life, but it surely does change everything. I do not claim to walk in your shoes or to know the challenges, injustices, abuses, hurts, or disappointments that are a part of your past. But I do know that God is aware of all that you have been subjected to. He is actively in the process of turning what was meant for harm into good, and he never stops doing that. He never will. Trust that in whatever difficulties you are facing, he is with you and he is for you. Choose to remain in relationship with him and live life from the position and benefits of the place that Jesus prepared for you. That's life to the full.

We have glimpsed the place prepared. We have tasted and seen that we can be in a place of family, a place of love, a place of peace. While we have focused on many of the functions or characteristics of the place that Jesus has prepared, as noted, the scriptures that we have focused on are not an exhaustive list of the characteristics of the place prepared. Without elaboration here, I offer a list to briefly review the qualities of the place prepared that we have considered through previous chapters and some possible elaborations for the Holy Spirit to personally quicken to you.

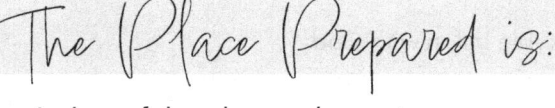

The Place Prepared is:

- A place of deep love and acceptance
    - *Peace with God and self, allowing you to accept others. Complete shalom.*
- A place of extravagant belonging
    - *You were made for such a place as this!*
- A place of everlasting purpose
    - *Life is good because God is good.*
- A place of sure salvation
    - *Being rescued and restored to wholeness.*
- A place of total forgiveness and cleansing
    - *Gratitude for accomplishing what is impossible for me to do.*
- A place of secure family love — in the family of God himself
    - *Attachment with a trustworthy and fully functioning caregiver, protector, provider.*
- A place of unfathomable plenty
    - *All that we truly need is abundantly provided when it is needed.*
- A place of total satisfaction and contentment
    - *Remaining in this place can reduce striving for and distraction of the things of life.*
- A place of everlasting freedom and victory
    - *Fulfilling the purpose for which you were created. Discovering unity and joy of the Lord.*

- A place of constant goodness
  - God is continually aware of your needs and delights to give you what is for your best.

- A place of increasing closeness and care
  - Becoming familiar with God's voice and tuning in to it, resting in his love, growing in trust.

- A place of absolute inclusion and refuge
  - Sheltered from the harm, injustice, and cruelty of the kingdom of darkness.

- A place of continual relationship with God
  - Not broken or distant. Filled and included and surrounded.

- A place of unshakable union with God
  - The God of love is with us and for us and in us.

- A place of oneness in love
  - Unity with God and others.

- A place of power for life
  - No obstacle is too great for God. Living life through him is radically different than trying to go it on your own.

- A place of life to the full
  - Invited to experience the depth of relationship that Jesus had in full sonship.

- A place of transformation and increasing maturity
  - Though we are accepted as we are, the love of God brings ongoing transformation and maturity.

- A place of divine destiny
  - Irrevocable giftings and callings.

- A place of absolute security
  - He is my rock, high tower, fortress, refuge. I am under his wing, in his shadow.

- A place of experientially knowing God's constant goodness toward me
  - Knowing through receiving — tasting and seeing what he has done.

The place that Jesus has prepared for you is incomparable. There is nowhere like it, nowhere else so perfectly suited for you.

Now that you have begun to see the place prepared for you, you must learn to hold to it. To prefer it, remaining in Jesus, seeking him above all other things. You must guard your heart against other things that you would place above remaining in Jesus — even good things that you would place next to it. Too many things can distract you from God's best, and his place prepared for you is the best. Renewing your mind and guarding your heart from this lens allows you to experience the presence of God, rest more fully and continually in your relationship with him, and live from the place he has prepared for you.

When you set your heart on plumbing the depths of the place prepared, consciously deciding not to push the boundaries God has placed for you, you experience more closeness with God. Staying centered in him and in the places he has prepared for you, you experience more of life to the full. The Holy Spirit in you, you in Jesus, and Jesus in the Father. And when you recognize that you have allowed yourself to be drawn out of the place that he has prepared for you, you can repent, which simply means to change your way of thinking, to turn around, to give yourself again to the mercy and grace of God extended to you through Jesus. Then you experience the restoration of God's presence in your life and once again enter the place he has prepared for you.

In every waking moment, many voices may come to you. Whose report will you believe? The scriptures converge to paint a glorious picture of the place prepared for you.

> **Why isn't the truth of these scriptures your everyday lived experience and continual reality? There are several possible reasons:**

1. You don't know what the Word of God says about the place prepared. If you have read this far, that should no longer be a stumbling block!

2. Through orphan-hearted self-dependence, you nullify the available spiritual blessings that children of God are entitled to. The antidote is trusting in the Lord with all your heart and not leaning on your own understanding, but acknowledging him in all your ways. This provides freedom from a culture and past circumstances that make self-reliance so alluring.

3. Lack of faith. Choose to believe and ask God for help with your unbelief. He delights to increase our faith. In reality, we don't have faith, he supplies it!

4. Believing the father of lies and his many voices from many sources. Ask for discernment in the Spirit regarding the voices that you hear. Be selective in the voices you choose to receive. Consciously reject those voices that contradict the truth of who you are in Jesus. Choose not to allow the accuser's voice to

echo in your mind. Know the place prepared and the unshakable nature of God's goodness and love for you.

5. Letting doubts rise in your mind and heart. Take thoughts captive and replace doubts and fears with the truth of his scriptures and the testimony of his past goodness toward you. It is the blood of the Lamb and the words of your testimony that allow you to triumph over the accuser of the brethren (Revelation 12:11).

6. Making choices to go your own way and be disobedient. Change your way of thinking and behaving. Quickly repent: Confess and ask for forgiveness, cleansing, and to be made new. When you become aware that you have "fallen," choose to get up again and walk on. Do the next right thing.

7. Being distracted by the worries of this life, deceitfulness of riches, and desire for other things. Take stock of things that bring you worries and submit them to God. Defer to his leading, provision, and goodness. Godliness with contentment is great gain (1 Timothy 6:6). Ask the Lord to increase your contentment and to increase his character in you.

Each of these potential stumbling blocks are old stories and strategies of the enemy of your soul, the thief who comes to steal, kill, and destroy. The good news is that he — and all that he intends for your harm — must submit to the lordship of Christ. As you mature in Christ, you will become less susceptible to the strategies of the enemy. Experientially knowing the love of God and remaining centered in it really does change everything.

The scriptures are filled with invitations to partner with God to do great things: extend the kingdom; set captives free; feed the hungry; bring sight to the blind; make disciples. When you live your life from the place prepared, you not only shift atmospheres, but through him, in him, and with him, you can shift relationships and circumstances. You do it by living your life in the fullness afforded to you in and from the place that God himself prepared for you.

Your challenge as a child of the Most High God is to remain in the place he prepared for you no matter what other places you are walking in or occupying. Can you remain in the place he prepared for you when you are at work, at home, in your community, and engaged in your daily chores and activities? You can experience more of life to the full as you invite him and depend on him in the places you encounter in your life: physical places, emotional places, and places in your mind.

Here is a practical example of being mindful of remaining in the place prepared. I have a goal to trail "run" twice a week (Actually, at this point in my lifespan, "running" might be an exaggeration; perambulating beyond walking speed is a better descriptor.). During the warmer months I run while wearing a ventilated runner's cap to protect me from the sun, to provide air flow around my scalp, and to protect me from biting deer flies in the woods. Often while I am running, if I haven't noticed any biting flies and if I am running in the shade of a wooded path, I will remove my hat to feel the breeze through my hair. Often while I am running, I am thinking about and processing many things from my life. Much of this book had its origin in my trail runs. Sometimes when I am lost in my thoughts, I become aware of deer flies buzzing around my head ready to bite me. Sometimes I even fail to recognize that I am shuffling along with my cap in my hand, that I have deliberately come out from under cover, and I have the ability to reestablish the protection I need. All I have to do is to replace the cap on my head to return to the place prepared for me. When I do, the flies are no longer a menace, allowing me to return from places of disquiet and distraction. Putting the cap back on returns me to the place where I am living from the presence of the Lord, communing in prayer and thought and having a whole different set of feelings than when I remove my hat. It's really that simple. Whenever you become aware that you have allowed your focus to be taken from the presence of the Lord, or you have done something to step out from under the cover of the Lord, simply do what you must to return to his presence. It changes everything! My practical example does not really address sinfulness; it is simply about leaving the place prepared and suffering the consequences of whatever you have immersed yourself into while out of touch with God's presence. Of course, if you find that you have left the place prepared in the Spirit and engaged in sinful attitudes, thoughts, words, or behaviors, repent — turn from what you are doing and return to the place prepared. There you will be welcomed, embraced, comforted, and equipped to move on down the road.

Another key is to choose to persevere. Persevere simply means "through the severe," choosing to stay steady through difficult circumstances, bringing them into the place he prepared for us — remaining and abiding in his presence — instead of allowing things of this fallen world to take our attention and focus. Faith-crushing voices of the enemy of our souls are distractions, tempting us to place the focus on the externals instead of the things above. Choose not to overly focus on the stuff of earth and instead focus on what our creator and the lover of our souls says about us in his indelible word.

The place prepared for us has been planned and generously provided. We are invited into it — now. We can live our lives on earth, to the full, from that place instead of stepping out of that place to live apart from spiritual blessings that have been provided for us. Why wouldn't we live from the place of unity and relationship with God as his lavishly loved child?

The place God himself prepared for us exists because of his great love for us, his desire for continual relationship, and his constant goodness. We see it now in a mirror dimly, but we have eternity to see with greater clarity. Scripture tells us that no eye has seen, no ear has heard, and no human mind has conceived what God has prepared for those who love him (1 Corinthians 2:9). Let us look at what we can't see with our eyes, because what is seen is temporary, but what is unseen is eternal (2 Corinthians 4:18).

More than anything, my experiences of living in relationship with the living

God have convinced me beyond reasonable doubt that Romans 8:28 expresses the nature and character of God. In all things, God works for the good of those who love him, who have been called according to his purpose. This has been his signature since before creation and will be for all of eternity. God transforms everything that was intended for harm into good — beauty for ashes, the oil of joy for mourning, a mantle of praise for a spirit of heaviness (Isaiah 61:3). God's presence changes everything. While all will be under his dominion when Jesus returns and establishes the new heaven and the new earth, we are invited to be with him now — kingdom now. We enter the place prepared for us through faith and asking him to increase our faith. As scripture says in Mark 9:24, I believe. Help my unbelief! God accomplishes all-encompassing, Romans 8:28 good in our lives for our good and his glory.

If at any point in your journey through the material in this book, you have felt overwhelmed or stuck, take heart. Growing in relationship with an infinite God and being conformed to his likeness is a lifetime pursuit; but it is one to which we are invited in the place that Jesus has prepared for us. If you are feeling discouraged, perhaps a good thing to do is to return to a "place" in the book that seemed somewhat familiar or easy to you in comparison to others. Revisit those meditations, prayers, and invitations from God to bring deeper relationship with Him in that place in your life. Sit in the encouragement of his love for you where it is familiar to you. The whole purpose of this book is to stimulate a deeper relationship with God, the Father, Son and Holy Spirit.

Perhaps after reading and praying through sections in the book where you felt the encouraging nearness of God, prayerfully revisit a section that you found to be more challenging. Reinvite the Holy Spirit to bring you to a new season of receiving more of His counsel, love and care in those places in your life. No matter what you decide, do it prayerfully, and do it in concert with and in dependence on the Spirit of God. Let Him lead your timing, your pace, and the order of your contemplations. When you hear a doubt rising in your mind, invite God to protect you from the voice of the accuser of our souls. Stay open to the presence of God, and keep going forward by trusting his lavish love for you personally. If you're still not sure what to do, simply invite God to guide you by his Spirit and do the next thing in love.

I pray that each day, in increasing measure, you will experience depth of relationship with our triune God, exploring the fullness of the places he has prepared for you, receiving all of the blessings of his presence and goodness into your life. I pray that you will see the goodness of the Lord in the land of the living. And that with increasing ability, consistency, habitual transformation, the transformation that comes from being a new creature in Christ, that more often than not, I pray that you will continually remain in the place that he has prepared for you and live from that place. I pray that your walk with the Father, Son, and Holy Spirit will be blessed thoroughly and filled to overflowing until streams of his living water pour from you into every situation you are in. I pray that those who come into contact with you would be drawn to his love, character, and goodness.

May the Lord bless and keep you and make his face shine upon you. May his road rise to meet you as you walk through the glory of his plans for you in his presence, living life to the full from the place that he has prepared for you. Amen.

Notes

100 Biblical Statements

Paraphrased and Personalized

100 Biblical Statements

Mindfully declare these 100 scriptural truths over yourself. Invite the Lord to minister his love to your heart and mind as you declare God's word about your true identity in the Father, Son, and Holy Spirit.

1. In love, I was chosen by God before the creation of the world (Ephesians 1:4).

2. I am set apart, called by God's grace (Galatians 1:15).

3. I am holy in God's sight (Ephesians 1:4).

4. I am blameless in God's sight (Ephesians 1:4).

5. I am a dearly loved child of God (Ephesians 5:1).

6. I am fully known by God (1 Corinthians 13:12).

7. I am accepted in Christ (Romans 15:7).

8. God loves me with the same love with which he loved Jesus (John 17:23).

9. I am not my own (1 Corinthians 6:19).

10. I belong with and to Jesus (Romans 7:4).

11. I was bought at a price (1 Corinthians 6:19).

12. God made me alive with Christ even when I was dead in my sins (Ephesians 2:5).

13. I was once in darkness, but now I am light in the Lord (Ephesians 5:8).

14. I am a chosen person, part of a royal priesthood, a holy nation, a people belonging to God, called out of darkness into his wonderful light (1 Peter 2:9).

15. I am a child of the light and of the day. I do not belong to the night or to darkness (1 Thessalonians 5:5).

16. I am holy, I share in a heavenly calling (Hebrews 3:1).

17. By grace I am saved (Ephesians 2:5).

18. I am saved through faith, and this is not from myself, it is a gift from God (Ephesians 2:8).

19. Christ dwells in my heart through faith (Ephesians 3:17).

20. In the Son, I have redemption through his blood (Ephesians 1:7; Colossians 1:14).

21. In the son, God forgave all my sins (Colossians 2:13; Ephesians 1:7).

22. I am reconciled, holy in God's sight, without blemish and free from accusation (Colossians 1:22).

23. I am washed, sanctified, and justified freely by faith in Christ Jesus and the Spirit of my God (1 Corinthians 6:11; Galatians 3:8, 3:24).

24. I am a child of God through faith in Christ Jesus (Galatians 3:26).

25. I am lavished in God's love (1 John 3:1).

26. Because I am his child, God sent the Spirit of his Son into my heart, the Spirit that calls out "Abba, Father" (Galatians 4:6).

27. I can receive the full rights of a child of God (Galatians 4:4–5).

28. Since I am his child, God has made me an heir (Galatians 4:7).

29. I am called to the riches of his glorious inheritance (Ephesians 1:18).

30. I am not qualified on my own; the Father has qualified me to share in the inheritance of the saints (Colossians 1:12).

31. Surely, I have a delightful inheritance (Psalm 16:6).

32. The Father has blessed me in the heavenly realms with every spiritual blessing in Christ (Ephesians 1:3).

33. I have been given fullness in Christ. I am complete (Colossians 2:3,10).

34. I was called to take hold of eternal life (1 Timothy 6:12).

35. I am a child of promise (Galatians 4:28).

36. I am called to be free (Galatians 5:13); It is for freedom that Christ has set me free (Galatians 5:1).

37. I am rescued from the present evil age (Galatians 1:4).

38. The Father has rescued me from the domain of darkness and brought me into the kingdom of the Son he loves (Colossians 1:13).

39. Because I have faith in Christ, I am a victorious overcomer of the world (1 John 5:4).

40. I am rooted and established in love (Ephesians 3:17).

41. God's power is at work within me (Ephesians 3:20).

42. I am God's workmanship, created in Christ Jesus to do good works, which God prepared in advance for me to do (Ephesians 2:10).

43. God works in me to will and act according to his good purpose (Philippians 2:13).

44. Jesus chose and appointed me to go and bear much lasting fruit (John 15:5,16)

45. Apart from Jesus, I can do nothing (John 15:5).

46. Now, in Christ Jesus, I, who was once far away, have been brought near through the blood of Christ (Ephesians 2:13).

47. My citizenship is in heaven (Philippians 3:20).

48. I am no longer a foreigner or an alien, but a fellow citizen with God's people and a member of God's household (Ephesians 2:12).

49. Through Christ, I have access to the Father, through one Spirit (Ephesians 2:18).

50. I am called to one hope, to one faith, to one baptism, and to one God and Father of all (Ephesians 4:4–6).

51. I have been baptized into Christ Jesus, baptized into his death (Romans 6:3).

52. I have been crucified with Christ (Galatians 2:20).

53. I died, and my life is now hidden with Christ in God (Colossians 3:3).

54. I died with Christ to the basic principles of this world (Colossians 2:20).

55. I was buried with Christ in baptism (Romans 6:4).

56. I have been raised in Christ through my faith in the power of God, who raised Christ from the dead (Colossians 2:12).

57. God raised me up with Christ and seated me in the heavenly realms in Christ Jesus (Ephesians 2:6).

58. I am clothed in Christ (Galatians 3:27).

59. I am included in Christ (Ephesians 1:13).

60. I am united with the Lord (1 Corinthians 6:17).

61. I no longer live, but Christ lives in me (Galatians 2:20).

62. In Jesus, I am being built together to become a dwelling in which God lives by his Spirit (Ephesians 2:22).

63. I myself am God's temple (1 Corinthians 6:19).

64. God's Spirit, whom I received from God, is in me (1 Corinthians 6:19).

65. I am one with God in Spirit (1 Corinthians 6:17).

66. Jesus is in his Father, and I am in Christ, and he is in me (John 14:20).

67. I am marked with a seal (Ephesians 1:13).

68. By the deposit of the Holy Spirit, my inheritance is guaranteed (Ephesians 1:14).

69. The anointing I received from him remains in me and teaches me about all things (1 John 2:27).

70. I love because God first loved me, and love comes from God (1 John 4:19, 7).

71. I am strengthened with power through the Spirit in my inmost being (Ephesians 3:16).

72. Like living stones, I am being built into a spiritual house (1 Peter 2:5).

73. I am a part of the body of Christ (1 Corinthians 12:27).

74. Grace has been given to me as Christ apportioned it (Ephesians 4:7).

75. His grace is enough for me. In my weakness he is my strength (2 Corinthians 2:9).

76. I can do all things through him who gives me strength (Philippians 4:13).

77. God has made known to me the path of life (Psalm 16:11).

78. He fills me with joy in his presence, with eternal pleasures at his right hand (Psalm 16:11).

79. The joy of the Lord is my strength (Nehemiah 8:10).

80. Jesus came so that I may live a new life (Romans 6:4).

81. Jesus came so that I can have life to the full (John 10:10).

82. God is pleased to reveal his Son in me (Galatians 1:16).

83. In Christ, I am a new creation, the old is gone and the new has come (2 Corinthians 5:17).

84. I am created to be like God in true righteousness and holiness (Ephesians 4:24).

85. In all things, I am growing up into him who is the head, Christ (Ephesians 4:15).

86. I am destined for glory. When Christ, who is my life, appears I will appear with him in glory (Colossians 3:4).

87. Christ in me is the hope of glory (Colossians 1:27).

88. God gives me the victory through my Lord Jesus Christ (1 Corinthians 15:57).

89. In all these things, I am more than a conqueror through him who loved me (Romans 8:37).

90. Nothing in all creation will be able to separate me from the love of God that is in Christ Jesus, my Lord (Romans 8:38–39).

91. God is for me, who can be against me? (Romans 8:31).

92. He provides me with plenty and fills my heart with joy (Acts 14:17).

93. God richly provides me with everything for my enjoyment (1 Timothy 6:17).

94. Apart from God, I have no good thing (Psalm 16:2).

95. God has assigned me my portion and my cup, he has made my lot secure (Psalm 16:5).

96. The boundary lines have fallen for me in pleasant places (Psalm 16:6).

97. God has plans to prosper me, not to harm me, plans to give me hope and a future (Jeremiah 29:11).

98. I will see the goodness of God in the land of the living (Psalm 27:13).

99. I will be like him, for I shall see him as he is (1 John 3:2).

100. I am confident that he who began a good work in me will carry it on to completion until the day of Christ Jesus (Philippians 1:6).

Notes

Notes

Notes

Notes

Acknowledgments

This book would not have appeared without the encouragement and support of many wonderful people. I am grateful to and for each of you!

About three years prior to this manuscript's completion, Bill Odders, a longtime friend, reading enthusiast, and lifelong bible student shared a lengthy list of "in Christ" scriptures with me. That's what got the whole thing rolling. I studied the list for use in a teaching, pared it down to 100 scriptural references, and organized them into a set of slides and handouts for a session at a men's retreat at The Barn Vineyard Church in February of 2020.

Shortly thereafter, the Covid-19 pandemic struck while traveling in East Africa on a mission trip with my wife, Judy, and Bob and Tam Mulrooney, friends and co-adventurers in living in relationship to our triune God. When we were able to arrange booking on the next to last Kenya Airlines flight out of Nairobi, we arrived back in the US and returned to Bob and Tam's home, where they graciously hosted us during our fourteen-day quarantine. It was during that period of time that I began to journal meditations on each of the 100 verses, and Bob and Tam's encouragement and discussions helped me to decide to try to turn this into a book. Over decades of living in intergenerational families with similarly aged members and doing life together, Bob and Tam have generously shared their home, their lives, and their pursuit of our loving Father with countless others. We have greatly benefitted from your wonderful hearts.

Thirty-nine years ago, I met Bruce and Lynn Latshaw, senior pastors at The Barn Vineyard Church, where I have attended ever since. They have provided vital teaching, pastoring, mentoring, counseling, and care for all these decades, and many of the meditations recorded in this book have been shaped by their teaching, ministry, and friendship over the years. Thanks for your hearts to pursue God and to equip people to encounter God, build community, have their lives transformed, and to live the adventure. We all benefit from your passion for God and your love. Your encouragement of my teaching and writing is invaluable to me.

In recent years, I have attended numerous Fatherheart Ministry events (A schools, a B school, weekend seminars) where Trevor and Linda Galpin, Leonard and Leslie Hays, and Mark Head have taught and ministered. In addition, I have read several Fatherheart books by Trevor Galpin, James Jordan, Stephen Hill, Ingrid Wilts, and Andy Glover. Many of the meditations in this book have been positively influenced by their sowing of the Father's love through their teaching, ministry, and writing.

Nina Groop provided insightful comments on a previous version of this book and professional and caring editing for this draft. Nina is a gifted writer, storyteller, and editor, whose insights and perspectives have been valuable to me and many of my family members over the years. This was not an easy edit, for sure, but Nina, your recommendations were excellent, and especially your precision in helping to ferret out much redundancy. The book would not have seen the light of day without your expert work. Thanks so much for the care that you invested in this. Felicia Murrell provided expert line edits and comments on the penultimate draft of the manuscript, offering greater consistency and clarity. Her attention to detail brought significant improvements.

Mark Ham, the only solutions architect I have ever met, brought inspired solutions for book design, publication, and coordinating websites, among other things. His ability to patiently listen to fuzzy ideas or big dreams, to ask the right questions, and to make connections with all sorts of gifted people, offered results that made this project come to fruition. Mark, your humble spirit, the depth and breadth of your expertise, your connections across domains with accomplished people, and your patience were invaluable to me. Thank you. The fact that this book is published is a testimony to your solutions.

Andrea Graver blended some literally sketchy concepts for the cover and interior design of the book and created a look that exceeded my hopes and dreams. Andrea, thanks for focusing your many gifts and talents in kingdom work.

Judy — your encouragement, love, patience, support, prayers, and excellent questions and comments are always foundational in any project I do. The ways that you continually show me and others the love of God is truly astounding. Thanks for your feedback on the earlier draft and the design and for fueling this project in so many ways.

About the Author

Rob Palkovitz has been a member of The Barn Vineyard Church (formerly Newark Christian Fellowship) since 1983 where he has served in various capacities: youth group leader, teacher, member of the pastoral team, member of the Global Outreach (missions) team, and as an elder for over thirty-five years. He is a son, brother, husband, father, and grandfather. He is also Professor Emeritus of Human Development and Family Sciences at the University of Delaware. His research and professional writing centered on fathering and intergenerational relationships and development, with a particular emphasis on the relationships between patterns of father involvement and developmental outcomes for men and their children. For over twenty-five years, Rob has done volunteer work alongside his family with urban foster and father-absent children. He has also participated in community development work in Togo and Kenya. Rob helped to launch Waterbrook Hills, a nonprofit organization that works to enhance social justice and facilitate positive life opportunities and family functioning for persons in challenging circumstances. He enjoys hiking, trail running, working in woodlands, and conversations over good coffee. He can be contacted at rob@aplaceprepared.net.

Made in the USA
Middletown, DE
08 June 2025